Tough Hope

by
Clifford Denton Schutjer

Tough Love
ISBN 1-887932-77-1
LOC: 00-102447

First Edition

Published by
New Concord Press
Zanesville, Ohio

Table of Contents

Understanding God's Way With Us
Through an Assortment of Ancient People

Revisiting Thanksgiving, Christmas, Epiphany, and Easter

Some Interesting Light From Other Sources

About the Title of This Collection of Sermons

"Tough Hope" is a transparent take-off on the concept of "tough love" that has been so well articulated in the teachings and writings that are a part of the various Twelve-Step programs of Alcoholics Anonymous, Narcotics Anonymous, Gamblers Anonymous, and others.

"Tough hope," like "tough love," that must sometimes go beyond warm sentimentality, endearing wishful thinking, and feel-good optimism, is hope that is tough enough to operate in the dark, to endure constant ambiguity, and keep a practical edge to its trust.

It is that tough kind of hope—hope for each of us as individuals, for our shared life, and for our world—that is a common thread through the majority of these sermons.

—*Clifford D. Schutjer*

In Memory of Dr. Carroll Damron
whose loving family made this book possible

Sermons to Help Steer Around the Potholes in the Road of Life

Loving the Mystery of It All

If one looks closely, we human beings devote a lot of thought and ingenuity to trying to make things fit into some kind of system or pattern or scheme. Maybe not quite all of us, but certainly most of us seem to hope that we can figure out the logic of living and, thereby, make it more predictable. After all, the sun reliably comes up every morning from the east; the seasons can be counted upon to remain in their proper order (with the possible exception of in Ohio). There are any number of other effects that always follow upon certain causes. So why wouldn't there be some such fully dependable system all across the board; a system that clever people should be able to figure out? So we do work at it. Even very young children seem confident that there must be a way that everything fits nicely together. If two plus two equal four, then all else should add up too—if one stays at it long enough.

One little girl, for example, asked her mother if she would please have another baby—another brother or sister for the family. The mother was surprised because the girl and her brother fought a lot. She asked her why, since she complained so much about being hassled by her brother, would she would want there to be yet another child. The girl replied, *"Because when a family gets three children, they get to have a van."* It was simple cause and effect: two kids plus one more equals a van.

Much of what we find endearingly comic about children is just that: childlike attempts to make predictable what is not. Another child—this one in a church school class— when asked by the teacher, *"Where does one find God?"*, replied with total confidence: *"God is in the bathroom at our house almost every morning."* The teacher asked why she would say such a thing. The girl replied, *"Because most mornings before I get up, I hear my dad by the bathroom door yelling, 'Good God, are you still in there?'"*

Yet one more example was an elementary classroom. As part of a lesson on substance abuse, the teacher held up a glass containing what she explained was vodka, a kind of liquor. She then dropped a worm into it. The worm immediately contracted and died. She asked the kids what this showed. The first to raise his hand answered, *"It shows that if you drink Vodka, you won't have worms."* See? Things are simple after all.

Those are no more than early attempts at what, for many, becomes a life-long struggle to figure out the system; to convince ourselves that we know just what works, what always fails, what are the secrets of success, and what explains the inexplicable.

We are able to figure out some of it reasonably accurately. But one of the toughest adjustments for many of us is learning to live with the fact that, while there is remarkable order in the physical dimension of life, there are other dimensions of life that do not submit to any dependable system or neat design.

Discovering *that* is a bit like the experience of yet one more child who came home from school, saying he was fed up with math. When asked why, he said, *"Because it took me a long time to remember that three plus three equal six and now the teacher is telling us that it's four plus two that makes six."* Right! And not only that: there'll be many similar frustrations ahead for him in life when other of his absolutes and simplifications and predictabilities crumble.

That, in a nutshell, is the tough one: learning to tolerate and live with life's ambiguity and randomness.

Here we'd thought that the world could be divided into good guys and villains, assumed that we knew what was always helpful for us and what was always bad for us, were certain that if one always avoided this and always chose that, then everything would be just fine. So colliding with blatant instances when it didn't work that way was infuriating, disorienting, or disillusioning.

Why get into all of this? It's because some people turn to religion in hopes of not having to accept this aspect of life. They hope that religion can show them the consistency, "absoluteness," and logic to life that they need. They don't feel that they should have to accept the fact that good things actually happen to bad people; and that bad things happen to good people; that terrible results can come from the best of intentions, while the stupidest of moves sometimes works out okay; that real courage, diligence, love, and other such virtues sometimes backfire for no apparent reason. So they hope to find a belief system that will satisfactorily explain all that. Maybe, for example, the horrible atrocity is just a difficult-to-recognize part of God's glorious plan. Maybe someone's excruciating suffering is merely God's strange way of testing that person. Maybe the dreadful epidemic is a perfectly sensible expression of God's infinite wisdom. Maybe, if they can shut their eyes, grit their teeth, and believe stuff like that, then the infuriating ambiguity will go away.

It's not difficult to understand why, when someone has been bruised and terrorized by odd or inexplicable experiences, he might long for such certainty. Unfortunately, though, there are no beliefs, no religious interpretations, and no holy explanations that can do that for us. Moreover, the ones that claim to provide such answers are not faith—at least not the Christian faith. They are only superstitions flavored with religion.

They are not a lot different from the superstitions that tell us that we must never walk under a ladder, step on the crack in the sidewalk, leave our lucky charm at home, let a black cat cut in front of us, break a mirror, tear up the chain letter, or stay in a room on the thirteenth floor of a hotel. At bottom, superstition (religious or otherwise) is a belief that there is a tight, knowable system of rituals, beliefs, and practices which, if followed, can magically affect or control destiny, luck, the accidental, and the unpredictable. It might be nice if there were some such cosmic gimmick, but there is not. And don't mistake anything like it for the Christian faith.

No, the Bible is right up front about the ambiguity of life, about our vulnerability and our constant exposure to the strange, the illogical, the disruptive, the bewildering and, yes, the tragic. It never claims, either, that it will show us how to make that go away or that it has a neat explanation for why such things happen to us.

In fact, the God we meet in scripture, isn't at all the neat and orderly deity that one might prefer. Talk about ambiguity—the Bible claims that God gets mixed up in god-awful situations, gets involved with a lot of people that no god ought to be caught dead with (for example, hotheads, cheats, philanderers, even a murderer), and describes a God who intervenes at one time and not at another, without a whisper of explanation.

Yes, anyone who can read this Bible of ours and come away thinking that now he knows God's system—knows just what God is likely to do next, or knows just how he can get all his prayers answered, or knows what is God's system of blessings and punishments, is either kidding himself or he's been smoking something he shouldn't.

One runs into the same thing in the New Testament Gospels. If you read what Jesus did and said, thinking you might be reassured that ours is that neat, moral universe (that is, that you'll find a pattern in which all is always reasonable, logical, and orderly) then you are going to be quite frustrated. Those stories of the miraculous immediately get in the way. As nice as some of Jesus' healings were, face it: they were random, indiscriminate, sometimes there, sometimes not.

Worse yet, if I am a "reasonableness-and-order" freak, what in Heaven's name, do I make of the story of Jesus walking on water? Or of his turning water into wine or of his shutting down a typhoon? Or of his sending into a stampeding herd of hogs whatever was demonic about some unfortunate fellow or of his bringing a particular friend back from the dead while doing nothing about the rest of the folks in the cemetery?

If we're honest about it, he taught that way too. One day he tells a fellow to sell all that he has and give it away. The next day he tells a story in which he is terribly critical of a man who failed to wheel and deal with money on loan to him. True, he says good things about loving, but only a short time later, he's saying that his way is likely to bring enmity between family members. And, yes, he commends righteousness and responsibility, but only to turn right around and mount criticism after criticism on the most disciplined, law-abiding, religiously devout people around: the Pharisees.

No wonder some people have always had problems with the Bible. Just about the time you think, *"Aha, now I know what it is saying, what it's all about, how to make it work!"*, it suddenly isn't about that at all any more.

But this is no accident. I, at least, have come to believe that this is precisely what the scripture, in general, and the Gospel of Christ, in particular, ought to do for us. It should "de-familiarize" me. It should keep causing cracks in every neat little system, every tidy set of surefire assumptions, and every collection of absolute certainties that I, in my infinite wisdom, think that I have proven to myself to be absolute.

For most of us, most of the time, an authentic encounter with God ought to do that to us: keep blowing the lid right off our most hallowed certainties, our most cherished opinions, our most comfortable ways of thinking—and leave us uncomfortably open.

The Bible does this to me from beginning to end. It confronts, for example, my neat little intellectually responsible world, where no miracles or mystery are permitted, and shoots holes in the satisfied feeling that I know just about everything I need to know, that my opinions and my ways are ninety-some percent right, and that I have God "down pat." Yes, it is very hard on my slick answers, my sacrosanct assumptions, my smug absolutes, and my comfortable dogmas and doctrines about what goes on and what never could.

It wreaks havoc upon my pious judgments about people and about what in them is forgivable and what is not, about which ones are really worth anything and which ones are throwaways. For it has the gall to tell me that God chose a con-man (Jacob) to be the father of a world-changing people; that God used Moses, a murderer, for a deliverer—when he was over 80 years old; that God would do something as off-the-wall as to cause edible substance to fall from the skies upon starving people. It tells me (jumping ahead) that a redeemer might be born in a barn, that grave illnesses could suddenly evaporate, that utterly worthless or throwaway human beings might be transformed in an afternoon, that even death wasn't what everyone had it cracked up to be.

So, for a scientifically oriented person like me and a lot of others, it can be a real stretch. I do think I know, though, what I am supposed to make of all that and of hundreds of pages more like it. The message is that God is more present, more active, and more directly involved than it may be comfortable to imagine; that life is much bigger and deeper than I make it when I think I have it all boiled down in my theories and certainties; that the future is more open than the experts and pundits would have us believe; that limiting our thinking and dreaming to what we can measure, weigh, and control is stupid and arrogant; that ordinary human beings have more power than they have begun to tap; that right along side of all of our good research, brilliant reasoning, careful exploration, astute defining, and systematizing, is this dynamic spiritual dimension that is not going to be organized or systematized by us.

We are presented with a world and a life, then, in which a powerful case can be made for our continuing to hope, despite there being NO logical basis for it; for our loving when it makes no sense; for our trusting when it seems unreasonable to do so—NOT because we know it works, but because in this mysterious world and life in which God has placed us, just about anything is possible and we don't get to know what all is really going on, except occasionally, on looking back.

To live like that requires a lot more tolerance for ambiguity than comes naturally to most of us. It requires our becoming comfortable with mystery, maybe even growing an appetite for it. It requires living with unprecedented levels of personal patience, of trust, and humility. But if you reflect on that, what it is, is: faith at its best. It is exactly what it is to be Godly in a complicated, unpredictable, convulsing, mystifying time like that to which God seems to have assigned to us.

Tough Hope ───────────────────────

The Will of God?

Matthew 26:36-39

> *Jesus went with the disciples to a place called Gethsemane. He said to them, "Remain here while I go over there and pray." He took Peter and two others aside. Deeply grieved and agitated, he asked them to stay nearby and remain awake with him. Going still farther, he threw himself on the ground, praying, "My Father, if it is possible, let this cup pass from me." Then he said, "Let it not be my will, but Yours that is done."*

It was the night of Jesus' arrest—maybe 15 hours before his execution. At this point, he could still have avoided being arrested had he so chosen. On the one hand, he believed that his arrest and likely execution were the only way to bring things to a head—to expose what needed to be exposed. At the same time, a very human side of him cried out against deliberately submitting to abuse, torture, and death. He described it as a contest between his own will and that which would best serve God—we call it "God's will." His decision, as we well know, was to permit the religious and political powers to do to him what they routinely did to whomever dared speak truth to power. His decision was to embrace the death, trusting that God would be able to use it; "*God's will be done*"! he said. As Christians, we believe that God DID take that terrible lynching and make it something eternally important.

So Jesus' decision on that night has been the primary Christian example of Godly commitment—of fitting oneself to "God's will." But still, as moving as that was, what God's will IS, what it is NOT, whether it's predetermined, or does it ever change, remain questions for a lot of us—bewildering, if not troubling ones.

If, for example, one listens much to what is sometimes offered as comfort at funeral parlor calling hours, one gets the impression that cancers, coronaries, cerebral hemorrhages, automobile collisions, and other cataclysms are all to be understood as God's will. One may hear someone say, for example, *"We know that you are going to miss your daddy, but God knows best in these matters and has a good reason for this."*

A number of years ago, Dr. William Sloan Coffin, a minister and teacher, lost his twenty-one-year-old son, Alex, in a one-car accident in which, on a very stormy night, his car plunged into Boston Harbor. After the memorial service, a woman who was trying to be sympathetic, said to him, *"I just don't understand God's will in this!"* Later, writing about it, the minister said that he found himself almost shouting at her:

> I'll say you don't understand God's will, lady. Do you think it was the will of God that Alex never fixed that lousy windshield wiper, that Alex was probably driving too fast in such a storm, that Alex had probably had too much to drink? Do you think it is God's will that there are no street lights along that stretch of road, no guard rail separating the road and the Boston Harbor? Why can't people get it through their heads that God doesn't run around the world with his fingers on triggers, his fist around knives, his hands upon steering wheels. God is dead-set against all kinds of unnatural deaths. I'm not saying that there are no natural-cause deaths. There are. But one thing that should never be said about any violent death like Alex's death is that "it is the will of God." My consolation lies in knowing that it was NOT the will of God that Alex died; that rather, when the waves closed in over the sinking car, God's heart was the first of all hearts to break.

Well said! Sincere though it may be, that brand of piety inclined to explain and label each tragic event, each happy coincidence, and all fortuitous successes or failures as being willed by God, ends up portraying God as monstrous at worst and capricious at best.

I recall once hearing a preacher say, with perfect certainty, that a proposed speaking engagement was obviously not God's will, because his flight was cancelled due to mechanical problems. Okay, but doesn't one have to ask: what about the others scheduled for that flight—ones who were on their way to a funeral or perhaps on some errand of mercy or were on their way to try to heal some terrible misunderstanding? As they drive back home from the air terminal, are they also to assume that their trip was counter to God's will?

Such glib God-talk gets very trivial and absurd. As some would have it, God willed the rapid run-up in a particular stock in order to bless them with a very nice profit. Think *that* through! While not getting around to willing enough food distribution to adequately nourish children in more than a fourth of the world, supposedly, the Almighty God WAS taking time to manipulate stock prices. I don't know how you feel about that, but don't ask me to worship a god like that.

If you've paid attention, you've seen some of the same kind of thing from a certain ilk of athletes; that is, that God wills the Christian quarterback's touchdown. To make that point, those quarterbacks kneel in the end zone and point heavenward. A month or so ago, Clark Morphew, in his Saturday newspaper column, raised sharp questions about God's will having anything whatsoever to do with pro-football team performance. Two weeks later, in another column, he described some of the hate mail he had received for daring to raise doubts that God would "will" certain outcomes in pro-football. It's odd stuff!

A couple of decades ago, Yogi Berra, who, while never receiving an award for eloquence, did address this issue remarkably well (for him). It was the ninth inning and the score was tied with two outs. The batter from the other team stepped up to the plate, piously genuflected, and then used the bat to make the sign of the cross in the dust on home plate. Berra, though a Roman Catholic himself, wiped the cross off the plate with his catcher's mitt and said to this pious batter, *"Why don't we let God JUST WATCH this game!"*

Of course, particularly when things work out well, there is a certain "holy coziness" and reassurance in believing that one's success, her good fortune, his pleasant circumstance all must be the precise will of God. That's an especially tempting interpretation when some failure, trouble, or catastrophe has been VERY narrowly avoided; that is, it's very reassuring to believe that God specifically willed my survival. If it is God's will to protect me, then the danger or the close call was not as close as it might have seemed.

As comforting as any of that can feel, it doesn't hold up at all under honest reflection. That is, one cannot have it both ways. If every narrow miss, every benign diagnosis, or every threat that went away was specifically, intricately willed by God, then doesn't one ALSO have to see every seemingly undeserved catastrophe, every meaningless cataclysm, and every random outrage that happens to us as *also* specifically willed by God?

It is obvious (as we've reflected on this in other sermons) that God has built a certain amount of order to the creation. There are all kinds of very real causes and effects. Misuse your body and it tends to sicken and deteriorate prematurely. Abuse the earth and there'll be dust storms, dead lakes, putrid streams, floods, and worse. Even be a selfish, abusive person and often (though not always) you'll end up isolated and lonely. But to infer from that—that there is some relentless, divine "intentionallity" behind all of the rest of whatever fortunate (or terrible) events and experiences that come along—is very bad religion. It is a form of superstition, not a form of faith.

Again, God did not "will" the death of the young man who skidded his car into Boston Harbor. God did not will the agonizing form of cancer that took your sister's life. God did not will AIDS to make a point regarding non-conforming sexual practices. It is not God's will that Ethnic Albanians be slaughtered. It was not God's exclusive, unalterable will that you married the person you did and not someone else. You did not end up in manufacturing rather than in teaching because that was scripted for you in the detailed will of God.

A hospital chaplain, who almost daily is confronted with people in angry grief, demanding to know from him why God would "will" the awful thing that is befalling them, says that his explanation to them is, that these things happen "not because they are a part of a PLAN, but because we are part of the PLANET." Just so! That's an important basic part of the picture.

Something else, though, that needs to be understood is that God takes very seriously our freedom; a freedom by which God allows us to build, destroy, risk, withdraw, prematurely wear ourselves out, experiment, improvise, and much more. So while, yes—God IS involved with us, is creating around us, is working through us, restores and heals us—NEVER is it as some kind of "celestial puppeteer" using us as the puppets. Much of our dignity as God's sons and daughters is, in fact, seen in that awesome freedom that we have been given, along with the scary vulnerability and the radical open-endedness of our life and history.

Another part of it is that the real will of God is not ever something to be turned into a means for browbeating ourselves or browbeating anyone else into or out of something. (*"Oh, Martha, I've prayed long and hard about this and I know now that it is the will of God that you marry me."*) Or better yet, *"God has revealed to me that God wants you to become a major contributor to our TV ministry."*

I recall that when my father decided to resign from his church in a Northwoods town in Minnesota, he received letters from other ministers telling him, amidst a lot of syrupy, spiritualized rhetoric, that they had prayerfully determined that it was "God's will" that they become the next pastor of that particular church (located as it was, in the middle of a northern Minnesota hunters' and fishermen's paradise). It couldn't have been much more transparent. God does not micromanage life that way. So be very wary of those who portray God as doing so. Typically, they have a personal agenda—not a Godly one.

Another principle here is that almost everything that we really know about the will of God has been learned chiefly in LOOKING BACK, after the fact. It is in looking back upon our personal pasts, as well as our shared history, that the hand of God can most easily be seen at work. Seldom, if ever, is it those nick-of-time rescues, extraordinary blessings, or mind-boggling coincidences. We'll see it more as a disposition, a weightiness, an overall direction, a quiet-but-definite movement toward your growth and mine—our healing, our renewal, our deepening. Yes, looking carefully back THAT WAY upon our own geography of grace, getting a sense of the drift of it and getting that larger-picture look at where God has been at work in us and around us, points the way toward where God is most likely to be moving in our future, or even what might be the meaning of strange inner stirrings that we are feeling right now.

To get at the last part of this—how God's will moves, touches, and creates—a word picture that someone came up with might be helpful. It has to do with the way the water from the melting snow on higher elevations forms streams, makes rivers, sometimes creates torrents and at other times, ponds and lakes as it moves among the valleys and plateaus.

James Freeman described it very well as he said,

> Rivers hardly ever run in a straight line.
> Rivers are willing to take ten thousand meanderings and
>   enjoy every one and grow through every one.
> When they leave a meandering they are always more than
>   when they entered it.
> When rivers meet an obstacle they do not try to run over
>   it; they merely go around.
> But they always get to the other side.
> Rivers take things as they are—conform to the shape they
>   find the world in.
> Yet nothing changes things more than those rivers!
> Rivers move even mountains into the sea.
> Rivers are seldom in a hurry.
> Yet is there anything more likely to reach the point to
>   which it sets out than a river?

The will of God moving in our world and history is something like that water. It takes more than one course. Its appearance is not identical in every situation. It has alternative ways of getting where it's headed. But there is an unmistakable overall power, process and direction to it. You and I are free to affect it, to bring our own creativity to the flow of it, to improvise within it—but we won't ultimately frustrate it. As water does find its way to the sea, so does God, in God's own way, weave a fabric of meaning and of good from the tangle of living, struggling, and aspiring that is you and me.

So this isn't as mystical or complicated or sweaty or arbitrary as some have made it look. Again, we are not God's puppets. We are joint creators with God, shaping life with God; we are the sons and daughters of God, free to have intentions, hopes, and passions of our own. And we have every reason, then, to feel at-home in it, to be confident as we go at it, and to be excited about what our own particular lives can come to mean: come to mean to ourselves, come to mean to our world, and, actually, come to mean to God.

Chasing Perfection

Matthew 19:16-22 (portions)

A man came up to Jesus and said, Master, what good thing must I do to have eternal life?" Jesus said, "If you wish to enter into life, keep the commandments." "Which ones?" the man asked...Jesus said, "You shall not murder; shall not commit adultery; shall not steal; shall not bear false witness; shall honor your father and your mother; and shall love your neighbor as yourself." The man replied;, I have kept all of those. What more must I do?" Jesus answered, "If you wish to be perfect, go sell all that you have and give the money to those in need, ... When the young man heard this he went away grieving for he had many possessions.

Doing THAT was going to make this man "perfect"? Divesting himself of everything he owned would turn him into a flawless person? I doubt it. Surely, giving away all of his assets wouldn't keep him from ever again being irritable over some trivial inconvenience, would it? Would the absence of wealth make it so that he never again would have a mean or prurient thought? Were the last of his mixed motives suddenly going to become pure with the closing of his last bank or brokerage account? Once he owned nothing, from then on, when he hit his finger with a hammer or spilled a gallon of paint on his carpet would he exclaim, *"Oh Praise God!"* instead of some of the more familiar things that are exclaimed at such a moment? It doesn't sound likely to me.

So why would Jesus tell this man that giving all that he had to those in need would make him perfect? And this wasn't the only time that Jesus said something like this. Right in the Sermon on the Mount, he says, *"Become perfect, just as God is perfect."* I didn't think that possible, did you?

Besides, if God expects human beings to live flawless lives, then someone has a lot of explaining to do in regard to the kinds of human beings with whom, according to our Bible, God became involved. Throughout his life, Moses had a problem with his temper; in one rage, he committed a murder. Jacob was a con artist, wheeler-dealer, and shyster. Gideon, though clever, lacked courage. Samson, King David, and King Solomon all created major problems for themselves because of their sexual appetites. The prophet Jonah was a bigot. The prophet Isaiah described himself as a man of unclean lips (and he probably wasn't talking about cold sores). The disciple Matthew joined Jesus directly from a line of work that entailed corruption and being a traitor to his people. Peter would shoot off his mouth without thinking— even did so that last night in the upper room. The apostle Paul was hardheaded, pushy, and often irritating. So, yes, flawlessness eluded those and all kinds of others of the people of God, both in and out of the Bible.

Let's face it: living flawlessly is a tall order. If we reflect upon it, all across the board it keeps eluding us. For example, what at first seemed to be the perfect job, the perfect wife, the perfect husband, the perfect marriage, the perfect circumstance, or the perfect location, always had flaws. To make it still more frustrating, when it comes to flawlessness in people, it turns out that those who try the hardest to be perfect, seem then to fall into a whole other set of faults and foibles, like egoism and self-righteousness.

A friend was questioning a man about a recent relationship. He asked him, *"You mean that, at your girl friend's request, you quit drinking?"*

"I did," he answered.

"And then, because she asked you to, you gave up smoking too?"

"That's right," he replied.

"And was it also for her that you quit going to the race track and quit coming to our Monday night poker games?"

"That's true," he nodded.

"And is it because of her that you cleaned up your language, finished your degree, and quit throwing money around?" The

man nodded

"Then WHY, *after all of that, didn't you marry her?*"

"Because," the man replied, "*after all of that reforming, I had become such a perfect catch as a husband, I realized I could do a lot better than her*"!

It often works something like that. At the point that a person believes he is close to one form of flawlessness, then delusions of grandeur, arrogance, haughtiness, or worse become the new defects and quirks.

So once more: what in the world was Jesus talking about when he said that we could, and we should, become perfect, even as God is perfect?

For that matter, how about God's perfection? Looked at carefully, it seems that even God stopped short of flawlessness in the very creation itself. The late Dr. Lewis Thomas—physician, scientist, philosopher, and author—wrote that, had creation been left up to us modern human beings, with our compulsion to try to make everything flawless, the creative process would have stopped cold very early on. He said that, for example, we never would have allowed the DNA molecule (the one that is the building block out of which all the wonders of life come about) to have flaws and imperfections. He said that, wanting it to be defect-free, we would have created that molecule to always make exact copies. Then he goes on to point out that, "*The capacity to blunder slightly is the marvel of DNA. Without this attribute, [this absence of perfection] we would all still be anaerobic bacteria and there would be no music.*"

You catch the implications of that, don't you? Our lungs that breathe air, our vertebrae that support weight, our legs and arms, our brains that reason and create, and so much more, all came about as flaws and blemishes to the DNA molecule. One might say that they were all lapses in creation's quality control. Apparently, it was God's openness to and coping with defect, blunder, and anomaly that brought us to be.

If, at this point, you are thinking that where this all comes out is some comfy little moral to the effect that "nobody's perfect," or that it's "all relative," or that "we're all predetermined to be what we will be, so don't sweat it," that's NOT SO. Not at all. The Bible is full of real concern about the errors, compromises, "cheapenings," "cheatings," and sins that can overcome and undo people.

Nevertheless, when Jesus spoke of being "perfect," he did not mean that God demanded and expected that you and I achieve total flawlessness.

No, Thank God! Jesus is talking here about the other meaning of the word "perfect." In our language, we have two possible meanings when we say "perfect." One does mean free of all defects. The other, the one meant by the word Jesus used in his own language, means "complete," "whole," "inherently comprehensible," or "having an inner coherence." It is "perfect," then, in the sense that one of us might say, "It happened at the perfect time," or "It was a perfect evening," or "It was a perfect solution," or "She was just perfect in that position." Said that way, it doesn't mean that no one spilled his coffee that "perfect evening" or used incorrect grammar. It doesn't mean that there was not the slightest glitch or irregularity about how things fell together. No, what we mean at such times is that it "fit," that it held together, or that there was a wholeness to it which was intrinsically right. That was what Jesus meant when he said, "You must be 'perfect' even as God is perfect."

I recall reading someone's reflections upon watching a house cat sunning itself. This writer said that the cat was managing to be "100% cat"—"perfectly cat," he might have said. And he went on to say, ruefully, that he couldn't remember ever being "100% anything."

I think I know what he means, what he is saying. It touches directly on this being "perfect" in the sense of being firmly-centered, integrated, and at one with oneself. It is something that cats and dogs may do better than you and I. It is too easily lost as you and I innocently take on conflicting demands, assume divergent roles, and become gun-shy after a few disorienting mistakes. Without my realizing that it is happening, for example, my public self comes to be unrelated to my private self. The motions that one goes through become just that: motions gone through, no longer connected to one's dreams, ideals, or values. That all-too-subtle loss of wholeness, loss of coherence, and collapse of the center of us—while not as obvious as the stupidities and flaws that show up on the surface of our living—is far more serious. In the long run, it is more destructive of the total person than whatever bad habits with which we may have to struggle or those nagging temptations, stubborn weaknesses, and other human susceptibilities that may haunt us.

So what does it take? What would it entail? What appearance would this kind of "being perfect," being an integrated, at-one-with-ourselves, "whole" have?

It starts with our fully affirming and accepting the individuals that we are, with all of our bewildering mix of chromosomes, hormones, and other God-given ingredients that have come together as "me." More than that, it is believing and knowing that God not only knows, cares, and values that unprecedented mixture that we are, but that God is *excited* about the particular piece of creation that is each one of us.

As to whatever may end up as my flaws, whatever those may be, it means refusing to believe that I am, therefore, one who had best hold back and tiptoe along in life until I overcome all idiosyncrasies, insecurities, and other annoying qualities that still trouble me. I musn't embarrass myself, upset God, or perhaps demonstrate that I am some kind of imposter in the picture.

It means, then, that I must allow to surface this person that God created, rather than some contrived version of me that I have tried to make work by adding a little of this and a little of that. You know, a smoke screen here, a facade over there, and assorted "posings" and pretenses until, rather than a work of God, I end up more like something invented by a committee.

It will mean not only becoming comfortable with that "soul of me" or "the soul of you," but also daring to disclose ourselves. That would mean, for example, reacquiring the grace of speaking directly from the heart, more like the way we did when we were children, before we took on overlays of sophistication, decorum, and elitism.

Part of this kind of being perfect will mean understanding and accepting the fact that you and I are beings who are permanently "in process;" that, at whatever stage, interval, or juncture I am or you are just now, it is not the final word. Once we believe that to be true, then we won't be nearly so likely to get pulled apart or fragmented by whatever is our current failure or success or dilemma or anxiety.

Above all, to be perfect in the sense that Jesus called for, is to know in faith that the whole unabridged, complicated, unfathomable being that you are, is, in the deepest sense, appropriate; is explicitly called for; is truly needed by God for this life and this world. It is knowing that your worth to God is not only your skill, your resources, certain endearing aspects of you, or your more marketable talents. What is needed is the full-blown living of the complete, undivided, maybe seemingly quirky YOU, as a "perfect" creation of God.

There is real freedom and peace in that. Get it right— become perfect in THAT sense—and with real confidence, you're ready to make coherent choices about what you are going to do, what you'll offer, what you want to say, as well as what you are going to drop, what you'll put on the back burner, or what you will simply say "no" to. You can even become comfortable deciding which of your weaknesses are worth worrying about and which ones you'll do better to develop a sense of humor about. You will find yourself free to quit torturing yourself with old guilts or neglects or failures—never mind what anyone else might think.

So: *"Nobody's perfect?"* Not so. *"Nobody is flawless,"* to be sure. But in this deepest, most exciting, holistic sense of "perfect"—the one that came through so stunningly in Jesus—being perfect is within the reach of every one of us. In fact, it is really the only way to live.

On Being Way Ahead of the Pack

Luke 18:9-14

Jesus told this parable for those confident in their own virtue and regarding others with disdain. "Two men went up to the temple to pray. One was a Pharisee and the other a collector of taxes. The Pharisee stood by himself and prayed, 'God, I thank you that I am not like so many others: the thieves, rogues, adulterers, and especially not like the tax collectors. I give away a tenth of my income. I fast twice a week.' The tax-collector, standing off in a corner could barely lift his eyes. He prayed, 'God, have mercy on a sinner like me.'" Jesus said, "It was that tax collector that went home right with God. The Pharisee did not. Those who exalt themselves will be humbled and those who humble themselves will be exalted."

Quite a few years ago, using that parable at a confirmation retreat, I asked the students what they thought it meant. The one who replied said that she thought it meant that, no matter how good a person is, he should always talk as if he were not all that great.

As she saw it, the Pharisee's problem was chiefly a public relations one: his failure to realize that one doesn't say things like that aloud. That tax collector, on the other hand, had learned to play "the humility game" well: *"O God, I am a terrible sinner, a real crud. But God, please note that at least I admit it."*

One could probably draw from that parable that, no matter how self-congratulating, how imperious, and how condescending one is, the important thing is to learn to act humble and modest. That doesn't sound much like something Jesus would teach though, does it?

The problem I have with the parable is that the Pharisee seems like an absurd parody—an overdrawn caricature, not a real-life person. The worst, most super-pious snob I know, is too self-aware to let himself come across as obnoxious as did this Pharisee in that prayer. He sounds almost as bizarre as that psychotic fellow suffering from severe delusions of grandeur who, at the first appointment with a psychiatrist, said, *"Doctor, If you will cure me of my delusions of grandeur, I'll grant you eternal life."* It is probably true that today's Pharisees are much more subtle about their self-congratulation, elitism, and arrogance than this one portrayed by Jesus.

But the fact that modern Pharisees may be much better at faking humility doesn't solve the problem that Jesus was addressing here. The problem was that, in his "heart of hearts," the Pharisee really believed that, by nature and attainment, he was someone who had risen above other people in his world—was utterly different from them. Were it now, his prayer probably would have sounded more like this:

> *O God, I am grateful that you have given me the intelligence, the motivation, the discretion, and the breeding to make my life one of which I can be justly proud. I thank you, God, that I am not like those others out there who live such pitiable and disastrous lives. Thank you, God, for helping me develop the self-discipline, the tastefulness, and the maturity that has made of me the person I now am. For you know, O God, that I've always worked harder and longer than most. I follow through on my responsibilities. While I may have some quirks, O God, even you cannot deny that I am nothing like the all-too-typical people are these days: living lives filled with irresponsibility, sins, and squalid dependencies.*

That sounds more palatable, doesn't it? Does it sound like little more than a good hunk of self-esteem? If I believe that, between God and me, I've steered clear of most of the dangers, the limitations, and the genetic problems that are the lot of most others, what's wrong with saying so—with celebrating the contrast?

There IS something wrong with it, though. Unfortunately, there is a subtle line that is all too easily crossed when one has lived awhile in fortunate circumstances, when things have gone smoothly, and when successes are coming close together. On the other side of that line, what may once have been humble gratitude, now becomes subtly, but horribly, twisted into self-congratulation, conceit, and—worst of all— a rationale for thinking oneself to be safely and inherently different from the mass of humanity.

In the case of the Pharisee, the key sentence was his first one: *"I thank you, O God, that I am not like other people."* In the remainder of his prayer, we quickly discover that he's not referring to his quirks or incidental differences in talent or resources. No, the man sees his status, achievement, style, and repute as evidence that he is inherently superior to other people. He is certain of it, and he is proud of it. His problem, then, was not that he was so boorish that he said it aloud. His problem was that he believed it to be so.

People do this to themselves in a whole variety of ways, each instance uglier than the last. The man in Jesus' parable did it with the list of virtues he'd attained. *"I always do so-and-so. I never do such-and-such."* (etc., etc.) The virtues WERE virtues. What became ugly and sick was what he inferred from the fact that he'd been able to practice them.

Unfortunately, there is no flag that goes down or any red light that comes on when one of us crosses that invisible line from good deeds, self-discipline, and ethical scrupulousness, pursued for their own sake, to where we begin to see them as evidence that we have climbed above the mass and the mess of ordinary human frailty. Thus, it is entirely possible for what, in early adulthood, was the finest, deepest, and most virtuous of individuals to go on to become imperious, smug, vain, and condescending by the middle years. This person still behaves well and has high ideals. But something has happened to the spirit of the person. There is now an ugly edge of self-righteousness and self-congratulation. Like that Pharisee, this person sincerely believes that she no longer has anything in common with the people "out there" who are so inferior by upbringing, so riven with weaknesses, and so lacking in character that they are prone to constant mistakes, inexcusable sins, and appalling values. Though she'd never say it, often she'll come to think of them as almost another species.

Don't assume, though, that being enthralled with one's own virtue is the only way this distortion of us comes about. Some still get that way as part of a fixation on their own personal ancestry. In ways difficult to understand, their "pedigree" becomes so inflated and distended in their minds, that some become convinced that, because of who they are related to, they are not "just your ordinary human being." Citing genes from a gene pool that may have included certain giants of history, captains of industry, founders of the country, or royalty can generate this fantasy of actually being a "breed apart" genetically. This is not to be confused with being in humble awe of the miracles and accidents of fate that worked together to bring you or me to a place where we have the opportunities and blessings that we have for the moment. No, this is to try to suck an identity, renown, and even nobility from one's great-great-grandfather, for example. It is absurd, but when, for whatever sad reason, one needs to feel that he is intrinsically different from most others, it can seem to work.

Who can forget that incident several years ago when a Chicago Bank contacted a Boston financial institution for references on a young Bostonian they were considering hiring. The two-page letter they received from Boston went on at great length about the fellow's lineage, detailing the fact that his ancestry included the Cabot family on his mother's side and the Vanderbilts on the other. The Chicago bank wrote a terse, but perfect, reply. They said that the information on the man's genealogy was fascinating, but that the Boston bank must have misunderstood the purpose of their inquiry. They hoped to hire the young man as a banker—they didn't anticipate using him for breeding purposes.

Then, too, some people have arrived at this spiritually-distorted condition by believing that what they own and what they control sets them apart and above. They believe that what they see on their own balance sheet adds up to clear evidence that they have achieved an inherent worth that doesn't even belong in the same sentence with the kind of people who have nothing to show for the years they've spent on earth. *"I thank you, God, that I have nothing in common with the likes of them. They've saved nothing, own no property, have been on and off welfare, live from hand-to-mouth."* One hears a lot of echoes of this form of Phariseeism. It happens when, enthralled with one's own financial success, he loses all track of the grace of God—of the fact that we live, survive, and succeed only by God's grace. The differences in financial status that get so much attention in our part of the world are incidental; that is, they indicate nothing more than the fact that a person has an appetite for, and skill at, acquiring money.

To mention one more, religion is also used this way: to create the illusion of being set apart from and inherently above others. *"Surely I am in a different category of God's love, God's protection, God's blessings, and God's help, having believed, as I have, everything I'm supposed to believe about God, Jesus, the Bible, heaven, hell, and miracles. I thank you, God, that I am a believer, unlike those doubters, heretics, heathens, and other wrong believers."* Obviously, it doesn't work that way. What someone has managed to believe can be mildly interesting, but is never important UNTIL and UNLESS we get to see what, if anything, that belief ignites in the way of loving, giving, caring, forgiving, and hope. To make one-self swallow every religious belief presented makes one a curiosity, not a religious hero or superstar.

In fact, our purpose and calling as Christians is not at all that of being superhuman. Rather, it is to become intensely human, in the deepest sense of the word "human."

To take myself to where I see myself as different from most of humanity has nothing to do with being Christian. That is not what Jesus did. He was quite the opposite: startlingly, thrillingly human. The wisest, most Godly people, then, are those who understand how similar they are and how inextricably connected they are to every life around them.

That's why the sweaty, tippy-toe brand of above-it-all goodness—no matter how scrupulous and conscientious—never seems to bespeak God's presence. No, the lives that have most deeply blessed our human adventure have been those that were the most at-home in the middle of the mess of it, honest about themselves, possessing a humble sense of humor about their own imperfections, and an unquenchable certainty that there are wonderful and exciting things that God can accomplish, even with all the quirks and weaknesses that we share.

The parable of Horville Sash may help sew up the principle here. Horville's job was the lowest, entry-level one in the company. He was a mailroom clerk in the basement. One day, he was about to step on a cockroach down there when the roach spoke up and said, *"Spare me and I will grant your fondest wishes."* Horville spared the roach, put it in a large jar, and wished himself promoted to the second floor. It immediately became so. But after a few weeks of hearing the footsteps above him from the third floor, he went back to the cockroach and asked to be promoted to the third floor as sales coordinator. That wasn't the end of it either. In the months to follow, he repeatedly returned to the roach for more promotions: to the tenth floor, the fifty-third, the seventieth. One day, from his office on the ninety-sixth floor, he was reflecting upon having reached the top in the company. To his amazement, he still felt a bit dissatisfied and wanted more. After some more thought, he formulated his next request. He went back to his roach and said, *"I want you to make me the closest that a human being can be to being God; that is, put me in the position that God himself would hold, were he here."*

Zap! Horville found himself back among the men and women down in the basement mail room.

That's the principle here: not drawing apart, but drawing closer; not being perfect, but being authentic; not what you possess, but what possesses you; and, not primarily your virtues, but, above all, your graces.

Taking Seriously What's Good About You

Mark 7:24-29

Jesus went with his disciples into the territory of Tyre....While there, a woman whose young daughter was possessed by a demonic spirit heard about him and came and fell at his feet. She was a Syrophoenician—a pagan. Nevertheless, she begged Jesus to cast the evil spirit from her daughter. But Jesus said to her, "The children must be fed first. It would be wrong to take the food meant for the children and throw it to the dogs." But she spoke again, saying, "That is true, sir," but even the dogs eat the scraps under the table that fall from the children's meal. Then Jesus said to her, "Woman, you have great faith. Go now to your home for the demon has left your daughter.

As a bystander, it would never have occurred to me to view that woman's behavior as a sign of faith. "Presumptuous" would have been my diagnosis—downright pushy. Jesus, though, seemed to think that she showed exceptional faith—greater faith than any he'd seen to date (according to one translation).

How so? It certainly wasn't that she was some great "closet" believer in orthodox religious principles. She as much as admitted that she was not. Apparently, he felt that it was indicated in her flat refusal to accept his attempt to dismiss her as being unworthy of God's help.

She reminds me some of the young woman who was having difficulty getting into college. When she received yet one more turn-down, she wrote to the admissions office of that school, saying:

Dear Admissions Officer,

I am in receipt of your rejection of my application to your institution. As much as I would like to accommodate you, I find that I cannot accept this rejection. I have already received five rejections from other universities and colleges, and five rejections is, in fact, over my limit. This, then, is to inform you that, even though it may inconvenience you, your non-acceptance of my application is hereby rejected. I intend to appear for classes on August 29th.

One could argue, of course, that this, too, was mere pushiness. Unlike either of those women, if you or I receive a rebuff from someone of stature or authority, aren't most of us inclined to back off—even to give up on whatever it was? Haven't we, as Christians, sometimes been taught that it is commendable to be "meek" and blessed to be "poor in spirit"? Or, that one must never harbor an inflated estimate of himself, etc.? The answer is "Yes, that's a common teaching within Christianity."

So why, then, is Jesus showing such enthusiasm for this lady who seemed so presumptuous, assertive, and obtrusive that she won't accept gracefully the fact that that she did not happen to qualify for his help? (That IS what he told her, at first.) By what twist of logic does THAT become "great faith"?

First, let it be noted that it certainly isn't always so. There are kinds of impudence, insolence, and brazenness that are nothing but the rawest form of arrogance—have nothing whatsoever to do with faith.

But haven't we also seen (and maybe ourselves been guilty of) a kind of prissy humility that is used as a reason for quitting when things get tough or frustrating, or when we encounter opposition? Isn't there a kind of "safe" tentativeness and reticence in which, having taken a stab at whatever it was, one's conscience is now cleared for giving up? Along with it goes carefully keeping one's dreams always in fuzzy shades of gray, not in sharp color. Hopes are kept safely general, always cautious, minimal, and somewhat indifferent. Prayers given by such a person have no teeth to them.

Speaking of that, I read only this week, a touching incident that bears somewhat upon this. The writer tells of taking his family to a restaurant. When the meal was served, his six-year-old son, who had recently become interested in matters religious, said that he wanted to "say grace" before they ate. So, there at the restaurant table, in a very audible six-year-old voice, he prayed:

God is good. God is great. Thank you God for our food, and I will thank you more if Mom lets us get ice cream for dessert. And liberty and justice for all! Amen.

The writer says,

Along with the laughter from the other customers at the surrounding tables, I heard a woman remark in disgust, *"That's what's wrong with this country. Kids today don't even know how to pray; asking God for ice cream! Why, I never!"*

My son heard it and burst into tears. He asked me, *"Did I do it wrong? Is God mad at me?"*

As I held him and assured him that he had done a terrific job and that God was certainly not mad at him, an older gentleman approached the table. He winked at my son and said, *"I happen to know that God thought that was a great prayer."*

"Really?" my son asked.

"Cross my heart," the man replied. Then, in a theatrical whisper, he added (nodding in the direction of the woman whose remark had started all of this), *"Too bad she never asks God for ice cream. A little ice cream is good for the soul sometimes."*

Naturally, I bought my kids ice cream at the end of the meal. My son stared at his for a moment and then did something I certainly will never forget. He picked up his sundae and, without a word, walked over and placed it in front of the woman. With a big smile he told her, *"Here, this is for you. Ice cream is good for the soul sometimes, and my soul is good already."*

Of all my children, he is by far my most trying: the quickest to anger, the first one to break something, and the last one to do as he is told. None of that matters though, 'cause like he said, his soul is good already.

That little boy's comment, as he presented his ice cream to that priggish and imperious woman, goes right to the core of this: *"My soul is good already."* Yes! While not overlooking any of the obvious dangers of inappropriate pride and self-importance, it is, at the same time, a major cop-out to trivialize or disparage or underrate the good that resides in you and me. It is sacrilegious to shrug off as inconsequential, the unique light with which each of us has been endowed. That's why it IS an explicit matter of faith to be able, in our most vulnerable and insecure moments, to speak and to act as one who knows that. *"I carry in me the very image of God. I am a full-blown bearer of God's presence; God has something unique to offer through me; and, by whatever passion and courage God gives me, I will not allow it to be discounted."*

That is what that ancient woman did. She said, in effect, *"Yes Jesus, I realize that I am a pagan and that I know much too little about matters spiritual. But I know that my soul is good. So, whoever God is, I'm daring to believe that that God cares about me and cares about my troubled daughter's problems."*

Do you begin to see what is at stake here? It is that, while most of us human beings are bothered by and worried about the most unfortunate sides of us (our stupidities, weak spots, bad motives), that leads much, much too easily to falling off the other side of the bed—denying or shrinking back from the best that there is about us. There is something seductive about mediocrity, "averageness," and self-deprecation. It usually seems safer and simpler.

Letting yourself off the hook, on the grounds that you are suffering from an acute case of "averageness," can be made to sound almost humble, can't it? Faced, for example, with someone who has given of himself sacrificially or who has poured herself out in tackling some horrible problem, haven't you heard it said, *"That's just wonderful, but I could NEVER be like that!"* That is not humility at all, nor is it honest. Had she said, *"I am unwilling to pay the personal price to apply myself as did he,"* or *"I am too protective of my own comfort and security to take risks or make sacrifices like that,"* then that would come closer to the truth. But the "I-could-never-be-like-that" statements are no more than denial of the best that there is about us.

That is also what it is when someone says,

"I could never forgive that."

"I could never live with that."

"I am incapable of making adjustments like that."

"I'll never understand that."

"I'm much too hurt to ever come back to life after this."

All that is, is a forcible pushing away of the best that there is to us, an implicit denial of the fact of God's image in us.

That is also what it is when I use my heredity, or my upbringing, or my former bad experiences, or yet other supposedly built-in flaws and God-given defects as a means to keep the lid on any high expectations of me. Humble as that can be made to sound, that's all it is: distracting or excusing ourselves from the best that there is in us and about us and to us. It frees us to give up after taking a timid stab at something and have it fail. It makes it seem okay not to be as effective, as powerful, as determined, or as loving as God has created us.

You may have heard the story about the woman who accompanied her husband to his physician's office for the report session, following his physical. The doctor called her into his office alone and told her, *"Your husband is suffering from a very serious condition, which will be substantially worsened by any stress, whatsoever. In fact, you are the key to keeping him alive. This is what you need to do or he'll be dead within a year.*

Each morning, cook him an elaborate, but healthy breakfast. During those early morning hours, always be pleasant and playful and accommodating. Similarly, make lunch and dinner not only delectable and nutritious, but also festive and blissful times.

Don't burden him with chores. Don't bother him with your problems. Make love with him daily and, in short, be right there to accommodate his every whim. If, for the next twelve months you do all of that, he'll recover from this and be well again."

As they were walking out, the husband asked, *"Well, what did the doctor say?"*

"That you're going to die," she replied.

Right! She'd already decided that she was not THAT good. And people do that. Whether it is the deepest of our capacity to love, or of our ability to feel empathy, or our determination to see justice, or a unique talent or passionate concern or special insight, so often it feels simpler and safer to keep the lid on it. For once a person gets out there, living close to the best of what God has made of him, there's no telling what will happen. Who knows what you'll get drawn into, what risks will tempt you, how it could change you, remake you, or even radicalize you!

There is an old, somewhat familiar legend that addresses this. It tells of a primordial time when people had so abused their wisdom and so twisted the good, that the angels met together and decided that, for the time being, the true wisdom and good needed to be hidden from human beings, lest they pervert them. The problem was, though, *"Where could they hide them?"*

One angel suggested burying them deep in the earth, but the others said that it would only be a matter of time before humans would dig down and find them. Another suggested the bottom of the ocean. That, too, was rejected, because the human fascination with bodies of water was bound to bring ocean exploration. For the same reason, outer space was also ruled out as a hiding place. They were stymied until a heretofore silent angel came up with the perfect solution. He said, *"We must hide the real font of good and the true wisdom deep inside of the human beings themselves. By everything I've seen of them and know of them, the last place they would expect to find good is in themselves."*

Good point! Oh, don't push it too far, or it becomes arrogance. But a real and vital part of faith is just this: the taking responsibility for one's giftedness, the owning of the particular formulations of good that are ours, and the making sense of that particular grace of God that has been allocated to each one of us.

That, again, is what that Syrophoenician woman was doing that day when she refused to be dismissed, saying in effect, *"Look, I, too, am a part of the family of God. Even though I'm not a Jew, I, too, carry God's image. I, too, am some of the salt of the earth and light of the world. Now, for God's sake, please help me!"* And an open-mouthed Jesus said, *"Woman, GREAT IS YOUR FAITH! What you ask will be done."*

So that isn't brazenness or impudence or lack of modesty. No! It is a person who knows that she is a daughter of God and is determined to proceed accordingly. Any of us can do that. But we do have to be willing to give up the safe, narcotic comfort of false humility, of calculated mediocrity, of intentional "averageness," and of protective indifference.

It is worth it, though. For a lot of us, this is the single most unexplored frontier—this one of discovering all that it can possibly mean to be the person that each of us is, as seen through the eyes of God.

Getting to Know You

Occasionally I give in to the temptation to read those "personal" ads in newspapers. I suspect that I am not the only one who sneaks a look at them out of curiosity. Typically, they will read something like:

Attractive, divorced, financially secure female chemical engineer, age 32, height, 5'4", weight, 110; loves music, the out-of-doors, good books, gourmet meals, travel, and sports; is good-natured, cultured, sensuous, and always a lot of fun. Seeking handsome gentleman who is warm, intelligent, and well educated.

Or:

Single man, widowed, middle-management executive, age 51 (but looks no more than 40), 6'3", 202 pounds; healthy, athletic, playful, adventuresome, bright, passionate, a skilled handyman, many interests, and very broad-minded. Looking for an attractive, attentive, classy woman in her thirties, with no children.

I don't read those ads, I hasten to say, because I am looking for a new relationship. I am drawn to them because I find it fascinating to see what it is that these men and women choose to disclose, when, in three or four dozen words, they set out to describe themselves. Typically, the ads manage to tell us very little—almost nothing of importance. What they do reveal, though, is what the writers assume is the most important information about them and/or what they think will be most important to other people.

If the question is, though, *"What of this man or woman is being revealed here?"*, most of the time the answer is surface stuff, window-dressing, packaging, nothing more. Nevertheless, the ads must get results because the number of them seems to be growing.

I did see a copy of one that, in a strange-but-delightful way, was a bit more revealing.

It said,

Loser seeks mate. I'm a lazy, spoiled, insensitive, irresponsible, insecure, desperate, single white male. I hate art, hate travel, hate reading and exercise. I love tuna noodle casserole, miniature golf, and tattoos. I love sitting, sleeping, drinking beer, and watching nature films on television. I am looking for a single white female, former cheerleader with amnesia, one who receives $100,000.00 from a trust fund, and would enjoy romantic evenings doing my laundry and cleaning my house. Sex is optional—only when I opt for it. My saving grace? A sense of humor.

In its strange way, that ad does tell us something. It's not only that he has a sense of humor, but that he has an acute sense of the absurdity of marketing oneself the way one would a used car; that is, by listing a lot of glossy, but superficial qualities. One might even guess that his zany ridicule of self-advertising, by seeming to do it, indicates some kind of depth to him.

So what, then, would be revealing or self-disclosing? Nothing that we'll likely see on a "personals" page. If one did get written, it might be something more like:

Divorced man, age 40; still trying to face up to, and come to terms with, my part in my marriage breakup. I am a life-long struggler with feelings of insecurity, and tend to need more encouragement than one should. I am a mixed success in my vocation, but am doing okay right now. I am carrying 20 pounds more than is good for me. I will probably end up as bald as my grandfather. I am cautiously hopeful, though, that I have grown enough in self-understanding and personal contentment that, if someone gives me a chance, this time I will be able to handle closeness without finding it threatening. I am looking for a relationship with someone willing to risk sharing that hope.

Or:

> Single female, age 36, member of Alcoholics Anonymous, and sober for nearly two years. I am considered quite attractive, but in my life, that's been more of a problem than a help. In the past I have tended to be a narcissistic person and somewhat inclined to self-pity. I am looking for someone—a close companion—who won't let me get by with that. I believe I have learned quite a lot about acceptance and forgiveness, and I think I finally understand what it might mean to love unselfishly. That's what I have to bring to a relationship.

Would anyone respond to an ad so candid, so unadorned, and so revealing? Probably not. Why knowingly become involved with anyone whom you already know is haunted by insecurities, is pursued by fears and anxieties, and is emotionally complicated?

Why? Because emotionally complex, insecurity prone, worry-haunted people are the only kind of human beings to be found anywhere. The only difference at all is between those who grow through it, are deepened by it, and become larger-spirited persons because of it, andthose who desperately cling to the illusion that, with a trim body, smooth social skills, sufficient financial resources and the right list of achievements, somehow "shallow" can be made to work for them.

So there is really no choice there at all. In our more thoughtful moments, we do know, don't we, that only the blindest, dullest, or most superficial person could seriously think that where he falls on the height/weight charts, how tastefully she dresses, which schools she attended, the prestige of his profession, his sexual prowess, her financial resources, his athletic ability, or any of the other stuff that we and our advertising industry keep pretending are important, have anything of real importance to say about who we are as human beings.

Think about it for a moment: what has gone into creating that which is best and deepest about you and, for that matter, those for whom you have the greatest respect and admiration?

If, for example, you are a person who, at this point in your life, has ended up with a lot of close relationships with others, the odds are that the capacity for that was forged in you through some tough times. It may have come, for example, when the life of someone very close—someone you loved deeply—was suddenly removed. Other times, it can have to do with a low spot in a person's life, one in which she discovered what a crucial gift she had in the support and empathy of others. A time of having been "marginalized," rejected, or isolated has created that capacity for closeness in yet others. The net effect, though, is coming to treasure and prioritize closeness to other people, above all else.

If you've turned out to be one of those people who seems to hold a Ph.D. in the matter of relishing life itself, in all of its dimensions—time, beauty, opportunity, awe—there is a good chance that you got that way when, at some point, you had to look squarely at your own mortality—stare your own death in the face.

If you are one with exceptional self-understanding and, therefore, as is often true, an uncanny perception of what is really going on inside other people, there is a good chance that it was created through an experience of personal failure, of embarrassment, or maybe of deep remorse. It'll do that—carve a depth that doesn't happen in a person in any other way.

If you are one of those somewhat rare persons who no longer has a facade, who couldn't care less about keeping up appearances, and who is unabashedly candid about his own errors and quirks, that grace can probably be traced to some unsettling time when every pretense and affectation was stripped away from you; so much so that, now, posing and putting up a front feels unnecessary and patently stupid.

The most creative junctures of people's lives do tend to be tied to their need for healing, need of forgiveness, need of support, need to reverse themselves, or need for comfort.

In fact, looked at carefully, those much-quoted, too often sentimentalized beatitudes from Jesus' Sermon on the Mount address this very candidly. Looked at carefully, what they really say is something like this:

Blessed—**not cursed**—are those who are poor in spirit, those who have known a lot in the way of pain, disappointment, and frustration. They, not the ones you might think, are where God's work becomes most apparent. Theirs is the Kingdom of God.

Blessed—**not flawed**—are the meek, the humble minded, the vulnerable. They are the ones who end up approaching life with awe and who have the deepest appreciation. They are, that is, the ones who inherit the earth.

Blessed—**not robbed**—are those who mourn. They are the ones who have had to learn what it is both to give and to receive strength, who now know how to accept the gifts of support and comfort from others.

Blessed—**not disturbed**—are those who have that radical hunger for what is just and right. They may seem driven, uncompromising, and too intense at times, but they will find meaning in it. That is, they shall be filled.

Blessed—**not dreamy-eyed and misguided**—are the pure in heart, the ones with that determined vision of all that could be and should be; those idealists who don't seem able to settle for being just practical and pragmatic. For all of the frustration with which they appear to live, *"They,"* Jesus said, *"are the ones who see God."*

It really does come down to this: that, should you wish to understand God's grace to you, God's touch upon your life, God's creative work within you, rather than sorting through award certificates, a list of current assets, achievement plaques, positions held, and letters of commendation, you must go back, instead, and look at the places where you had to do a lot of healing. Those places where you were NOT delivered out of the trouble in the nick of time, where you were unable just to "think" the frustration or hurt away, where you wrestled desperately with your doubts or with the cynicism encroaching upon you; or where you felt terribly cut off and alone.

While one could wish it were otherwise, the un-mistakable truth is that the majority of what has humanized you and me, what has deepened us, and made large-spirited persons of human beings, has come packaged as struggle, frustration, daunting complexity, grief, remorse, and a lot more of what seemed, at the time, to be God's absence rather than God at work.

The late theologian, Paul Tillich, said it beautifully in one of his sermons. He said:

> God's grace strikes us when we are in great restlessness and pain. It strikes us when we walk through the dark valley of a meaningless and empty life. It strikes us when we feel that our separation is deeper than usual, because we have violated another life—a life which we love or one from which we are estranged. It strikes us when our disgust for our own being, our indifference, our weakness, our hostility, and our lack of direction and composure have become intolerable to us. It strikes us when, year after year, the longed-for perfection of life does not appear, when the old compulsions reign within us, as they have for decades, when despair destroys all joy and courage...
>
> It is as though a voice were [nevertheless] saying, "You are accepted." You ARE accepted; accepted by that which is greater than you and the name of which you do not know. ....
> It is such moments that make us love our life, that make us accept ourselves, not for our goodness or in self-complacency, but in our certainty of the eternal meaning of our life... We

receive the power to say "yes" to ourselves. Peace enters into us and makes us whole. Self-hate and self-contempt dissolve and we are at one with ourselves. Therein has God's grace reached us.

The Shaking of the Foundations by Paul Tillich

All this could require reworking some of our thinking about what have, thus far, been our real assets and blessings. It could require reconsidering what have been the most important experiences in life, suggest a new way of looking at our own histories and understanding of where it was that God was most specifically at work in us. But make no mistake about it, this IS the way meaning is brought to life in us most of the time. And, as odd as it would be to see it included in one of those "personal ads" it—NOT height, weight, age, financial condition, educational level, or being photogenic—reveals the important truth about you and me.

"What has life taught me about my own finiteness and fallibility?"

"How much have you had to learn (and how many times) about recovery, repentance, and being reinvented and reborn?"

"Does the person understand how fortunate he was that time when he was stripped forever of his former ego-fantasies and delusions of superiority?

"What, in her life and about her life, is it that she give thanks for when she gives thanks?"

Those, and some others like them, are not merely interesting questions about who we really are. They are the ONLY truly important ones.

Untangling the Piety Puzzle

Some time ago, there appeared on our cartoon bulletin board, a cartoon which showed a wife saying to her husband,

When people ask me what you are like, I tell them that you are a saint. That usually shuts them up!

It probably *would* be a "conversation stopper." People don't always know what to make of it when it is said, for example, that someone is a paragon of virtue, is really righteous, is pious, or, as in this case, is a "saint." Words like that, as you've noticed, are used both positively and negatively. *"She was a wonderful, devout, pious woman,"* someone will say in high praise. But just as often, one will hear statements like, *"It is his insufferable piousness that makes my flesh crawl!"* Describing someone as "very Christian" will at one time, indicate respect and admiration, while at another time, it will mean that it is time to head for cover. *"Please don't seat me next to her!"* So, there seems to be something of a love/hate relationship when it comes to the matter of personal devoutness and piety.

It is not that we are against piety. Officially, most of us are in favor of earnestly trying to be a good, righteous person—of being devoted, reverent, and dutiful. AND YET, just let it get back to us that someone has referred to us as "pious," and it may very well send us looking for some way to prove that we are NOT pious. That's because it so easily conjures up images of being tight-lipped, disapproving, scripture-quoting, sallow-faced, and otherworldly—not the way most of us prefer to be viewed.

My father (himself a clergyman) used to tell of an incident in which a woman was sent to an airport to pick up a visiting minister. Unfortunately, she had never met him and had no idea what he looked like. After most of the arriving passengers had dispersed, finally she approached one of the remaining men that she thought might be the right one. *"Excuse me,"* she said, *"but might you be a Christian minister?"*

"Oh, goodness no!" the man replied. *"I'm recovering from a bad case of hepatitis. That's why I look this way."*

Apparently to her, the pasty, fragile, undernourished appearance was the very "hue" of piety—not a great advertisement for goodness.

Another expression of this common ambivalence toward "being good" is there in the little poem that says,

> I keep the rules for being good,
> Behaving just the way I should.
> My mother taught me not to smoke, and I don't;
> Or listen to a dirty joke, and I don't.
> At church they taught me not to wink at pretty girls or even
> think about intoxicating drink, and I don't.
> To sow wild oats I know is wrong, and I don't.
> Some guys chase women, wine, and song, but I don't.
> I don't kiss girls, not even one—in fact, I don't know how it
> is done.
> You wouldn't think I'd have much fun. WELL I DON'T!

And yet, underneath all such perplexity and all mixed feelings, we become part of Christian churches, hoping that one, nevertheless, can truly be a good person without being sanctimonious. We believe (or at least hope) that there is a way of being righteous without being self-righteous, that one can hold strong convictions without becoming closed-minded, that it is possible to be devout without religious haughtiness, and that being spiritual doesn't have to mean being unrealistic. The hope is that, despite all aberrations and pitfalls, there can be for us a coherent, unself-conscious, non-ponderous way in which you and I can be the presence of God, perhaps something along lines of what we saw in Jesus.

Speaking of Jesus, this was no less confusing in his time. Then, too, people struggled to make sense of the fact that there were some charming, attractive—even fascinating—sinners and there were also some stale, irascible, insufferable saints.

To further "stir the pot" on this matter, is the fact that there were a substantial number of Jesus' contemporaries who saw HIM, not as virtuous (as, after the fact, we perceive him), but as blatantly sinful. He was criticized, for example, for what they saw as his playing loose with Biblical standards, including a couple of the Ten Commandments. They also thought him to be much too cavalier about longstanding religious practices and principles. They felt that he showed appallingly bad judgment in some of the individuals with whom he chose to associate. At times, he did and said things that were really disruptive. Yes, respectable people (including religious leaders) saw Jesus as one of those charming-but-dangerous people that come along from time to time, unnecessarily confusing people and undermining discipline, order, and respect for authority.

So, where does this all leave us in the matter of what it is to be good, to be virtuous, to be Christ-like? Will doing all I can in order to be as nearly perfect as I can, or always being as nice and respectable as is humanly possible, or scrupulously following every rule of which I am aware, or relentlessly pursuing and attacking sinfulness every chance I get possibly lead to my becoming stuffy and obnoxious? AND YET if, at the same time (as I think we all know), being immoral, shameless, disreputable, crude, and lawless are wrong and are ultimately self-destructive, AND IF ON TOP OF THAT, moral mediocrity and spineless "averageness" are also appalling, what in the world can it mean to be Christian?

Another cartoon seems symbolically to portray it. It shows two frightened-looking little Boy Scouts, obviously lost in the woods while on a hike. They are trying to control their panic by repeating the Scout Law, saying: *"I am trustworthy, loyal, helpful, friendly, courteous, kind, obedient, cheerful, thrifty, brave, clean, reverent, ... and LOST, LOST, LOST in these damn woods."* Trying to live an effective and yet intelligible Christian life can sometimes feel that way: *"I am devout, believing, pious, obedient, careful, respectful, and responsible, but nevertheless uncertain, disoriented, and often way off the path."*

Most of you will recall the encounter of Jesus with the wealthy young ruler. In a way, that fellow seemed to show some of the distress of those Boy Scouts. The passage says:

> *A man of the ruling class put this question to him: "Master, what good thing can I do to attain eternal life?" Jesus said to him, "You know the commandments: 'Do not commit adultery, do not murder, do not steal, do not give false evidence, honor your father and your mother.'" The man said, "I have kept all of those commandments since I was a boy." Hearing this, Jesus said, "There is still this: go sell all that you have and distribute to the poor...."*
> *When he heard this the man's heart sank, for he was very wealthy.*
> Luke 18:18-23

It was an important and revealing exchange.

The first thing to note about it is that Jesus did not devalue or discount in any way the importance of following the commandments (as the man said he had done all of his life). Not here or anywhere else does Jesus ever shrug off as unimportant, the personal ethics, practices, and disciplines that have to do with being humane and with maintaining personal integrity.

At the same time, however, note that Jesus did not say to him, *"You've followed all the commandments? That's amazing! That's as much as God expects of anybody. If you can just keep that up, you will have been everything that is humanly possible."*

No. Instead Jesus shocks his socks off with this crazy-sounding suggestion that, after all of that, in his case it would be a good idea to now begin using what he owned to assist the poor. Hearing this, the man was upset and left—and understandably so. He had come to Jesus sincerely looking for some additional sacred disciplines and practices, or maybe additional kinds of belief to supplement his many virtues and his admirable ethics. What he is told is to do something that would disrupt, unsettle, and rearrange what he considered to be a very good, if not exemplary, life. What possible merit could there be to a suggestion like that?

But right there is a clear example of the goal toward which Jesus was always pushing people (you and me included). Diligently performing admirable good deeds and avoiding bad behaviors turns out, in the Christian Gospel, to be only the basic minimum—the elementary part of the good for which God created us.

When one stops to think about it, we didn't need Jesus to reiterate the minimums: to tell us, for example, that stealing, murdering, lying, and exploiting are not good. We didn't even need a Jesus to point out that treating people with the kindness and mercy with which we ourselves would like to be treated, is a pretty good idea. That had been around for centuries before him. It was and is important, but it is NOT anything close to the main event. And THAT is what we are hearing in his final words to this fellow who was, again, a solid, ethical person. *"Good!"* Jesus says in effect, *"You've mastered the basics. Now if you really want abundant life, do something creative, something exciting, something that makes a difference, something extravagant with what you have become and what you have."*

Unfortunately, that was more good, more Godliness,

more purpose than this very nice man could stomach. He excused himself and went home to settle, we suppose, for continuing to behave himself—being law-abiding and being respectable.

An analogy for this was suggested to me by someone years ago. It related it to composing music. The idea was that, as important in music as are the principles of harmonics and rhythm, one cannot create a beautiful musical composition merely by never violating the principles of harmony, by scrupulously obeying the principles of rhythm, by tenaciously believing in the bass clef and the treble clef, or by being loyal to a key signature. Those are part of the basics in music, but the beauty and the power of a musical composition are something far more than that.

Similarly, good ethics, good conduct, and good manners are vital, essential under-girding; but where the image of God is truly revealed in you and me, where God becomes incarnate in you and me, is where we take it from there. That "Kingdom of God" to which he kept inviting us, requires our imagination, improvisation, creative hoping, generosity, spirituality, empathy, and spontaneity—all of which is far more than the sweaty kind of piety that we have sometimes seen grow so brittle, rigid, and repugnant.

It was what was so refreshing and startling about Jesus' way with people. One can get a feeling for it, not only in his telling this particular man to liquidate his assets and go use them in a way he had never considered. Another time, he tells what would have been a barely believable story about a Samaritan who spontaneously risks his life in a robber-infested wilderness for a man who normally would not have even spoken to him. The Samaritan even pays the man's medical expenses.

Another time, Jesus not only defends, he commends a woman who actually wasted several hundred dollars' worth of perfume in an exuberant, extravagant demonstration of deep caring and love.

On another occasion, he becomes really excited about a poverty-stricken lady who gave her last coin away when she should have been on the receiving end of charity, not a contributor.

"When someone slaps you on the cheek," he says in effect, *"I would hope you would have the imagination to come up with something better than slapping him back. Try turning the other cheek. See what that might do."*

On and on it goes like that. And again, none of it is the kind of thing that you can turn into a commandment or code of ethics. NOT AT ALL was he saying, for example, *"Should anyone become wealthy he must always immediately sell everything that he has and give it away,"* or *"If you are poverty stricken, as was the widow, you, too, must always divest yourself of even what little you do have,"* or *"In all cases, you are hereby commanded to keep turning the other cheek for as long as your attacker continues to wish to abuse you."* No, these were not new rules or ethics. They were Godly improvisations. The message was, *"For God's sake, bring some imagination, some spontaneity, some creativity, some innovative forgiveness, and maybe even some playfulness to the struggles, the work, the pain, the needs, the upsets, the opportunities, and the possibilities that swirl around you every day of your life. There are whole other dimensions of "rich" beyond the scrupulous bean-counting, the playing everything safe, the striving for perfection and for always being right, and the preoccupation over the mistakes and sins around us."*

Do you begin to get the flavor of it? Among other things, it turns out that you were probably right to wonder whether some of the rigidly pious, judgmental, fiercely righteous, sanctimonious Christianity that turned you off, was Christ-like. Almost certainly it was not! Had Jesus been anything like that, you never would have heard of him.

No, a big part of the "good news" that unfolded in Jesus is that each one of us being a son or daughter of God is so much more free, more flexible, more exciting, more spontaneous and, yes, more fun than many of us imagine, much less explore.

So get out there and live it that way!

About Those Quirks & Eccentricities

Numbers 20:1-12 (in summary)

In their first month in the wilderness, there was no water for the community of Israel. In their discontent, the people came to Moses saying, "Why have you brought us out into this wilderness where we and our livestock shall all die because there is not even water to drink?"

God then spoke to Moses and said, "Take your shepherd's staff in hand and stand before the assembled people of Israel. Then you shall speak to the rock that is there and the rock will yield water for them and for their beasts to drink."

So Moses gathered the people as the Lord had commanded him. With the whole assembly present, he said to them, "Hear this, you rebels. Must we bring water out of a rock to quiet you?" Then he took his staff, raised it in his hands, and began to strike the rock with it. Water gushed forth and all drank from it.

But God said to Moses, "Because of what you just did in the sight of all the people of Israel, not upholding my holiness before them, you shall not be allowed to lead them into the land which I have promised to them."

One wonders what was so terrible about Moses losing his temper that day? For many weeks, he has put up with the constant complaining, whining, ineptness, and self-pity of this motley mob of ex-slaves. During that same period, there had been very little food or water, no shelter, and not enough sleep. Wouldn't that wear down anyone? One's patience could erode—especially if, like Moses, you are the one in the hot seat.

But as this story has it, because Moses becomes somewhat testy in front of the people and then irritably beats up on a certain rock, rather than talking nicely to it [*perhaps a case of his taking the rock for granite*], God decides to punish Moses for that by not allowing him ever to set foot in the promised land.

Is that unfair or what? Despite what for Moses will be decades of stress, of risk, and of frustration as he prods the people of Israel toward maturity and nationhood, and because he got a bit impatient that afternoon, Moses won't be there for the culmination of it all.

For God to do that would be picky, mean, and trivial, and I don't believe that it happened exactly that way, nor should you. I don't believe that God ever vengefully pounces like that upon someone's weak moments or bad episodes to clobber him with punishments such as forbidding that Moses ever enter the promised land.

BUT, as I have pointed out before in regard to other Old Testament stories, though the theology is sometimes primitive, nevertheless, there usually turns out to be several layers of wisdom, insight, and truth to them that can shed important light on our human adventure. Don't ever write them off because they don't conform, at every point, to modern thought.

How could that be so in this story? It has to do with the fact that, despite the wonderful, amazing, courageous things that Moses did (as sometimes turns out to be true of human beings), he had his own troublesome internal barriers to joy and fulfillment. As much as they revered him in their memories, they also remembered something about him that frequently got in the way—a flaw of his which, in effect, kept him out of his own promised land. For someone else, it could have been perfectionism; for yet another, pessimism; for still another, timorousness. What it apparently was for Moses, though, was a fretful, irritable, chronic impatience.

Seen that way, the story suddenly goes from being an all but incomprehensible one (in which God badly over-reacts to Moses' moment of ill-humor) to a parable that inquires about your and my impatience—whether, by any chance, we are tolerating in ourselves something that might be keeping us out of our own promised lands.

Just as some of you can, I also can easily imagine how good it felt that afternoon to stand in front of that sullen, complaining mob and rain down multiple blows on that rock until the water gushed forth, shutting up their whining for at least awhile. In fact, I could make the case that his intolerance of how long all this was taking, his being appalled at the lack of progress, and his determination to get something to happen one way or another was actually a kind of "righteous impatience"—something of a virtue. Mine always is, isn't yours? At least that's the way it feels at the time. It feels righteous, even through all the aggravation of it.

I strongly suspect that, like me, my brother Moses was a compulsive wrist-watch checker. I'd be willing to bet that when he shopped at the nearest supermarket there in the wilderness, that he seethed with fury when the person ahead of him had obliviously wheeled a whole cart full of groceries into the express lane. I'd be willing to bet that Moses was a finger-tapper, a horn-honker, an engine-gunner, and a finisher of other people's sentences for them. I'm sure that he was one who regularly worked himself into a lather when Mrs. Moses took longer getting ready to go out than, in his mind, he had planned. Surely some of you recognize him— in fact, may know him embarrassingly well.

A feeling for it is described in a book entitled *The Sidelong Glances Of a Pigeon Kicker*. The principal character is a college dropout who now drives a taxi. At one point, he says,

> The woman in the back seat of my taxi told me that my honking the horn would not make the traffic jam go away. I asked her how it was that she knew so much. She said I was young. As I grew older, I would learn the virtue of patience. I told her that patient people were people who were dead; that honking the horn was my inextinguishable voice of outrage, and if it didn't make the traffic jam go away, it certainly made me feel better. She said that I was a disgrace. I said I was glad.

You caught there, didn't you, that rather than being

apologetic, the man was openly militant in his impatience. One gets that way when he or she is certain, beyond any shadow of a doubt, that the interruptions and digressions are intolerable, that this misuse of time is atrocious, that the slow pace of things is inexcusable, that the lack of efficiency is outrageous, and that the failure of others to share your sense of urgency is a flaw in their character. Do you see? *"All I am asking is that things be kept moving at a good pace, that the stuff getting in the way of quick progress be ripped away, that the pressure be kept on so that this doesn't take all day. If that's impatience, so be it. I'm proud of it."*

Yes, impatience can have a very righteous feeling to it, can't it? What could possibly be wrong with insisting upon saving precious time, overcoming indolence, and demanding some efficiency?

What is wrong is that it becomes, for some, an utterly graceless way of life—a driving impulsion that (to use the imagery of those ancient Hebrews in telling Moses' story) keeps a person out of his own promised land. Yes, the person ends up barred from the promised land of joy because, *"How can one feel joy when surrounded by exasperating people and sluggish circumstances?"* She is barred from the promised land of personal inner peace because of that nagging sense that if, at every moment, she isn't making sure things keep moving, no one will. He is kept out of the promised land of what should be today's beauty and joy because, mentally, he is already way on up ahead worrying about getting to tomorrow "on schedule," if not ahead of schedule.

So, again, for all of the genuinely superb and admirable qualities of one like Moses, he, nevertheless, carries within him his own barrier to personal fulfillment and peace, and, to some extent, thus becomes his own enemy.

Bruno Bettleheim wrote something that touches firmly on this. He wrote:

Our modern infatuation with speed is a very real handicap. Our new yardstick of time tends to be the machine, not the living cell. Our image of time no longer rests on the slow growth of trees nor in the nine months it still takes before a baby is ready to be born. ... There ARE time tables in human development that can only be hurried at a painful and deadening cost. Violence is the behavior of the person who cannot wait.

What he says rings disturbingly true, doesn't it: both the "painful and deadening cost" of our impatience and the fact (when one reflects upon it) that violence is the behavior of those who are unable to wait. So-called "road rage," about which we frequently read, comes to mind as a particularly lurid, modern example.

In *Zorba The Greek*, Kazantzakis gets at it when he puts these words in the mouth of one young character:

> I remember one morning when I discovered a cocoon in the bark of a tree, just as the butterfly was making a hole in its case and preparing to come out. I waited awhile, but it was too long in appearing and I became impatient. I bent over it and breathed on it to warm it. I warmed it as quickly as I could and the miracle began to happen before my eyes, faster than life. The case opened, the butterfly started slowly crawling out. I shall never forget my horror when I saw how its wings were folded back and crumpled. The butterfly tried with its whole trembling body to unfold them, but in vain. It had needed to be hatched out patiently, and the unfolding of the wings should be a gradual process in the sun. My breath had forced the butterfly to appear, all crumpled, before its time. It struggled desperately and, a few seconds, later died in the palm of my hand.
>
> That little body is, I do believe, the greatest weight I have on my conscience. For I realize today that we must not hurry, we should not be impatient, but that we should confidently obey the eternal rhythm. Oh, if only that little butterfly could always flutter before me to show me the way.

Perhaps that is a tad bit overly-sentimental, but it does

beautifully pick up on Bettleheim's point about a certain kind of violence subtly lurking in our unwillingness to wait.

So not unlike that butterfly experience, when one puts on enough pressure, trying to speed up the unfolding of a personal relationship, the odds are, he'll kill it. It works that way because human relationships unfold at their own unique speed.

Continue to impatiently increase the pace of your living and, without exception, you WILL destroy the peace that was meant to be there in your living.

Impatiently rant, rave, fume, and snarl to build fires under those around you and, notwithstanding the fact that they'll probably humor you and indulge you—whether you sense it or not—you will have exchanged their respect for mere deference or, worse yet, for apprehension.

Always push headlong for quick, measurable, bottom-line results—for the "quick fixes"—and, while you may force some kind of results that way, don't expect lasting ones or creative ones or ones that have much meaning to them. It just doesn't work that way. In fact, here too, in all sorts of ways, it deprives us of our own promised lands; NOT because God inflicts it on us as a punishment, but because, unlike what one might think, a certain "holy patience" happens to be the price of getting to where we need to be in life.

I think it is instructive to note that, according to our Christian Gospel, when God set out to express God's love, God's hope, God's good will, and, in general, shed some light upon human life, it happened the long, slow way. There were, with Jesus, thirty-some years of emerging, growing, unfolding, and revealing. And even then, it was ONE encounter, ONE incident, ONE awakening, or ONE thought or insight at a time.

I seriously doubt that that has been amended and now "the pace on earth," not "peace on earth," has become God's will for us.

Impatience is not, as you know, everyone's problem. But for those of us who have it, let's not shrug it off as normal or as a sign of motivation or of healthy ambition. Not only is that *not* what it is, it actually turns us into bulls in life's china shop. It deprives us of the very joys, the fulfillments, and the graces, ... again, the "promised lands" that God intended for us.

Afraid, Yes–But Without Terror

A woman awakened her husband one night at 2:00 a.m., telling him that THIS TIME she was absolutely certain she had heard a burglar moving around downstairs. The husband, who had been through this many times before, was doubtful. Still, he dragged himself out of bed and stumbled down the stairs. Suddenly, there was a flashlight in his face and the muzzle of a handgun pressed against his ribs. In a menacing whisper, the burglar warned that if he wished to continue living, he had better not make a sound or try anything heroic.

The husband readily assured the burglar that he would give him no trouble whatsoever on one condition. The condition was that the burglar come upstairs with him for a moment. He explained, "*My wife has been expecting you every night for more than twenty years. I want her to meet you now that you are finally here.*"

You can see where this husband was coming from, can't you? As unpleasant and menacing as was this real-life, flesh-and-blood burglar, he was nothing compared to the disembodied specter of "burglarness" that his wife had made a part of their nights for twenty years. The real burglar would merely grab a few things and soon be gone. This husband's hope was that, if his wife saw the real thing, then the "other burglar"—the one that, for all of those years, had terrorized his wife's fantasies and tormented her soul from within—might go away.

It probably didn't work, but it does touch upon the distorting hold that fears and anxieties so often have upon our lives. And it is not, obviously, that there aren't some things in life of which to be afraid. Aggravated burglary, for example, does happen. To be a victim is frightening and terribly unnerving. Even so, at some point, it is over and the victims move on with their lives. That lady had, in effect, made burglary a long-term, fully-nourished dread that haunted her life, and her husband's sleep, for two decades.

Though its forms are usually less bizarre and less comical than hers, overfed fears that cripple our spirits are terribly common. The amount of thought, anxiety, imagination, and, yes, lost sleep that are invested in worry over possible illnesses that haven't happened, but theoretically could; terrible embarrassments or humiliations that could be waiting in the wings, about to happen; tragedies and disasters that might suddenly overtake one; or possible old mistakes that could be about to catch up with you, is downright awesome. Chronic, delusional, and illogical fears do seem all too easily able to rob us of personal peace, suck away our confidence, and smother our joy. Often starting when we are quite young, our catalog of fears begins to grow and expand, along with our knowledge, to become a daunting and debilitating disease of the spirit.

In one of his children's poems, Shel Silverstein vividly reminds us of how some of us started torturing ourselves like that in our early years. It says,

> Last night, while I lay thinking here, some "whatifs" crawled inside my ear, and pranced and partied all night long and sang their same old "whatif" song:
> What if I'm dumb in school?
> What if they've closed the swimming pool?
> What if I get beat up?
> What if there's poison in my cup?
> What if I start to cry?
> What if I get sick and die?
> What if I flunk the test?
> What if green hair grows on my chest?
> What if I tear my pants?
> What if I never learn to dance?

Everything seems all swell and then the nighttime

"whatifs" strike again!

> *What if nobody likes me?*
> *What if a bolt of lightning strikes me?*
> *What if I don't grow taller?*
> *What if my head starts getting smaller?*
> *What if the fish won't bite?*
> *What if the wind tears up my kite?*
> *What if they start a war? ... etc. etc.*

Surely you recall some of those, don't you? Many of them seemed to "come out of the blue." We hadn't lived long enough yet to have anything close to direct experience of what, nevertheless, terrorized us as children.

Then too, a lot of the habit of fearing is deliberately fed to us and awakened within us in order to control us or exploit us. When one reflects upon it, how much of advertising is based on just that: creating negative possibilities in our minds, then selling us protection from whatever it is? Garrison Keillor, on his Prairie Home Companion show, used to have a regular segment in which he advertised for an imaginary store catering to fear-haunted people. It was called "The Fear-monger Shop." One of the ads for Fear-monger products said:

> Yes, the world is full of big, hairy spiders with large hairy legs. They move all over through the world—mostly in places where we never see them, so we never really know that they are there. Even if you keep your house really clean and you brush away all those cobwebs up in the corner of the dining room, they're there! They're down the basement. You probably know that when you go down there. But that doesn't mean that they always STAY in the basement—especially when you go to sleep at night. They know you're asleep. And that's when those big hairy spiders with their hairy legs come slowly crawling up the stairs and through the living room and into the bedroom and up (shudder)—up right on to your covers and over your arm, crawling right up on your face.

THAT'S WHY you need a bed net from the Fear-monger Shop. It's a tight steel mesh net that fits right over the bed. You tuck it in when you go to bed—all four sides. Only then will you be safe all night. Stop in, first thing tomorrow, at The Fear-Monger Shop.

Beneath the bald absurdity of that spoof lives the fact that, in addition to self-generated fear, much of our advertising industry works full time on ways to make us afraid, insecure, and uncertain. Silverstein could easily have written a parallel poem with lines like:

What if my breath is bad?
What if my teeth don't shine?
What if bacteria are wildly breeding in some
*   unattended corner of the kitchen or bathroom?*
What if I run out of money before I die?
What if I am deficient in some obscure vitamin?
What if my salad oil contains carcinogenic additives?
What if my clothes look out of date?
What if harsh shampoo is ruining my hair?
What if I'm under-insured and get sued?
What if I no longer appear youthful?

So we part with our money to purchase the supposed protection because it seems better to use a few dollars to go through the charade of buying off any fears that can be bought off.

But now we are here as people of faith, right? One might think, therefore, that we would have no such problem—that faith is an automatic, sure-and-certain antidote to any fear.

It would be nice if it were, but it really isn't. Faith is not an antidote to anything that is real in life. That is the first matter to be faced. The fact is, scary things do happen in our world. There are genuinely frightening dangers, threats, and ordeals that do become a part of human life. Religious gimmicks that are supposed to wipe away all fear are just that: gimmicks. Our capacity for fear is part of our self-preservation instinct. It is for our own good that we have the capacity for fear, and nowhere does the Bible try to browbeat us out of it.

Not only is our ability to be afraid, at its best, important and necessary to our living. Often it is a vital part of the truth about what is happening—a part to which you and I need to listen. So don't assume that to be afraid is an automatic failure of courage and character, or that bravado is an automatic sign of character. Our fear of what is right now threatening, dangerous, or terrifying is no more than our minds working and reacting in precisely the way God intended.

The problem comes at the next level of fearing—in the things that we infer from what we fear. Once frightened for good reason, how do I know, for example, that this isn't only the tip of the iceberg, that there aren't mystical, unseen, mysterious, relentless, forces with a lot more in store for me? Burglary had become just that for the woman in the opening story: a dark, omnipresent force out there in the nights of her life. She fed it until it became much larger, more powerful, and more ominous than any two-bit burglar could ever be. Burglars take silverware and furs. She had managed to rob herself of more than 7,000 nights of her adult life.

There is a line in that familiar old 23rd Psalm that has to do with the difference. It is the one that says,

"Even though I walk through the valley of the shadow of death, I will fear no evil."

Did you catch that? It didn't say that I will not be afraid.

It said, *"I will fear NO EVIL."* THAT's the principle here. It is avoiding what you and I do when we take fear to the next level. It happens in several common ways.

For example, another instance of "fearing evil" is when whatever frightened you or me is taken to mean that our luck is now changing, or that that our astrological situation has become negative or that we're out of sync with some numerology or bio-rhythms that pull the strings governing our lives. That is a whole lot more than only fearing what is fearful. It is being self-terrorized by specters of larger, darker forces astride in the universe poised to victimize us.

The more religious equivalent of that brand of fearing evil is the all-too-familiar fear that what is coming toward you is quite likely God's punishment for your past sins. This is an especially nasty form of fearing evil, because it makes God the enemy. For those who do that to themselves, God then, is the "terrorizer," imagined to be just now getting around to "getting back at you." It, too, is a next-level form of fear, borne partly of guilt, but also out of an asinine concept of God.

In addition, to not imagining secondary, behind-the-scenes, insidious forces, there is another important part of managing fear. It is learning not to act our way into embellishing it. For example, every time that wife made her husband get up and go downstairs to look for an intruder, she fueled her fear, rather than quieting it. It works that way. When, in our alarm, we pile on protection upon protection, when caution and safety become an overriding obsession, when, in panic, we react by throwing money at what we fear, by withdrawing, or by running scared, we empower it. To empower the very demon that haunts us is pretty stupid.

A last part of the matter is that which has the most to do with our faith: the absolute importance of cultivating a strong sense of God's presence with us in all of life—not only the pleasant, rewarding, inspiring, or religious ones, but every bit as much in the disconcerting, unnerving episodes. Once more, it won't get rid of any fear that is there for solid and legitimate reasons. It will, however, prevent that awful sense of desperation, despair, and dread that makes fear become so crippling and disorienting. Knowing that, as the 23rd Psalm says, God is still involved with you and with me in even the most terrifying times of life, is the difference between feeling trapped like an animal in some black hole and merely traveling for a time through a dark valley. Whether it is the fear of possible failure, being frightened by a serious illness, dreading an approaching divorce, terror of dying, humiliation, cataclysm or whatever, the sense that you and God are living and moving through it together is a totally different experience than that of imagining that everything has now gone out of control or turned against you, or that you're on some relentless course toward disaster. It doesn't require being a spiritual hero—only mustering enough faith to trust that there will be sufficient courage and light when and as needed.

Yes! If we don't get in its way, there is a strange internal calm—the one that the Bible describes as a peace that passes understanding—that allows us to get our sleep until the night the burglar actually shows up. It is a holy confidence that enables a person to fully embrace today's good and today's joy and not have it sucked away by fearing what tomorrow could conceivably bring. It is to trust that the dark valleys are only incidents and events, not tragic endings or humiliations—unless, in panic, we make them that way.

So, are you and I going to continue to be afraid amidst the crises, dangers, threats, and precarious situations that come our way? I hope so. Fear is important. Without it we'll imperil ourselves and everyone around us.

But will our fears demoralize us, paralyze us. and plunge

us into some kind of neurotic, paranoid siege mentality? I would hope not. If that happens, it is because we let it happen. We do so by borrowing trouble from a future that isn't here yet, by fearing the work of evil forces that aren't out there, and by assuming that the God who created us didn't bother to equip us to deal with the very life and time given to us. To believe that is an insult to God and can make you really crazy.

When Love Misfires
(Scripture: Luke 19:1-10)

A "Dear Abby" column some time ago included a poignant letter, the painful bewilderment of which touched me, and maybe it did you, too.

Dear Abby,
   I am a 38-year-old college-educated woman with a successful career. I have traveled all over the world and enjoyed a variety of life experiences. You are not going to believe this, but I have never been asked out on a date!
   I have gone out socially (I asked the son of a family friend to the junior prom) and have gone out with groups of friends for years. I have even used escort services for business functions. But I have never had a boyfriend or the chance to turn down someone I didn't like.
   Mother and Father told me that there is a lid for every pot. Lately they haven't mentioned the subject.
   I have a good sense of humor and have been told I'm interesting to talk to, but no man has ever shown a romantic interest in me. I dress well, and some people have told me I am pretty. (I have seen some extremely unattractive people who are part of a couple.)
   Two years ago, I adopted a child. I live a full life and don't sit at home or get depressed. However, what I really want in life is to meet a man who shares my interests and wants to build a life with me and my daughter. I can be alone, but I would rather not. Do you have a solution?
—Single In Seattle

It is not difficult to sense that the underlying longing there is to be loved. It is a familiar kind of agony and bewilderment of those for whom, for whatever reason, it doesn't happen. And as you know, sometimes it doesn't.

That fact was echoed in the conversation of two single women; one was telling the other of an acquaintance who had just gone through the death and the cremation of her fourth husband. The other replied, *"That's the way it goes.*

Some of us can't find a man, while others have husbands to burn."

That random aspect of finding loving companionship was the first part of Abby's reply to "Single in Seattle": that is, that for no perceptible reason, and though it is unfair, sometimes people do not ever find the loving relationship for which they long. But Abby did go on then to suggest that it might be worthwhile to have what Abby called "truth sessions" with her most trusted male and female friends, to see if they could offer any insight. Did she, for example, come across to people as unapproachable or emotionally unavailable? Whether something like that was true in her case, we don't know; but the possibility that a person is unwittingly creating barriers to his or her own need and longing to be loved is very real.

Whether for the married or for the unmarried, for the young or for the old, for the popular or for the isolated, remaining unloved (and/or believing oneself beyond the reach of love) can become a source of emotional, social, and spiritual problems. But the fact that the gift or blessing of being loved is often so unpredictable, illogical, and uncontrollable makes this a very frustrating matter. For it IS true that loveable, loving, deserving people, nevertheless, do sometimes end up in life alone and/or emotionally starved in ways that make no sense whatsoever. Others who are selfish, emotionally distorted, and devoid of character are sometimes loved beyond what they either appreciate or deserve.

Yes, that's true. And still, being loved is not ENTIRELY a matter of chance. It can, in fact, be because he or she does not allow himself/herself to be loved. While there is a side of her that wants love, for any number of reasons and through a variety of means, she may barricade or vaccinate herself against really being loved.

One very typical such case in the Bible seems to have been the man Zacchaeus. You probably remember his story.

He was a small man, a wealthy one, but had amassed his wealth working for the Roman oppressors, squeezing arbitrary taxes from his own people. For that and maybe other reasons, he was unpopular. Like many of his brothers and sisters down through history, his social isolation and his feelings of rejection fed on each other. That is, since people disliked him, he thickened his skin toward them. To avoid the pain of further rejection, he would reject and repel others before they could do so to him. It is a common survival strategy for one like him: *"Maybe I won't feel your spurning and exclusion of me if I reject you first."* Had you asked him about it, he would have undoubtedly assured you that, yes, he definitely wanted people to like him and love him, but that he knew it would never happen, since everyone he knew was much too mean and judgmental.

On the day of his well-known encounter with Jesus, he has ignominiously climbed a tree, hoping for a glimpse of Jesus, but without having to be down on the street, subject to the real or imagined glares and whispers of the crowd. Jesus apparently reads the situation as soon as he sees Zacchaeus hiding up there. He asks him to come down, saying that he wants to spend the day with him (which he does). The impact of that day upon this isolated, lonely, emotionally starved man is astounding. Whether it is because Jesus has caught him off guard, with his defenses down, or because he is just so overwhelmed at anyone actually caring enough to want to be with him, in no time at all, Zacchaeus is a different person. With no preachings or scoldings or arguments from Jesus, he's now brimming with enthusiasm, is excited about reaching out with his considerable wealth to the underprivileged, and has decided to give double their money back to those of whom he had taken unfair financial advantage.

Admittedly, his case was extreme, but the personal

miracle that happened when he risked letting someone in through his long-accumulated barriers and defenses is not at all an uncommon miracle.

But it can be very difficult for a person to allow that to happen. For whatever reason, human beings often have a whole repertoire of stances in life that, without their ever realizing it, get squarely in the way of being loved.

One very common and prevalent one—especially among men—is that which says, in effect, "*I want to be loved for what I believe is lovable about me, but don't you dare get close enough to know more about me than I wish you to know.*" In other words, he wants to be admired, respected, and maybe worshipped, but that's all. He wants no part of real closeness or emotional intimacy. That stance makes it very difficult, if not impossible, for love to reach him.

If you have scanned the "Dateline" page (or something similar) in the local paper, you may have noticed that some of those personal ads, though advertising for relationships, actually belie just that. Some of them are the human equivalent of a used car ad. The ones I am referring to list admirable accomplishments, skills, and matters of appearance and, sometimes, even go on to prescribe what those need to be in any person that responds to the ad. Glaringly absent, though, is anything that even hints at an appetite for closeness, for sharing, or for anything close to a nurturing companionship.

The back pages of *The New York Review of Books* have similar ads, all very artfully done and exquisitely well worded. But in many of them, too, there is the same hint of persons who would obviously like to be admired and maybe worshipped, but who, I suspect, are not interested in anyone who might wish to really know who the person is, rather than what he does or what all he has accumulated.

A chilling example:

> Hardworking, cynical, pragmatic, Ernst & Young audited 8-figure guy looking for similar doll with no mental or physical problems...

It then goes on to give his weight and height and to say that he is bald and wears glasses. It's not exactly self-disclosing, is it? Another says,

> 45-year-old female choreographer and filmmaker; elegant, exotic, macrobiotic, interested in metaphysics, and in world culture; seeking long-term partner. Please send photo.

She doesn't seem to understand the difference between material for an obituary and that which might reach out for a living, loving relationship. Given the fact that such ads need to be brief, it makes it even more telling when they are so scrupulously unrevealing of anything humanly significant.

Real love rarely, if ever, works under those conditions. One can acquire admiration—even awe—through attractively packaging oneself. People get hired or elected that way. But to be loved virtually always demands self disclosure—a willingness to risk being known behind the public image, where it is not possible to conceal quirks and insecurities.

Another formidable barrier to finding one's way into a loving relationship, though, is narcissism. The stance is this: *"I love ME and I WANT you."* Overtones of this are also sometimes there in some of the personal ads. It is the person who, having acquired all else that has to do with being a success, sees himself as now needing "the right person" to complete that attractive picture of him. It is a "marriage shaped" hole in his or her life; one which, as a competent, motivated, can-do person, he or she "deserves" to have filled and is going to fill. He may succeed. There are people quite willing to reduce themselves to being an extension of another's ego. But he shouldn't expect to find emotionally evolved, genuinely loving persons because such individuals are not looking for a niche to fill as an add-on, wholly-owned subsidiary to someone's life. They are looking for a relationship—for a mutually nourishing, loving companionship. And they do know the difference.

The other major barrier to being loved is off in almost the opposite direction. This person scares love away because of his wild expectations of what love should and will do and be. It is the person who has never formed her own identity, doesn't really know who she is and so is looking for someone to whom she can turn herself over; one who will then fill the emptiness, will single-handedly bring meaning to her life, and, above all, will rescue her from the tough process of functioning as an intentional, confident, mature, adult person in her own right. One would have to be crazy to knowingly take that on in another's life since it is something that cannot be done. As desperate as that person may be for love, the chances are not good. Worse yet, what may happen is that she will mistakenly hook up with someone like her who is also looking for love as an answer to insecurity and lack of identity. When two such people link up, a mess of tragic proportions will follow. One writer describes what he feels is really taking place in some marriage ceremonies where this is the problem.

> [Such] couples inevitably find themselves standing before a minister to be married. Minister: *"Do you take this woman with all her immaturity, self-centeredness, nagging, tears, and tension to be your wife forever?"* The dumb ox, temporarily hypnotized by the prospect of being able to sleep with her every night mumbles, *"I do."* Then the minister asks the starry-eyed bride (who is all of 18), *"Do you take this man with all his lust, moods, indifference, immaturity, and lack of discipline to be your husband forever?"*
>
> She thinks that "forever" means all of next week, because

she has never experienced one month of tediousness, responsibility, or denial of her wishes, so she chirps, *"I do,"* in the thought that now she has become a woman. ...

They are now legally permitted to breed, fuss, bully, spend each other's money, and be held responsible for each other's bills. It is now legal for them to destroy each other, so long as they don't do it with a gun or a club.

—(*Married for Good* by Paul Stevens)

That is overly harsh, but, even so, it makes the point: love can do a lot of wonderful things, but when it is sought as the perfect, all encompassing answer by someone who doesn't yet know himself—has no idea what his life might come to mean—it degenerates into total disillusionment.

You do see, then, how intricate is this matter of opening oneself to being loved. When someone seeks and hopes and prays to be loved, or prays for more love, he needs to understand what all it requires.

To ask to be loved is to ask to be vulnerable. It means to drop the facades and masks. The prayer, "God, let me be loved," must not secretly mean just, "God, let me be admired," or "God, let me be respected," or merely "God, help me be useful," and not even, "God, help me be enjoyable and likeable." No, to pray, "God, let me be loved," is to open myself to being frighteningly exposed to another, awesomely available to another, to be more understood than I thought I wished to be, and to be subject to hurt, loss, and disillusionment that I might otherwise avoid.

So love is not a certainty, not a science, nothing that can be forced, and certainly not an entitlement. But letting down the barriers, opening oneself to others, cultivating an appetite for all kinds of people, and having a humble-but-solid understanding of who one is and what are one's own gifts and limitations as a person, adds up to a grace that is well worth the trouble, no matter whether it gets the results one wants or not. Happily, it virtually always turns out to make a person quite loveable.

Unavoidable Conflict

Matthew 5:24-26

If, as you approach the altar with your gift, you suddenly remember that your brother has a grievance against you, stop where you are and first go and make your peace with your brother. Only when you have done so, then come back to make your offering. If someone sues you, come to terms with him promptly before you get to court. Otherwise he may hand you over to the judge; the judge will turn you over to the constable, and you will remain in jail until you pay every last cent.

Conflict makes many of us uncomfortable; in fact, it is a real embarrassment to us. Particularly for those people who try the hardest always to be kind, to be reasonable, to be understanding, or to be amiable persons, ending up as part of some interpersonal conflict can feel like a personal failure. For a devout Christian, those feelings may be exacerbated by what Jesus said about turning the other cheek and going the second mile. It adds guilt to what is already the discomfort that conflict causes for many of us. So, for a variety of reasons, people run from, hide from, or simply deny conflict when it comes close to their lives.

You may remember the story about the devout Quaker gentleman who shunned all confrontation and conflict. One day he was cheated by a man who was blatantly taking advantage of the fact that it was relatively safe to cheat Quakers because they wouldn't fight back. The old Quaker did his best to control himself—to take it quietly. Nevertheless, as he departed, through gritted teeth, he did say to this crook, *"Sir, when thou gettest home to thy kennel tonight, I do hope that thy mother bites thee!"* Do you see? It was the Quaker equivalent of calling him an s.o.b. Despite the devout gentleman's heroic attempt to squelch it, the conflict bled through. The inescapable fact is that, to be a human being among human beings is to be a part of conflicts. The belief that it shouldn't or won't be a problem for truly good people or for "real" Christians is misleading and naive.

Someone suggested that the very first episode of human conflict was in the Garden of Eden when, after the "forbidden fruit incident," Adam and Eve realized that they were naked. To cover their genitals, they immediately picked leaves from nearby plants and sewed them together. It was when they couldn't find enough suitable leaves to cover both of them that they had their first argument. It was about "who is going to wear the PLANTS in this family."

In any case, as you could hear in our scripture, Jesus did not assume that we human beings could or would overcome conflict in our life together. In fact, as you read through the things with which he grappled in his ministry, it is clear that his time, like ours, was replete with every variety of human misunderstandings, estrangements, quarrels, disputes and fallings-out involving family members, neighbors, and friends, political conflicts, religious ones, and all the rest. Jesus himself repeatedly was embroiled in conflicted situations.

So while he had much to say about how it is handled, about not letting it grow and fester and destroy, and about reconciliation, in no way did he commend ducking conflict as being a form of goodness. True, he speaks of the need to love our enemies, but never does he suggest that Godly persons never have any enemies. When, in our scripture, he uses the example of a dispute erupting between two people, he does not say that the dispute never should have happened in the first place. Rather, he warns against the often-seen stupidity of nourishing it until it grows into something that sickens and destroys.

And that, right there, is the part that easily gets away from us in the clinches. It is where legitimate conflict becomes distorted as our tempers rise and our egos intrude, making it horribly illegitimate and sick.

How? One common problem arises from the fact that some of us cannot seem to keep from bringing a compulsion to blame into every clash and disagreement. It comes from a childish and patently stupid belief that in every unpleasantness, someone is the good guy and someone is the villain. It's the inability to accept the simple fact that two very healthy, whole, intelligent, good people can, nevertheless, for a host of reasons, be in awesome and passionate disagreement without its meaning that one or the other of those in conflict lacks wisdom, lacks character, or lacks integrity. Blaming, then, always deepens and muddles the conflict. The reason is simple and obvious. Blaming, even when accurate, has to do with what WAS. Reconciliation and healing are about what NOW needs to be. So while the blamer (and they are a dime a dozen) tends to believe that he is proving that he is not the problem, his very need to blame becomes the principal barrier to getting beyond whatever the problem was.

Something else that sickens conflict is the need to triumph. The need to triumph is actually a disorder—a character disorder of sorts. It is to be stuck somewhere back in some early stage of development where not to win is experienced as being a failure as a person. If I am emotionally arrested in the childish stage where for me, not to come out on top in contested matters, always leaves me feeling humiliated, devalued, disgraced, and depressed, count on it; I'll be a nasty person in any conflict. I'll do, I'll say, I'll try anything in order to triumph, because it feels as if my very dignity and worth as a human being is at stake. Meanwhile, the goal when in conflict, contrary to what some may think, is NOT to win. The real goal is to understand enough and open oneself enough to discover a way to move forward and beyond the conflict.

Similar to the need to triumph is the need to punish. An obsession with punishing is not only another need that makes conflict mean, but it keeps it going on and on. The feeling seems to be: "My *adversary must be made to pay for challenging my opinion or my authority—for the 'sin' of confronting me. I won't let go of this until he's been punished.*" Thus, long after the actual conflict would seem to be over, he or she is secretly still looking for an opportunity to exact that punishment.

Still another of the many ways in which legitimate conflict often becomes contorted and unhealthy has to do with the sneaky and dishonest strategies that people will sometimes use to transfer elsewhere the conflict that is legitimately theirs.

One nine-year-old boy found himself on the short end of that. He arrived home from the playground with a bloody nose, a black eye, scratched up, and totally disheveled. While cleaning him up, his father asked what had happened. He replied that there was a boy at school with whom he had never gotten along, so—having heard how they settled feuds in olden days—he challenged him to a duel. He went on to say, "*I gave him his choice of weapons for the fight.*"

"*That sounds fair,*" his father said.

"*Yeah, I thought so too,*" the boy replied. "*But the weapon he chose was his older sister.*"

Typically, it's a little more subtle than that, but you get the idea. "*There must be some way that I can get someone else to carry on the conflict while I remain above it all.*" One man tried to pull this with Jesus, asking in effect: "*Jesus, how about your telling my brother that he has to give me a larger share of our inheritance.*" The more modern equivalent might be someone saying, "*Doctor, now that I have told you how it is, how about YOU phoning my wife and straightening her out on this matter. She'll take it from you.*" Another is the one who thinks,

"I bet that if I can just get to his employer (or to her mother, or two of those guys he golfs with) they'll soon shape him up for me." For awhile, I had a cartoon on my office door that showed two parents saying to their pastor, *"Reverend, we want you to talk to our son about his substance abuse, about the slut whom he's dating, and about all of his unpaid bills. But you mustn't tell him that we told you."* Conniving to arrange surrogate conflict not only never solves anything, it is cowardly and contemptible.

Yet another troublesome kind of conflict avoidance is "displacement." If I have no stomach for dealing with the conflict where it really is, I'll fight, but I'll have the fight instead over something in which I feel more comfortable and/or more likely to prevail. For example, a marriage conflict might be over money, but instead of money, the couple fights over sex. Or maybe the actual conflict stems from in-law problems, but to avoid bringing that out in the open, they fight instead over child-rearing. It sounds crazy, but people do it.

The most common contortion of conflict, though, is simply "sweeping it under the rug" for as long as possible. One can get by with that for awhile, but this, too, is ultimately very destructive—mostly self-destructive. Having seemed to acquiesce enough times, having pretended that all was fine when it was quite the opposite, or having pretended that the various issues were not important when they were, one becomes a caldron of free-floating anger and frustration. When this happens, it will either eat the person from within, or will explode one day in some nonsensical, out-of-proportion way that is infinitely more ruinous than having faced the conflict where it was when it first surfaced.

But still, notwithstanding the strange things done to avoid it or that pervert it, conflict remains an intrinsic part of our shared life. It can, moreover, be a good and important thing. How?

The first principle is simply that of admitting to oneself that it's there when it is there, and THEN having the argument, having the heated discussion, having the disagreement openly. Though it may get a bit unpleasant, it is far better than the sneaky alternatives that we come up with when we don't do so.

The second vital principle is often the most difficult: that of being strong enough to NOT always have to come off the winner. Needing to triumph is a spiritual deformity that turns healthy conflicts into disasters. The fact, meanwhile, is that no matter how sure of myself I may be and how firm I think is my grasp on the truth of the matter, it is NEVER absolute. No matter what it is, looked at carefully, there will be dimensions and nuances that still support some part of the other side of it. So rather than the ugly brand of winning that humiliates the other contender and/or crushes her ego, be certain that the other side comes out with something. Otherwise, we've merely sowed the seeds of still more conflict.

Another important principle of conflict is simply listening. That sounds easy, but it is not. Far more typical is to listen only enough to hear the errors and weaknesses of the adversary. Do that and you doom the conflict to a bad outcome. Again, the purpose of conflict is to find the path by which to proceed from here, NOT to play some stupid game of "gotcha" with the other person's vulnerabilities.

Not allowing conflict to become adulterated with extraneous material is also vital. To bring in ANYTHING that is not a part of THIS issue—whether it's previous failures, personal quirks, baggage from previous disagreements, or whatever—always turns legitimate conflict into dirty fighting. It is what one man was describing when he reported that every time he and his wife argued, she became completely historical. The counselor corrected him saying, *"You mean 'hysterical' don't you?"*

"No, 'HISTORICAL' is just what she becomes! She goes back over the whole HISTORY of our marriage."

Overarching all of that, though, is the need to know and believe that real good comes from conflict. It is to know also that, far from its being a defect, more often than not it is a sign that there is some substance to the persons involved; it indicates that they care; it indicates that they have convictions, values, and spirit. Only an extraordinarily insipid person would never have any conflict. Know also that two very healthy, whole, moral, intelligent, good persons can be in passionate, deep disagreement without it meaning that either one lacks wisdom, principles, or character.

The bottom line on it goes something like this: conflict is merely one more dimension of the intricate and complex way in which God has placed us here to grow and unfold as individuals. You and I are called, then, to be wise, responsible, hopeful and imaginative in handling disputes and confrontations, just as we are called to be that way in the more pleasant, comfortable, less-loaded parts of the human adventure.

One of the central affirmations and principles of our Christian Faith applies as fully here as anywhere in our walk with God; that is, that all things—even conflict—can come together to work for good with those who love God and work within God's purposes.

Neighbors? No Way!

Matthew 22:36-40

> *In an attempt to entrap Jesus, one of the lawyers in the crowd asked him, "Teacher, which commandment in the law is the greatest." Jesus replied, "You shall love the Lord your God with all your heart, with all your soul, and with all your mind. That is the greatest commandment. Just like it is the other one which says: 'You shall love your neighbor as yourself.' From those commandments come all of the law and the prophets."*

Until Jesus went on to say the part about loving one's neighbor, his listeners were with him all the way. Loving God with heart, soul, mind, and strength had (and still does) the nice, warm, sentimental religious sound to which people easily cozy up. To feel love for the creator of gorgeous sunsets, lofty mountains, flower-strewn meadows, star-spangled skies—that is, the God who inspires noble thoughts, glorious poetry and soul-stirring music—was (and is) not particularly controversial. It's an easy virtue, a low-cost piety.

But, as on some other occasions, Jesus couldn't let well enough alone, could he? He goes on to tell them that another commandment said the very same thing in a different way: that one must love one's neighbor as oneself.

And now we see some of his listeners turning away in disgust, muttering, *"There he goes again with that mawkish, mushy, bleeding heart, wishy-washy, liberal claptrap of his. Why did he have to go and say that? What does loving neighbors really have to do with loving God? Nothing! Loving God is 180-degrees away from loving the human trash that infects so much of the earth."*

Then, too, there would be some who were not so surly, thinking, *"Okay, maybe I can buy that as long as I am the one who decides who are my neighbors and who are not my neighbors. I'm quite willing to love those whom I consider to BE my neighbors."*

And that is probably the way many of us get around this central commandment of the Christian faith. *"Respecting, caring about, feeling affection for, and being enthusiastic about those good friends and enjoyable acquaintances who are such delightful companions is just fine. Those who are so supportive in difficult times, who accomplish admirable things, who are always improving themselves, who handle life admirably, who are possessed of such solid wisdom, who, in short, feel like real brothers, sisters, aunts, and uncles to us, are very acceptable. Love them? Absolutely! Jesus, it's a joy to do so."*

"But Jesus, you can save your breath if you thought to persuade me that a lot of those others are my neighbors; that I'm supposed to waste my love, concern, interest, or consideration, pouring it down the 'rat holes' that many of them are. No way. It's not going to happen. Look at them, Jesus. They are not 'neighbor material.'"

>*That one had every opportunity in life—far more than I ever did—and he completely squandered it.*
>
>*She not only has no morals and no scruples whatsoever, but seems actually proud of it.*
>
>*He works overtime at being boorish, rude, and deliberately vulgar.*
>
>*She is lazy, indolent, absolutely unmotivated—is a militant loafer.*
>
>*There's one who is fickle, disloyal, insincere, evasive, devious, and a double-crosser. He always has been and always will be.*
>
>*She has made her life one of gossiping, backbiting, maligning, humiliating, and slandering every chance she gets.*
>
>*He is hoggish, greedy, mercenary, self-seeking, and stingy; and that's his GOOD side. The rest of the time he is a cheat, a thief, and a swindler.*
>
>*They are pagan, primitive, and heathen. It's that simple. They believe all the wrong things, have distorted practices, and perverted values.*

C'mon, she was caught selling drugs to school kids. [or]
He is the father of three children from three different women,
none of whom he supports. [or] She embezzled money from
her own elderly mother's meager funds.

Yes, and not only are there all of those. Beyond them are our powerful revulsions at the Saddam Husseins, the Timothy McVeighs, the Theodore Kaczynskis, and the Fidel Castros, or even an O.J. Simpson. *"Jesus, such people are NOT my neighbors and don't try to tell me that they are. It's difficult enough to see those who have descended to such abominable levels as being a part of the human race. My principles are such that they don't allow me to see them as neighbors—as anyone whom I should love as I love myself."*

A very devout saintly, elderly lady was being challenged on this matter by her daughter regarding a relative of theirs who was causing terrible trouble within the family. The daughter asked, *"Mom, do you think that God actually loves even someone like Uncle Fred?"* This sweet elderly lady thought a moment and said, *"I am certain that God loves him. ... But remember, God probably doesn't know him the way we do."*

There you have it. If God knew as much as we know about some of those people out there, SURELY God would despise them as much as do we, right?

I am sorry to report that Jesus left us no "out" like that. To the contrary, both by what he said and even more so in what he did, he kept zeroing in on that rogues gallery of persons who would NOT have appeared on anyone's "list of neighbors." There were prostitutes. There were traitorous men who worked for the Roman oppressors against their own people. There were people with illnesses of a type believed to be a direct result of their sin. There were people who were so horribly dysfunctional and anti-social that they were considered to be possessed by devils. There were unpleasant foreigners. There were chronic whiners, hypochondriacs, and more. There was nothing endearing or attractive about them, nothing to tempt a person to identify with them. They were precisely the sort who are easily dismissed from one's mind and concern because they were way "off the bottom of the chart" in virtually every way: social behavior, morals, motivation, and respectability.

What we are running into "head-on" here in this very tough teaching of Jesus, is that the kind of loving that is truly Godly has almost nothing to do with those warm, positive sentiments with which you and I react to people who are friendly, helpful, loyal, kind, and forgiving toward us. Not that there is anything wrong with that kind of loving, but apparently it is only the most elementary kind of love. As Jesus said at one point, even the heathen do that much.

As the saying goes, where "the men get separated from the boys" in the matter of loving, is in the love that does NOT come at all "naturally," may not "feel right," and often won't seem to "make good sense;" that is, love that can even feel as if, by pursuing it, we are lowering our standards and principles.

What would this not-very-romantic, unsentimental, non-instinctive kind of love look like? If I understand correctly what Jesus was saying and demonstrating, it might include such things as,

- setting out deliberately to make contact with people with whom I am LEAST at-home and LEAST comfortable, not because I owe it to them, but because I happen to have the chance to do so;
- staying at it, perhaps against all my instincts, until I am able to see behind or under or over all of that about him which I find troubling—not giving up until I am able to see that which he and I hold in common as human beings;

- forcing myself to be as accepting of his or her idiosyncrasies, incompetencies, and failures as I have had to learn to be of my own most troublesome quirks;
- keeping before me the fact that her terrors, frustrations, angers, and despairs—while they seem trivial to me—are just as daunting, disorienting, disillusioning, and distressing to her as have been some of what I am inclined to think of as my very serious and important difficulties;
- approaching him firmly, believing that whatever there is about him that I find obnoxious, destructive, or irresponsible, it is NOT there because he sets out each morning to be as aggravating, hateable, disagreeable, or disgusting as possible, that as self-defeating and misguided as I think him to be, it is no more than his way of trying to cope with what has been dealt him;
- being as tenacious about her freedom and her right to unfold in her own unique way as I am about my own freedom to do so, even when I really don't approve of the directions in which she is exercising her freedom;
- being as forgiving of their outright sins as other people have had to be of mine, back along the way in life.

Those give only a little of the flavor of what Jesus seems to have meant by loving one's neighbor as oneself. So there is nothing natural about it. It requires all of the imagination, determination, presence of mind and raw empathy that most of us can muster. It seldom, if ever, carries the warm, fuzzy, instantly rewarding feelings that we may have thought should always be there with authentic loving.

AND YET, as Jesus repeatedly demonstrated (and

perhaps you have discovered a time or two when you have risked it), it can be an astoundingly powerful thing.

Years ago, *The Village Voice* reported an incident at The Circle On The Square Theater in Greenwich Village. It was back when the stage play, *The Night of The Iguana* was being performed. Dorothy McGuire was starring in it. It was close to time for the curtain to go up and for the performance to begin. In the front row was a strangely-dressed woman, her hair a hopeless, greasy tangle and her manner one of open agitation. Suddenly she yelled in a coarse voice, *"C'mon, start the show! Start the show! I wanna see Dorothy McGuire!"*

The other theater-goers giggled and laughed at her boor-ish outburst. She got louder: *"Let's get this thing going. I want to see Dorothy McGuire! Start the damn show!!"* And she kept it up like that. The crowd was now laughing derisively. Some of them began clapping whenever she would start to yell. She clapped back at them. Some of them booed her. She booed back at them. Others shouted loud, ridiculing com-ments. The woman was losing control and working herself into a seriously agitated state, as the crowd continued to treat her as a kind of "side-show."

At this point, Dorothy McGuire came from behind the curtain and walked down to where the woman was sitting. She smiled at her, then sat down on the floor in front of her and spoke quietly with her for a few moments. Finally, they both stood up. Dorothy put her arm around the woman and they both walked across the front toward a stage door. But first, after a few steps, Ms. McGuire stopped and, with her arm still around this strange, disheveled, disruptive woman, said to the crowd, *"I just want to introduce you to another fellow human being."*

There was total stunned silence. And then, after a moment, thunderous warm applause. Someone, you see, had risked what Jesus commended as "loving" this heretofore unidentified "neighbor." So, at least for the time being, there was redemption and healing, both for the woman and, in some sense, even for the crowd.

Now, if you are thinking, *"That's fine for a Jesus or for a Dorothy McGuire, but I don't happen to be put together like that. I could never do something like that."* WRONG! DEAD WRONG! True, it won't come naturally or easily, but you and I can do it. In fact, it is the most exciting and powerful of the miracles that God turns over to you and me to perform.

Surviving an Enmity

Matthew 5:43-48

You have heard it said, "Love your neighbor and hate your enemy." What I am saying is this: Love your enemies and pray for your persecutors. Only in that way do you become the sons and daughters of God. ... If you love only those who love you, what reward is there in that? Tax-collectors do that much. If you embrace only your brothers and sisters, in what way is that extraordinary? Even pagans do as much. There must be no limit to your goodness, just as the goodness of God is boundless.

It is scriptures just like that one that sometimes leave people frustrated and despairing over ever being able to be as Godly as they aspire. Why couldn't Jesus have just settled for the way it was in the Old Testament? There, while making it perfectly clear how important it was with one's friends, family, and allies, to be forgiving, forbearing, and charitable, when it came to one's enemies, it was "open season" on them. Since they were enemies, one was free to hate them. But then along comes Jesus and replaces that with this baffling, daunting, unrealistic-sounding command that we must also love the enemy—that we are not free to hate him or her with impunity.

It's not that anyone believes hating to be a great virtue. But as we all know, hating does happen. When someone deceives you, uses me, slanders her, humiliates him, or attacks them, to hate that person for it seems logical and deserved, and it comes naturally. *"So, Jesus, with hate being such an inborn, instinctive, customary part of human beings, why would you meddle with it"?* It's straightforward, unambiguous, and it feels right.

To love one's enemies, on the other hand, goes against instinct and intuition. It feels contradictory, and at times it can even feel like a lack of character—feel as though maybe one lacks the courage to react the way he ought to after what's been done to him. So, loving one's enemies has always been one of the most unpopular things Jesus commended to us.

Some part of the problem with it is what the word "love" is automatically assumed, by most of us, to include. Loving someone is almost totally associated, in this part of the world, with feelings of affection and fondness for him or her. That is NOT what Jesus meant when he spoke of loving one's enemy. No, after gross mistreatment, hurt, duplicity, injustice, or whatever, if we thought we were required to perform some kind of mental and emotional gymnastics through which we'd feel affection, admiration, or endearment toward the perpetrator, that would be crazy. It doesn't work that way. One's feelings and responses won't be manipulated that easily.

"Love," as Jesus uses the word here, is not merely a sweet, sentimental fondness for someone. As the scripture says (in effect), "*Anybody, even the most shallow, can feel affection, enjoyment, or attraction to someone who is likeable, helpful, and pleasant.*"

The loving that Jesus asks for the enemy is something one does quite apart from whatever are one's feelings just then. Perhaps while still being barely able to stand the sight of him, this kind of loving means taking specific steps inside yourself (but also having to do with *him*) that remove the barriers to eventual healing and, in general, lead to shifting to hatred of the ENMITY rather than the ENEMY. That IS tough to do. It doesn't feel at all natural. But it is possible.

What is particularly difficult for most of us to believe at the time, though, is that it is primarily for the good of the hater rather than for the sake of the offender or abuser. Hatred consistently damages the hater more than it does the hated. It doesn't seem fair that it works that way, but it does. Hating is a little like what is the cost to a honey bee of stinging you. It is unpleasant for the "stingee," but it kills the bee who does the stinging.

I don't recall which premier or president it was, or even which little country he was from, but he obviously understood this when he said that he felt less anger and grief over the hostile and aggressive things done to them by their enemy than over the fact that the enemy had succeeded in turning his people into haters. Good point! To make people hurt is terrible, but that can heal. To make them into haters is to inflict damage to them that will go on and on, affecting every aspect of life.

There is a bit of an analogy for it in what became the fate of a certain Swedish warship. Sweden, determined to crush her enemies, spent seven years building and armoring an awesome warship. It was outfitted with 240 tons of cannons—an unheard of 126 of them! Sure enough, in its first battle encounter, it was able to inflict unprecedented damage to the enemy. But on the second combat outing, as she made a sharp turn, the sheer weight of the incredible weaponry she carried caused her to capsize and, in only minutes, she had gone straight to the bottom.

Hating, for us human beings is a lot like the top-heaviness of that extraordinarily well-armed ship. Even when it seems utterly justified and appropriate (as I'm certain, did all those cannons), hating will eventually sink you. One cannot do it and remain unaffected by it.

In one scene from the film, *Godfather III*, this was touched on unexpectedly. Michael Corleone, the head of the Mafia family in that story, warns a certain younger, hotheaded gangster-colleague, *"Never hate your enemies. It always affects your judgment."* It was a strange context, but it's right. Hate is too heavy for anyone to carry around and not be damaged by it.

So then, if one were to try to do as Jesus says, *"love one's enemies,"* what would it mean? While not liking someone, while still being appalled at her actions, and with the experience of his malice or deception or exploitation still jangling you, how does one "do" this kind of love of which Jesus speaks?

One part of it is hinted at in that haunting novel, *All Quiet On The Western Front*, by Erich Maria Remarque. An Allied soldier accidentally stumbles into the foxhole where Paul Baumer, a German soldier, is crouching. Baumer immediately drives his bayonet through the body of this enemy soldier, killing him. But he is then left in this small space with nothing to look at except this man that he has killed. As he sits there staring for the first time at an actual face of the hated enemy, he begins to think about it and starts to cry. He talks to the dead allied soldier, saying,

> Comrade, I did not want to kill you. If you jumped in here again, I would not do so if you would be sensible, too. But you were only an idea to me before, an abstraction that lived in my mind and called forth its appropriate response. It was that abstraction that I stabbed to death. But now, for the first time, I see that you are a man like me. I had thought only of your hand grenades, of your bayonet, or of your rifle. Now I am seeing your wife and your face and our fellowship. Forgive me. We always see it too late. Why do they never tell us that you are just poor devils like us, that your mothers are just as anxious as ours, and that we have the same fear of death, the same dying, and the same agony. Forgive me. How could you be my enemy?

You do see what happened there, don't you? As Baumer described it, this enemy was transformed before his eyes, was transformed (albeit, a little late) back from being an abstraction to being another vulnerable, flawed, struggling human being.

That's a big part of what is involved in loving an enemy despite the fact that, in certain ways, he or she is yet an enemy. It entails "rehumanizing" the person in one's own mind. Charles Lamb, the English writer and poet, touched on it when someone tried to get him together with a person who had been a truly nasty critic of his writing. But Lamb said, *"No! Don't introduce me to him. I want to go on hating him and I can't do that to a man I know."*

There is another feeling for it in that incident reported from the streets of New York City in which, on a sweltering day at rush hour, traffic was held up at a green light because of a horribly crippled elderly man inching his way, unassisted, across the intersection. Two cars back, a taxi-driver was leaning on his horn and screaming obscenities. At that point, the driver of the front car got out and walked back to the taxi, offered the driver his keys and said, *"Here, if it is that important for you, you take my car and run over him. I haven't got the heart to do it!"* One hopes that at that moment, for the taxi driver, the disabled man again became a fellow human being, rather than only an abstract obstruction to despise for being in his way.

Again, this isn't easy, but getting oneself back to recognizing that the enemy is a human being (not an embodiment of pure evil) is possible. But you will likely fight your way through a jungle of contrary emotions before understanding, for example, that ninety-some percent of what is the enemy's total life actually has little or nothing to do with the particular matter that has made him your enemy just now. There will be a strong side of you that won't wish to see that, behind his belligerence or meanness or contentiousness, is a whole array of more-or-less standard uncertainties, fears, weaknesses, and hungers not substantially different from yours and everyone else's. It will also require (even if you don't believe it at first) some hard talking to yourself about the fact that, as wrong and hurtful as she's been behaving, nothing is permanent with us human beings and that change is always going on. So, no more than you would wish to be seen forever in terms of what you were like at your very worst awhile back, should she be permanently frozen in your mind as being the way she's acted these last few months.

To have forced oneself to look again at all of that does not excuse anything that an enemy has done, nor will it probably cause you to like him or her. It IS, though, to "love" him in the sense that God loves us: that is, as complex human creations of worth, even when the worth is badly obscured from time to time.

As you can see, this is not "feel-good" stuff. No, it is definitely easier to go with the simplicity and the deliciousness and antiseptic abstractness of hating. And if you do, few, if any, will blame you. People understand hate. Even the enemy may not blame you for hating him. But you will be damaged by your hating.

And there is yet more to this than only changes in thinking. There is also the part that has to do with that principle or fact about us that says that, when one cannot feel his way to acting differently, it is still possible to act one's way to different feelings. One of Jesus' suggestions, for example, was, *"Pray for those who despitefully use you."* That, too, may be needed at some point as part of this kind of loving one's enemy. So might making yourself act toward him or her with simple civility, courtesy, or graciousness. Overtures from you of reconciliation might be another way of approaching it, even when he spurns them. Will that feel authentic or right? No, probably not. But such things ARE the low-key ways of taking charge of one's own recovery from hate—acting one's way out of it when the feelings seem unchangeable. If it makes a difference in the one whom you hated, so much the better. But even if it doesn't, again, it halts the damage that hating will otherwise do to you.

And, yes, at some point forgiveness needs to be a part of

it. Here, too, forgiveness doesn't mean your becoming fond of that enemy, doesn't mean that you may not still have to protect yourself from further hurt by him, or that you no longer recall the things that happened. It only means that from your side, you declare your war over against him or her.

That, briefly, is what is required to survive an enmity—that is, it is what is required to love the enemy in the manner of Jesus. It does not come naturally. It feels inappropriate—seems totally counter-intuitive. But it is still profoundly right, mainly because it prevents you and me from being sucked down, and spiritually mutilated and distorted by hating.

So, whoever it is in your life that is making it very easy to hate him right now, please don't let him do that kind of damage to you. You don't have to turn him into a friend. It may not be possible to stop disliking him or her for what he's done, or for what she's failed to do, or that for which he stands. Nevertheless, determine to love him in this healing sense of which Jesus spoke. Failing that, your enemy will have succeeded in taking you down to his level—something far worse than anything else he has done to you.

Getting Sucked In

John 8:1-11

Jesus was at the temple and many people gathered around him. He was seated there teaching when the Scribes and Pharisees brought in a woman who had been caught in an act of adultery. Placing her in the middle, they said to him, "Teacher, this woman was caught committing adultery. Our law, as given by Moses, prescribes that she be taken out and stoned. What do you say about it?" They hoped that his answer could be used to bring a charge against him.

Jesus bent down and wrote with his finger in the dirt. They continued to press their question. After a time he sat up and said, "That one of you who is without fault shall throw the first stone." Then he bent over again, continuing to write in the dirt with his finger.

Hearing this, the members of the crowd departed, one by one, beginning with the oldest. When all had gone, the woman was left standing there. He stood up and asked her, "Where are they? Has no one condemned you?" She replied, "No one, sir." Jesus said, "Nor do I. Go now and sin no more."

Executing this woman for adultery was only part of what the Pharisees had in mind that morning. What they were really relishing was this chance to put Jesus in a double bind—in a classic "no win" situation.

Today they were quite certain that, one way or another, he was going to be in trouble. For in the book of Deuteronomy (Deut. 22), it decreed that anyone caught committing adultery must be stoned to death. If then, you were a Bible-believing Hebrew who was concerned about family values, there was no doubt as to what must happen to this woman. She must be taken out and stoned. The scripture prescribed it not only for adultery, but for quite a number of other offenses, including that of your son being unruly.

But then, there was also this. Currently, it was against the law to obey this law. Not long before, Rome had made it illegal for Jews to carry out any executions on their own.

Only Roman officials could now hand down a death sentence. Since Romans could not have cared less what the book of Deuteronomy or any other part of the Hebrew Bible said, they would not have allowed this execution. Thus, if this death sentence, as prescribed by the Bible, were to be carried out, it had to appear to be a spontaneous lynching. It would have to be orchestrated from behind the scene. Participation, then, was purely voluntary for everyone except the victim.

So do you see? If Jesus consents to the stoning of this woman, he can be arrested for consenting to and encouraging the breaking of Roman law. If, on the other hand, in front of his own people, he takes a position against it, he has publicly discounted part of their Holy Law and has sided with the hated Romans (in effect, sided with the Federal government), preventing his own people from doing what their Bible and their beliefs dictate.

So, in addition to the matter of whether this particular woman would momentarily become a bloody pulp under a pile of rocks, there were issues of law and order, of local control versus federal interference, of strict versus liberal understanding of scripture, of church versus state, and maybe of capital punishment itself. Some of that sounds oddly familiar, doesn't it?

Had I had been the one (instead of Jesus) on the hot seat that morning, my mind would have been frantically searching for a safe middle-ground, one of those "unhappy mediums," something—anything—I could say or do without really saying or doing anything at all.

For example, perhaps we could give the woman the alternative of committing suicide with a cup of hemlock. That would certainly seem more humane than death by stoning, but would still get the job done.

Or, how about charging her with something for which

the Romans themselves would be willing to execute her: treason or fomenting public disturbance, for example.

Maybe we could stone her as the scripture says, but make everyone stand a hundred feet away and use only small rocks. That would still be "a stoning" as the Bible required, but who knows? She might survive.

As you heard, though, Jesus did not get into any such plea-bargaining, maneuvering, rationalizing, or hedging. No, his perception of what needed to happen and his way of approaching it was something startlingly different and, thus, something very much worth reflecting upon.

Without doubt, he felt grief for this woman—this guilty, terrified, humiliated person having gotten herself into what was probably a fatal predicament.

(Incidentally, one cannot help but wonder where the man was with whom she had been caught. One would think that, even way back then, adultery would require two people.)

Apparently Jesus also felt sadness and real concern for the members of the mob. They were a gathering of people anxious to do some hurting and killing, perhaps hoping that doing so might relieve and release some of their own internal frustration with life and with the world. So, the woman was not the only one in danger. Each mob member who would end up taking a personal part in killing her and, for his having done so, would himself become more hardened, less human, and spiritually shriveled in the process. Without exception, that happens to people who fall for the temptation to seek out victims on whom they can safely dump their anger. Worse yet, having done so, they will typically look for a chance to do it again in order to prove that it was justified the first time. Between the woman and the mob members, for Jesus, the moment was loaded with enormous potential for tragedy and loss—both loss of life and loss of soul.

Jesus sits there for a moment, looking at the ground, idly

scratching at the dirt with his finger. When he finally speaks, it is to take a huge gamble. As we all know, the gist of what he said was, *"Do what you have to, BUT let the one who is faultless begin the stoning."*

Some have chosen to view that as Jesus' plan to shame, ridicule, and humiliate those people into backing off by exposing them all as hypocrites. I don't think so. Nowhere else was that Jesus' way with people.

Nor was he establishing the principle that only perfect people should ever be part of dispensing justice. He knew, as do we all, that there could be no law and justice system whatsoever if everyone in it was held to a standard of complete personal flawlessness.

No, the enormous gamble that he took was that, somewhere underneath the intoxicating fury and the bloodthirsty indignation into which these people had whipped themselves, they might still be put back in touch with their own humanity.

It might not have worked. Had only one or two in that crowd been one of those pathetically dwarfed souls who believe that the world can be made safer, that life can be made better, and that satisfaction could come through killing, disgracing, or employing other expressions of hatred, the stones might have begun to fly. Sweat must have poured down Jesus' neck for a minute or two as, silently praying that no such "sickie" was there to trigger the tragedy, he went back to scratching the dirt.

What it says next is especially interesting. It says that one by one they began to go away, BEGINNING WITH THE OLDEST! Why begin with the oldest? Because often (not always) it is the people who have lived the longest who, at some deep level, do understand how much forgiveness, forbearance, mercy, and benefit-of-the-doubt have gone into their own survival. True, some refuse to see that and only become more arrogant and judgmental with age. Happily, though, many do come to understand God's grace more clearly the longer they live. Fortunately, some such older ones were there that morning, and the healing in that situation began with their lead.

Make no mistake about it. It was not that, as they left the scene, they now approved of what the woman had done. It was not that they were now pro-adultery or even anti-capital punishment. It was only that they were now looking at this woman with different eyes. She was no longer an embodiment of depravity, was no longer a symbol of all that was wrong with society and the world, and was no longer one of some awful "them." They had returned to seeing her as an ordinary human being—one who, for having handled temptation very badly, was now in a lot of trouble and pain. As serious, though, as was the charge against her, individually they no longer relished being instruments of vengeance against her. Something like, *"There, but for the grace of God, stand I"!* had resurfaced in their souls, making it feel like a pretty good time to go home. They went home, and in much better shape than they almost did.

So, it worked that time. It was a nice result. Don't get too cozy with it, though. Unfortunately, it looks far easier than it is. It is, in fact, extraordinarily difficult to do what Jesus did that day; that is, to love, to care about, and to be a source of healing to BOTH sides of a "brokenness," a conflict, or a hurt.

What he did is "counter-intuitive," as they say. Far from coming naturally, at the time it can feel and look like a lack of character or principle. *"What's wrong with Jesus, anyhow? Has he become soft on adultery? Doesn't he believe in obeying the scriptures? Has he lost sight of the importance of demonstrating to our children the consequences of such wrongdoing? Has he become afraid to take sides in matters of morality?"* None of us would relish being accused of such, would we?

That is why it is so tempting and compelling to always jump onto one side or the other in the face of any sticky problem, contention, or alienation; tempting, for example, to throw in with the Pharisees, since they had the full weight of religion and law with them. For others, it is just as tempting to side passionately with the "underdog," fiercely attacking the false piety, the sanctimoniousness, and lack of mercy of her accusers. Getting sucked into coming down quickly, firmly, and unequivocally on one side or the other, not only happens easily, but the emotional momentum of doing so feels so right and even exhilarating!

What was demonstrated here, though, is a Godly alternative to turning knee-jerk passions loose against one or the other side of pain, of wrong, or of conflict. What Jesus did here was care genuinely and worry imaginatively about what was to become not only of the "stonee," but also of the stoners. That is far from typical. It takes real grace, requires a holy kind of empathy, and demands a type of love that is truly and unmistakably of God.

Scott Peck tells of a Sufi teacher strolling through the streets with his students. They come to the city square, where a vicious battle is being fought between government troops and rebel forces. Appalled at the bloodshed, the students turn to their teacher, asking, *"Tell us quickly, which side should we help"*? *"Both!"* their teacher answers. The students are confused and a little appalled. *"Both? Why would we help both?"* He replied, *"We must help the authorities learn to listen to the people, and we must help the rebels learn not to despise and reject all authority."*

When one's blood is boiling, the possibility of doing that may sound neither satisfying nor intoxicating. Moreover, it is difficult, risky, and stressful. But it can be done. For example, some of you may know that from having tried stubbornly to understand and work at loving BOTH sides in the divorce of friends. Others know it from daring to try to remain close and to be a source of healing to both sides of a bitter hatred. Another time, it may have been no more than your refusal to declare "open season" upon the sinner as part of hating his sin. In general, it is to be willing to wade in as a determined healer, despite shallow people calling you unprincipled, accusing you of lacking conviction, and condemning what they see as your complacency. It is to risk walking that narrow, lonely line between what really is no more than cowardly "fence-sitting" and, on the other hand, risking others' disapproval in making yourself a source of God's peace.

Anyone can select and climb onto whichever seems the safest of the passing ethical, political or ideological bandwagons, and then mindlessly parrot the "accusings," "despisings," condemnations, "ridiculings," and other savagery that is so easily mistaken for a sign of character or principle (and may even feel like it).

We are called, though, to something much better than that: to remain stubbornly loving, always imaginative, constantly improvising and determinedly hopeful. Hopeful that there are kinds of good, that there are still means of healing, and that there are untried ways of understanding the anger, the "brokenness," the conflict, and the hot-button social and political issues that so often turn people into haters, thus making a mockery of the very image of God within us.

Again, it is not easy, but with a little imagination and by keeping our wits about us, with God's help, it is something that every last one of us can do. And when it works, there is nothing more satisfying.

Tough Hope ─────────────────────────

Keeping a Comfortable Distance

Luke 16:19-31 (portions in summary)

There was once a rich man who dressed in purple, wore the finest of linen, and who enjoyed magnificent meals each day. His name was Dives. At his gate lay a poor man named Lazarus who was covered with sores. Lazarus was glad to satisfy his hunger with the scraps from the table of this wealthy man. The dogs would sometimes come and lick the sores that covered his body.

The time then came when Lazarus died and was carried by the angels to be with Abraham. Dives died also and found himself in torment. He looked up and there, at a great distance, was Abraham with Lazarus close beside him. "Father Abraham," he called out, "take pity upon me! Send Lazarus with water to cool my tongue, for I am in agony." But Abraham said, "My son, remember how things were in life for you and how they were for Lazarus. Now there is a great chasm between us and no one can cross it from either direction."

Dives then called out again, "Then, Father Abraham, at least send Lazarus to my five brothers to warn them." But Abraham said, "They have the law and the prophets. Let them take heed of them."

Probably no parable of Jesus is more likely to be wrongly interpreted, distorted, or misapprehended than this one. Maybe it happened for some of you just now; that is, what you thought you heard was the well-to-do man, Dives, being damned for having been wealthy in life, while it seemed that Lazarus, on the other hand, was being commended and rewarded for nothing more than having been poor and miserable. It's a common impression of this parable, but is not really what is there.

It does not say, for example, that Lazarus was a saint-in-rags who had a heart of gold, or that his bad health, for example, was because he had worn himself out caring for others, or that his generosity had made him poor, causing him to give away all that he had.

Nor, for that matter, does it imply that Dives' wealth came from evil sources: from illegal insider trading on camel futures or from manufacturing shoddy or unsafe sandals or from extortion or from selling opium at the high school.

All it really does say is that Dives' life was financially secure, very pleasant, and comfortable. He dressed, it says, in the finest fabrics and he ate very well. His home was apparently fenced or walled in, since the parable mentions that it had a gate. It does not, however, say that all that was evil. No, his being an able man of good-taste (being one who appreciated a good cut of beef or the right vintage of wine), being a man who could dress well, decorate well, and landscape well, was not the issue. A person could certainly be and do all of that without being un-Godly, stingy, mean-spirited, or unscrupulous.

In fact, couldn't one just as easily conjecture that Lazarus' life would have been even more miserable had Dives not made certain that his cook put leftovers out by the gate for Lazarus to eat? It is conceivable that the coat with which Lazarus covered himself may have been one that Dives had given to the Volunteers of Israel Clothes Closet. Dives' annual contribution to the Nazareth United Jewish Appeal probably helped fund services which, even if unused by Lazarus, could have helped him and may have helped others of his ilk.

And while we are still conjecturing, it is also conceivable that Lazarus may in some way have brought his poverty upon himself by squandering good opportunities, for example, or from lack of motivation, or because of an earlier alcohol problem, or just from being undisciplined.

We just don't know any of that, one way or the other. No, Jesus was very careful, in creating this story, not to give any information that might help you or me deflect his point by making either Dives or Lazarus sound so extreme that they had nothing to do with us or with matters pertaining to our lives.

We come, then, to the second act of the parable. Both men have died and, for reasons which we are not told, Lazarus ends up with Abraham (considered a good place to be). Dives, on the other hand, was way off in the distance in a kind of torment. Some part of his torment had to have been his shock—his incredulity at the way things worked out. Maybe he hadn't been perfect (*who is?*), but he certainly hadn't been depraved either. So, he makes what seems like a very reasonable request. *"Father Abraham,"* he pleads, *"please send Lazarus to bring me some water."* Note that he even asked for Lazarus by name. Though they had been from very different parts of society, to Dives' credit, he did know who Lazarus was. That is, Lazarus wasn't only a nameless, faceless social problem. Moreover, Dives must have felt that, at least indirectly, he had done enough for Lazarus back in life that it was reasonable to ask for a return favor—a minor comforting gesture. (I would have thought so too, wouldn't you?) *"Please! I am miserable. Send Lazarus with just a little water for me."*

Now we get to the real meat of the parable. Abraham does not claim that Dives' request is brazen or inappropriate. His words to Dives are not at all taunting. In fact, he sounds compassionate. In a matter-of-fact way, he says:

> *My son, there is now a great chasm between where you are and where Lazarus is. It can no longer be crossed from here or from there.*

THAT is what this story is about. It is not about the nature of any heaven or hell, or about what good deeds or which stupidities might land someone in either place. No, it is about creating chasms, about carefully keeping distance, and about comfortable remoteness.

And here is where the matter of Dives' wealth and/or

position and/or power—while not THE direct cause—do come into play. Apparently, in his case, they did have something to do with the chasm. For as we know, while there are many things, that money cannot buy (things like love, respect, serenity, joy), unfortunately, one thing that money often can purchase, and too often does, is distance.

Whether for Dives or you or me, one of the options that is always there, once a person has some financial resources and personal power, is arranging a comfortably oblivious remoteness. That seems to be what happened here. Dives arranged his life and controlled his exposures so as to be out of any direct touch with ugly human realities or any upsetting misery and struggle (of which Lazarus was a close-at-hand example). It probably wasn't all that difficult to do it, either. He could set his life up so as to be able to go for weeks, maybe months, without ever actually looking Lazarus in the eye, or anyone like him. Whether it was Lazarus-the-failure, or Lazarus-the-underprivileged, or Lazarus-the-lonely, or Lazarus-the-social-outcast, or Lazarus-the-minority, or Lazarus-the-troubled, or Lazarus-the-abrasive, or some other disconcerting, or maybe disgusting, or possibly depressing Lazarus, Dives digs a mote around his life, one comfortable shovel-full at a time. Abraham called it a great chasm, this deliberate distance that protected him from "people like that."

It is a subtle thing, but all too real. Moreover, it insidiously becomes far more than only the absence of direct personal contact. It is the separation that then grows in one's mind that becomes the worst of it. Maybe you have noticed how easily it grows. Though it sounds upside down to say it, the greater the distance and the less the contact, the more of an expert Dives believes himself to be in regard to Lazarus and others whose troubles and problems make one upset or uncomfortable. Stand back and watch sometime, if you haven't already. Those who are most remote, most antiseptically out of direct contact, and who most carefully control what they are exposed to seem to be the ones who are most certain and completely comfortable saying things like:

Lazarus could get out of the mess that his life is if he really wanted to. He likes being a social parasite.

Lazarus wouldn't appreciate a better situation if he were given one. In six months, he'd be right back as he is.

Lazarus isn't really sick. He is a hypochondriac. He prefers having people feel sorry for him to being well.

Lazarus' health wouldn't be so awful if he would take care of himself the way you and I do.

I can't prove it, of course, but I'd be willing to bet that Lazarus really is of very marginal intelligence.

I know now that I have made a mistake in putting leftovers out for Lazarus. He doesn't need food. He needs to get hungrier so that he'll get motivated.

I happen to know that not only was Lazarus' mother a beggar, but so was her father. One would have to be crazy to believe that anything will ever change with him.

As Dives carefully turns off his own empathy, do you see how the chasm is built? The greater the distance, the more easily come those generalities, the discounting, and sometimes even derision. Dives may even commend himself on how much clearer, wiser, and more realistic his thinking has become from this distance.

What further muddies and complicates the picture is that some of those analyses of Lazarus may be accurate—at least to some extent. There is a good chance that Lazarus DOES have some real problems. Even so, what Dives failed to understand is that when such conclusions about someone's problems, mistakes, or predicaments are made by someone from the safety of the other side of the chasm, it is not really information on Lazarus. NO, it is very grim information on the person doing the talking—information on what deadly thing Dives has allowed to happen to his own soul. The underlying function of those glib generalizations, party lines, social cliches, and pontifications of the elite is to create the distance that protects the mind and emotions from what might otherwise interfere with one's self-interest, comfort, and insular way of looking at life.

And let there be no mistake about this: chasm-building is not only the problem of the wealthy. Wealth obviously can make it easier to do, but it is an option and a temptation to a lot of us. What makes it alluring is that it promises simplicity and a way to emotional tranquility and imperturbability in the face of the very upsetting kinds of struggle and pain and injustice with which our world is unfortunately infected. But it exacts a terrible price! C. S. Lewis caught the principle magnificently, as it has to do with loving (which is, of course, one component of this). He wrote:

> To [care] at all is to be vulnerable. Love anything and your heart will certainly be wrung and possibly be broken. If you want to make sure of keeping it intact, you must give your heart to no one, not even an animal. Wrap it carefully round with hobbies and with little luxuries; avoid all entanglements; lock it up safe in the casket of your self interest. But in that casket—safe, dark, motionless, airless—it will change. It will not be broken. It will become unbreakable, impenetrable, irredeemable. The alternative to the risk of complication and even tragedy is damnation. The only place outside Heaven where you can be perfectly safe from all the dangers and perturbations of love, is Hell.

Exactly! That's what makes this really a tough little parable—a disturbing one. What that isolated, spiritually dwarfed, tormented character, Dives, ends up revealing is that what we don't know CAN and DOES hurt us. What we manage to keep from letting ourselves feel definitely DAMAGES us. Insulating ourselves from depressing aspects of humanity erodes OUR humanity. In short, the very chasm that we put there to protect us and to keep things nice, turns out to be the grave where the image of God within us gets buried.

"What if we are not aware that we are doing it"? is the remaining question. At the end of the parable, Dives is protesting that he never had a chance to know any better. But Abraham says, in effect, *"Uh uh. Not true. You had every opportunity to know better."*

He's right, of course. We are all intelligent enough to catch ourselves if we want to, parroting generalizations about people of whom we have no personal experience, but have only heard about from professional chasm builders. Everyone of us is insightful enough to recognize that we (in most cases), never having been homeless or never having been without adequate food or never having been chronically ill and unable to get decent health care or never having been on the short end of bigotry, are on dangerous ground when we philosophize and pontificate on what all is wrong with those who have ended up stuck in those kinds of misery or deprivation. Yes, at some level we do know what we are doing when we push from our minds what is unpleasant to know and when we are contriving not to get close to what could complicate our thinking. We do know! It is just that staying with our empathy is emotionally expensive. Mercy and forgiveness are often controversial, particularly these days. Allowing oneself to get directly and personally involved is unpredictable and difficult to control. To be one who cares a lot is often to be labeled a "bleeding heart" (particularly by those who have shrunk their own). That's why it can be so very tempting to buffer ourselves from unpleasantness, to severely limit the scope of our concern, and to intellectualize rather than sympathize. There will probably always be a side of us saying, *"In times like these, if a person can afford it and arrange it, WHY NOT keep everything around him just as simple and as undemanding and undisturbing and 'nice' as possible? I can't solve all the world's problems or make everyone's pain go away. What's so bad about buffering my emotions and my morale?"*

If I understand correctly this parable about this unfortunate man, Dives, the answer is that those perfectly reasonable, practical chasms are the major way in which you and I are likely to separate ourselves from God.

If you haven't figured it out, then, this particular parable is not told to get more help for Lazarus. It is for the sake of the rest of us. Apparently, we need to be doing everything we can come up with to stay closely, personally in touch with what life is and what it means for every kind of human being that surrounds us. To fail to do so is to begin to die spiritually.

The Child Stays

Mark 10:13-15 & 9:36-37

People were bringing little children to Jesus for him to touch them. The disciples tried to turn them away, but when Jesus saw this, he was indignant and said to them, "Let the children come to me. Do not stop them, for it is to such as these that the kingdom of God belongs. I say this in all seriousness: whoever does not welcome the kingdom of God in a childlike way, will never enter it."....

Then he took a little child, placed him in front of them and, putting his arms around him, said to them, "Anyone who welcomes one of these children in my name, welcomes me, and anyone who welcomes me, welcomes not only me, but also the one who sent me."

Some years ago a tour group traveling in a Middle Eastern country found themselves terribly hounded by child-beggars. As perhaps you know, impoverished parents in third world countries have been known to train their children as beggars because tourists are often more susceptible to children than they are to adult beggars.

After a couple of days of being subjected to this, the members of the tour group complained to their guide about how unpleasant it was to be faced at every turn, with the persistent cloying, shrill harassment by these children. With a twinkle in his eye, the guide responded, *"Aha! Now maybe you understand the real reason they crucified your Jesus. It was for his saying, 'Let the children come and forbid them not.'"*

Interesting reply, wasn't it? Religious artists and illustrators have, as you know, created many dozens of sentimental depictions of this incident with the children. In the background, they show these stuffy looking men with frowns on their faces, while in the foreground, Jesus is smiling warmly as he hugs the children (who look like miniaturized adults)—all of them clean, orderly, docile, and gazing with abject reverence into Jesus' face.

When I was a child, it never occurred to me to question

the realism of those pictures. It was only after I became a parent myself that I realized that those portrayals were not much like any situation I could imagine, in which children wound up at an adult gathering. In fact, I found that I had gained at least a little bit of understanding of those adults in the pictures (and in the scripture) who weren't too wild about turning this event into a "kid thing."

Maybe young children were totally different back then, but I doubt it. I suspect that they had the same short attention spans, the same irrepressible energy, the same impatience, the same explosive emotions, the same shrill voices, and the same ability to exhaust their parents that children do now.

I read about a mother who was registering her youngest child in a new school and was filling out a routine questionnaire regarding him. He was, as it turned out, a wildly energetic, rambunctious boy with some degree of attention deficit. After all the usual questions on the questionnaire, there was a space for "other remarks." The school administrator said that, in bold letters this mother had written, "YOU'D BETTER BRACE YOURSELF!"

Something similar is echoed by the kindergarten teacher who described teaching her class as being like trying to keep twenty-two corks under water at the same time.

The late Phyllis Diller claimed that she found the key to emotional tranquility written on one of her medicine bottles. The label said, "Keep away from children."

Another such dour quip came from a parent who said, "Anyone who says that money can't buy happiness, has never sent his kids away to summer camp."

Among the most biting of such obviously jaundiced comments was that of the third grade teacher who said that, if there is such a thing as reincarnation, she hoped to come back as a childhood disease.

In short, to have said to the parents of these kids (as did Jesus), that the Kingdom of Heaven is just like this bunch of children, might well have found them thinking, *"Easy for him to say. He's single. He's not parenting twenty-four hours a day! Wait till he has kids."*

So, no, unless this was intended to be a miracle story, that is, unless Jesus was showing off the fact that, not only could he walk on water, calm storms, cure leprosy, and raise the dead, he also could magically turn primary-age children into sedate, orderly, placid, and reverent miniature adults, there had to have been something more he was saying here.

The subject matter at the time had to do with struggles with sin and temptation, with the matter of divorce, and other complex issues. These, obviously, were adult matters and needed rational adult discussion. So why, in the midst of that, would he suddenly allow the focus to switch to these kids with their runny noses, sandals untied, skinned knees, and peanut butter smears on their cheeks?

But he does so, saying, moreover, that until and unless we can accept the child—that is, that whole childlike aspect of our humanity—we are out of touch with the kingdom of God.

You can bet that *that* was not what they expected to hear. If anything, they would have hoped to hear Jesus share their impatience at those not "grown up" enough to become more practical and "suitable" in their living; not only kids, but the ones who get their feelings hurt at age 35 as easily as they did at age 5, the ones who stubbornly don't tone down their expectations to fit the practicalities of the real world, or the ones who aren't as solemn about adult matters as a serious adult ought to be. For after all, our decorum, our respectability, our composure, and keeping some semblance of refinement is difficult enough, without Jesus coming along and saying that, not only do we need to take another look at the child that is among us and within us, but that until we do, the very kingdom of God remains out of our reach. *"Whoever cannot welcome the Kingdom of God as would a little child, cannot enter it,"* was his comment.

What are we supposed to make of that? Maybe you have already figured it out. It has to do with the fact that, despite how smooth, how chic, how urbane, how well put together we become in adulthood, there is still an active child in us that won't really go away and cannot be completely hidden.

Frighten some of us badly enough, suddenly drop others of us into surroundings where we are terribly lonely, hit certain ones of us with biting criticism or ridicule, arrange for yet others not to prevail a few times, when our hearts were set on winning, yank away from us our usual sources of protection and security, and it can be stunning to see what can become of all that cool, adult reasonableness, the controlled detachment, the seamless aura of self-sufficiency. To a shocking extent, it can suddenly be replaced with cringing, whining, hiding, pouting, tantrums, and other behavior all-too-reminiscent of the six-year-old whom we preferred to believe is no longer lurking in us.

I am quite certain that that is why Jesus wouldn't let them send the children away that day when they were being so respectably and sedately adult about some very serious matters. It was an acted-out parable that said, like it or not, the child remains right there in the midst of things. That's because authentic life isn't the smooth, dispassionate, adult-appearing, perfectly appropriate, flawlessly executed matter that we sometimes imagine it to be when trying to be sophisticated in the living of it.

In fact, we do well to recognize that most, if not all, of our disdain, irritation, impatience, and indignation with certain others who don't seem to us to show the maturity they should, bothers us because at some level we recognize that their very childishness also lurks somewhere not far below the surface in ourselves.

She is so emotional about things! She cannot seem to control her tears, her anger, or her enthusiasm. It makes everyone uncomfortable.

He is so self-centered, so preoccupied with what HE'S been doing, with what is upsetting to HIM, with what it is that HE wants. He's like a little kid! (True enough; a kid I know all too well.)

She's impulsive and doesn't stop to think about how her actions look, or of what are the implications of what she says or does. Where is her sense of appropriateness?

He's so indecisive, so dubious, always so uneasy about anything new. His fears and misgivings make no sense. When's he going to outgrow that?

Her sticky, sweet, little-girl manner drives me, and everyone else I know, up the wall. I'd expect it in a six-year-old, but it infuriates me in an adult.

His perpetual cowering, fawning, waffling, and trying to ingratiate himself to anyone and everyone is disgusting. He needs to grow some backbone and stop worrying about being liked by everyone.

Yes, people who exhibit those and other insecurities, anxieties, and quirks that we consider childish often "get to us" disproportionately. *"Keep him/her away from me. I can't stand that sort of thing."*

But Jesus said, "No. The kids stay!" And I don't think it was just his attempt to be nice and indulgent toward them. It was because he knew that their efforts to dismiss or push out all childishness and immaturity were, at least partly, a denial of that aspect of themselves. He knew that they (and we) quickly become brittle and stuffy when we succeed in denying that about ourselves. He knew how much we need to be in touch with the "littleness" of us, the insecurity that still haunts us, the loneliness that we fear, the wish for attention that is very alive and well within us, the uncertainty about whether we are really loved, or even liked, that is still there in every last one of us. Yes, if you and I are honest in remembering our own least admirable and most childish moments in the last three months, we know that our having become grown-ups is a "sometimes" and "on-again-off-again" thing.

Leo Rosten touched on the principle of it when he said,

> You can understand and relate to most people better if you look at them—no matter how old or impressive they may be—as if they are children. For most of us never really grow up or mature all that much. We simply grow taller. To be sure, we laugh less and play less and wear uncomfortable disguises like adults, but beneath the costume, is the child we always are.

Exactly! Even though right now we may feel more secure, less afraid, or more confident than some others do, that doesn't mean what we may have told ourselves: that those others are, by nature, childish while we have outgrown all of that. The child in us may be under somewhat better control for now, but none of us outgrows it.

In fact, depend upon it. That the very immaturity, impulsiveness, dependency, attention-getting ploys, or other childishness that we most wish to get out of our sight stands an excellent chance of carrying in it this vital, if painful, source of truth about ourselves.

Then there is this, too. There are also positive graces in that child that need to be kept alive in you and me. One could take from this that God is not totally enthralled with our solemn adult "posings" and assemblages of discreet, antiseptically correct, always scrubbed and combed, decent and ordered "niceness" as we may have thought God would be. The spontaneity of the child, the playfulness of the child, the unselfconscious capacity for wonder of the child, and the emotional openness of the child are all gifts of God that, in adulthood, easily get misplaced or traded for dull pieties and cautious stuffiness. There, too, as Jesus said, the kingdom of God will not be yours or mine unless, and until, we can embrace the child in our midst.

So, there was more than we may have thought to this little incident where Jesus reacted so strongly that afternoon to the attempt to get the children out of sight. The message was not that it's our Christian duty to grit our teeth and bear with a certain amount of foolishness and immaturity, as we try so hard to keep intact as an orderly adult world. No. Rather, I am pushed here to take another careful look at whoever it is that I'd like to send away, at whoever's immature behavior is driving me crazy, at the whining or complaining or childish blustering that feels so mature to condemn.

If I understand this correctly, while I don't have to like or even excuse childishness, I do well to examine what drives my irritation with it. There is usually important truth to which we need to attend in whatever most aggravates us. In fact, only when I finally am able to recognize my own reflection in another person's struggling, or in her paralyzing uncertainty, or his inept way of coping, or her clumsiness in her encounters, or his overreactions when scared, will I really understand enough about myself to be an effective forgiven and forgiving son or daughter of God.

So don't, then, try to hide from the child. In all that childlikeness, he or she embodies some of the very truth about ourselves that you and I need.

Getting Permission

Luke 14:1-6

One Sabbath day, Jesus was on his way to the home of a Pharisee for a meal. They were watching him closely. In front of him appeared a man who was having trouble breathing. Seeing that he was being closely watched, Jesus asked the Pharisees and lawyers, "Is it lawful to cure a person on the Sabbath Day?" They did not answer.

After healing the man and sending him on his way, Jesus said to them, "If one of you has a child or even an ox that has fallen into a well, do you not immediately rescue it, even if it happens on the Sabbath?" To this, they did not know how to reply.

For the Pharisees, this incident was about whether Jesus (or anyone else, for that matter) was free to help this man—a man who apparently had congestive heart failure. What they discovered was that, though it had directly to do with disobedience to one of the Ten Commandments, Jesus didn't wait for anyone's approval or permission to go ahead and do what he saw as needed.

Couldn't he at least have humored them—tried harder to get their permission first? I think that's what I might have tried to do. He might have said, for example:

Gentlemen, it looks like we have one of those gray-area situations here. On the one hand, it IS the Sabbath and keeping the Sabbath "holy" is important. On the other hand, the way this man's breathing sounds, he might not make it until the end of the Sabbath. As devout, but also reasonable people, I assume that you would all agree that God will understand if I go ahead and do a little something for him right now. I'll feel a lot better about it, though, if I have your support to do so.

Jesus didn't do that. Not only here, but throughout his ministry, he wasn't very good at waiting for approvals and permissions. It is almost as if he subscribed to the contemporary saying that, *"It's a whole lot easier to get forgiveness for something afterwards than it is to get permission ahead of time."*

What we're talking about is that confusing, often loaded, matter of approval—of that common wish for someone to give us permission or consent for what we do and how we live.

I loved the bit of ersatz history that Dave Barry tells in his book, *Claw Your Way To The Top*. He claims that Attila The Hun had a brother, Bob The Hun, who got lost in history. Bob the Hun is not remembered because he was a more cautious and accommodating person than his brother, Attila. In fact, whenever Bob The Hun and his bloodthirsty followers arrived at the edge of a new town, Bob would always ask the townspeople for permission to steal everything, to rape the women, and to burn the houses. When the people said "No!", Bob The Hun would apologize and leave. Barry points out that it was because of his need for everyone's consent before doing anything, that Bob The Hun was lost in obscurity. Actually, that's a somewhat flawed example of what we are talking about here, but the problem is, nevertheless, real.

Undoubtedly, much of what turns out to be a powerful need for all the consents and approvals we can possibly get, dates back to when we were young children and we were required to ask permission for virtually everything. Rightly so. Getting it was an important part of avoiding childhood perils. Unfortunately, some of us never learned to feel okay without it. We simply switched to other larger permission givers.

If, with this in mind, one listens to us carefully, it is revealing to discover how many kinds of permission people just assume that they DO NOT have.

I just couldn't! People wouldn't understand.

My family would think I was losing it.

I'd have no problem with it, if I knew for certain that a lot of others had tried it.

Oh, I'll ask my husband and my sister if this would be a good idea for me, but I already know what they'll say.

I could never make a move like that while Dad is still alive. It would kill him.

And on and on goes the catalog of *ad hoc* authorities from whom it feels necessary to obtain at least tacit permission. Thus, a lot of energy and ingenuity is spent trying to obtain permissions that we really don't need, fishing for pre-approval before each decision, and refusing to commit without the consent of what we have allowed to be the authorities over our lives. What that adds up to is nothing less than a refusal to embrace the inner authority that God has given to each of us.

Examples? How about the millions of us who can't feel like successful and worthwhile individuals in life without all, or most, of the approved possessions or status symbols that we've been led to believe need to be there for anyone who is really "okay." And from whom does that approval come? As absurd as it may seem, when we are forced to admit it, the approval-givers are clothing designers, automobile manufacturers, real estate developers, ad agencies, and any number of others just as inappropriate to ever be allowed to hold the key to a person's sense of worth. Empowering such trivial, banal authorities to furnish or withhold from us the approvals and acceptances that are then allowed to shape our living makes no sense, but, to an embarrassing extent, they do.

Applying the same quirk in a whole different arena, the permission to forgive ourselves is one that a great many of us seem to have farmed out to external sources.

Now it is true that, by its very nature, forgiveness does have to do with our relationship with others. Nevertheless, in the final analysis, no one outside of us should ever have veto power over our feeling that we're forgiven. Nobody outside of us should be able say whether it is okay now for you or me to let go of what is done and over with. There is no one in your or my world whose approval we should need before moving on, after some remorse and repentance. That's because it's a matter between each one of us and God. And there is a second reason. It is that, in addition to all of the wonderfully forgiving people around us, there are also those pathological grudge-holders and life-long "resenters" to whom, if it is left to them, we'll grovel in regret and guilt forever. So, as important as the forgiveness of each other is, the responsibility for and the permission to be a forgiven person finally has to rest with you and me.

Yet another way it is easy to see that this troubles our life is in those who lack the permission to take the pressure off themselves. They don't feel they have the right to do it. It is not even clear to whom that permission is turned over, but it IS clear that some don't have it. At its worst and most absurd, the permission to "let up" finally has to come from a heart attack or some other grave, stress-related disability or disintegration. Only when, physically, they cannot go on, does it feel all right to quit being "productive," to no longer be "achieving," to not have to be demonstrably "useful," and, in general, to quit trying to manage the universe. Until the day that the machinery collapses or some other circumstances conspire to call a halt, the permission isn't quite there.

Then, too, are those of us who, if the truth be known, are uncomfortable allowing ourselves a strong, self-generated viewpoint that hasn't first been validated and approved by the social circle of which we are a part, or perhaps consented to by one's husband or wife, or maybe checked out with his religious group or, as in many cases, shown to be consistent with her political party. These are often the same ones who don't know whether or not they liked the film they just saw, the concert they just attended, or the book they just read—until they read the reviews. As an "ordinary person," they believe it to be presumptuous, if not dangerous, to have convictions and passionate concerns purely on their own.

Also common are those tortured souls who, lacking the ability to ever be approving of themselves with their particular flaws, imperfections, and susceptibilities, spend their lives role-playing, maintaining a facade and, in general, running from the unique individuals that they are. Some of the luckier ones, after spending thousands of dollars on therapy, find that approval, but it's a tragically overdue embracing of the personal authority with which God endowed us.

Those are enough examples to identify the phenomenon, aren't they? The sources of it are fairly obvious.

Sometimes, as I've already suggested, it's a matter of never having moved beyond the time in our childhood and youth when consents were still needed. So, instead of discovering themselves as freestanding, adult centers of thought, of intention, of power, of decision, they merely find new authorities to whom they subject themselves. Some, in fact, cling to those early approval sources. Millions of adults—though way up in mid-life—still remain stuck, immobilized, and disoriented in the absence of their parents' approvals. But whether that, or a replacement authority like a spouse, a friend, or a therapist, it needs desperately to be understood how unnecessary and inappropriate it is, and then to drop it and move out of it. The habit (and habit is all it is) of granting others the power to overrule or second-guess or give a final okay to the choices and wisdom God has given us, profanes the very image of God in us.

Another source of the problem is even worse. It is the not-at-all-noble need (as some are fond of describing it) to "always cover our own rear ends" in our acting and deciding. That's what's behind it when someone says, *"Well you know, it's not just me. I know a whole lot of people who feel just as strongly as I do,"* or *"I'm only telling you what all the recognized authorities say,"* or *"I'm not going to say anything until I've had a chance to discuss it with people who know all about this sort of thing."* It's not, you see, that there's anything wrong with considering the perspectives of others in forming one's own perspective. There is nothing wrong with that, UNLESS, that is, we do it in order to keep from speaking or acting on our own personal authority. In that case, it is cowardice.

Finally, the other major source of a runaway need for the approval and consent of others is the simple refusal to believe that God has not only given us full authority to think and decide and question and act, but has also given each one of us a unique set of understandings, intuition, imagination, and creativity that is unlike that of anyone else. Refusing to trust and embrace that truth about us is to discard what is most important and exciting about us. What gets thrown away are the distinctive insights, the vital "yes's" or the "no's," the particular wisdom that has unfolded in each of us, and the experiences and "comprehensions" peculiar to each one of us. It's not that our inner authority is always perfectly accurate on all matters, but it is nonetheless always important because it is part of the fabric of God's presence and truth being woven into our shared life.

Think carefully about it, then. For example, what two or three permissions might you or I have farmed out to someone or something else?

What is there that we have not pursued or not offered that we should have because something or someone hasn't yet indicated that it is okay?

Where, if anywhere, have we not yet forgiven ourselves for something, because some unforgiving person is withholding permission for us to do so?

What contentment or self-esteem continues to elude us because certain external indicators seem to tell us that we haven't achieved enough yet or accumulated enough yet to be validly content and at peace with ourselves?

What strong conviction or concern are we keeping under wraps because, since we are not approved experts, we don't feel that it is proper to express it?

Maybe there are none. That's great, if so. But again, think about it. Each of us has more personal authority and freedom than we have likely begun to explore. Moreover, it's God-given. If by any chance we are seeing it otherwise, that's a nasty form of sacrilege that we are committing upon ourselves.

Possessed

Acts 7:51-52 & 57-60

Stephen continued speaking. "How stubborn you are," he said, "cynical at heart and blind to what is true. You always resist the Spirit of God. You are so like your ancestors. Was there ever a prophet who your fathers did not persecute? They killed those who foretold the coming of The Righteous One. Now you have become his betrayers and murderers."

At this the crowd covered their ears. They screamed at him, rushed him, and dragged him out of the city and proceeded to stone him. While doing so, they laid their coats at the feet of a young man named Saul. As the stones began to strike him, Stephen called out, "Lord, receive my spirit." As he fell to the ground, he cried aloud, "O God, do not hold this sin against them." Then he died. The young man, Saul, was among those who approved of Stephen's stoning.

A stoning was an ugly thing—possibly seeming especially so when the person being stoned was so young, handsome, and obviously intelligent. What a waste! But the feeling, even among some good, responsible people was that, though unfortunate, this stoning was necessary. In fact, had there been a local newspaper, undoubtedly the editorial the next day would have spelled out why. It would have pointed out that the stoning was only a tragic symptom of what had become a dangerous infection. It would have gone on to explain that no society can afford to sit by and allow young women and men to be radicalized by teachings like those of the martyred carpenter, Jesus. It would have concluded saying, *"Sincere as he may have been, people like Stephen undermine the faith of our fathers and our beloved Hebrew way of life. Their very passion makes them a clear and present danger to themselves, to religion, and to society."*

So the talk around the tables, the next week at the Jerusalem Rotary Club, would go something like, *"Who do people like that think they are, anyhow? Being fervent, being ardent, and being enthusiastic is okay to a point, but not when a person gets carried away as he did."* A few would speculate that Stephen's parents were partly to blame, having failed to teach him proper restraint, discretion, and gentility while he was growing up. Those with kids would go home to tell their teenagers to let Stephen's execution be a lesson for them.

What lesson? What moral? It was that, "Above all, one must stay 'cool'!" Never forget that you are merely one person. Remember that there are many people who are older, wiser, and more experienced than you are. Sure, you have a right to strong feelings, but keep them personal and private. Restraint and self-control are the keys to getting by in life, so don't get carried away. You could end up like Stephen: quite literally have to be carried away. That would have been the conventional wisdom among the onlookers.

There is more to the story, though. As you heard, a young man named Saul was entrusted with guarding the coats, umbrellas, and briefcases of those who actually got in there and threw the stones. Saul was also a young man—also a person of considerable passion. Watching Stephen's grisly death affected him deeply. So, while most of the crowd went home vowing to be still more careful about not rocking the boat, yet more determined to measure their words and ride herd on their feelings, Saul was inflamed and incensed by what happened that afternoon. *"What contagious kind of sick religion was it that could so horribly infect this fellow, Stephen, that it brought it to a point of his having to be put to death? Whatever Christianity was, something needed to be done about it before it destroyed anyone else!"*

Saul was so upset that he decided, then and there, to drop all else that he was doing, to acquire the necessary authorization, and to then make it his personal mission to stamp out these Christians and their poisonous beliefs. Shortly, he had become as dedicated a persecutor as Stephen had been as a teacher—awesome in his pursuit and imprisonment of Christians.

It is well known what subsequently happened. One day, chasing down some Christians who had gone to Syria, Saul had an experience that stopped him cold. He said he heard the Lord speaking to him, asking him why he was persecuting Christians. Saul was dumbfounded, bewildered, and aghast. He had thought he was doing the very work of God. If this experience were real, it called for a total reversal in his thinking and believing.

It WAS real and he DID reverse himself. Not only did he quit persecuting, but within a very few days, all of the passion that he had poured into persecuting was now focused upon spreading Christianity. He changed his name to Paul, came to be called the Apostle Paul, and would eventually write much of what is our New Testament.

That was certainly odd of God, wasn't it? By then, there were many hundreds of Christians—good, circumspect, even-tempered, self-possessed people—people, moreover, who had never persecuted anyone. So why would God choose Saul? Why someone so impulsive and so vulnerable to his own intractable fervor—someone whom many would consider to have more enthusiasm than good sense?

Obviously, I don't know why. What I do know is that, from its beginning to its end, our Bible is full of accounts of God becoming present in persons just like this. They are the sort of whom their critics routinely say such things as,

I really like him—love his enthusiasm—but he needs to chill out a bit.

Her fervor is endearing and charming, but that passionate impetuousness of hers makes me and a lot of others uncomfortable.

Saul, for God's sake stop and look at yourself. Last month you were arresting Christians. This week you're one of them.

Stephen, no one doubts your sincerity or your commitment. It's your intensity, your zeal, and your extravagant way of expressing yourself that scares people—even makes them downright hostile.

Sometimes, feedback like that is precisely what that person needs. There certainly are those who intoxicate themselves with their own emotions the way someone else abuses drugs. They work themselves into artificial emotional "highs" over anything and everything—passion for passion's own sake.

A reporter discovered a prime example of that, while doing a human interest story on a weekend political campaign rally in a very rural town in the Ozarks. He noticed that every candidate was receiving the wildest of yelling, whistling, and clapping from the entire crowd. Everyone seemed to explode with enthusiasm, no matter which side of which issue the candidate supported. Confused by this, the reporter buttonholed one of the loudest and most exuberant and said, *"Sir, you're obviously excited about all of this. But tell me, what do you really think about what they're saying on these issues?"*

The man replied, *"Mister, I didn't come to town today to think. I came here to holler!"*

That, I submit, is cheap enthusiasm—the kind that constantly oozes out of some for no significant reason and to no particular end—full of sound and fury, but of no significance. It's whipped up merely to mask boredom and to make themselves feel more alive than they are.

Such synthetic passion notwithstanding, though, we need to remember that the word "enthusiasm" is derived from a Greek word which means "possessed by a god." And there is a very real sense in which "possessed by a god—by THE GOD" should be the working definition of you and Ibeing Christian.

And it does not mean, as some seem to think, merely getting all emotional about God or about Jesus or about matters religious. No, this is a much broader and deeper definition of enthusiasm than any gratuitous religious cheerleading.

This is enthusiasm that has overtones of "appetite"—an appetite for living. One sees it in the kind of person who is pulled along by a sense of purpose, not just herded along by circumstance. It is to be caught up by a vision of what all could come to be. It is to be willing to risk turning one's full energy and imagination loose upon something that everyone else considers idealistic or impossible.

A California resident reported answering the door one afternoon, to find a seven- or eight-year-old boy holding a can with a slot in the top. After a polite greeting, the boy said, *"At school I found out that there are millions of boys and girls in the world who are starving to death right now, so I am collecting money for food to feed them."* The resident was amused at the naivete of the boy, and condescendingly replied, *"So you then, young man, all by yourself, are going to collect the money to feed all the world's hungry children?"* But without flinching, the boy replied, *"No, not by myself. I've got another boy helping me."*

Impractical, naive, and childlike as one might label that boy, there is a quick glimpse of holy enthusiasm—that very "being possessed by God" that caught up the Abrahams and the Moseses and the Stephens and the Sauls and the Martin Luthers and the Gandhis and countless others who became incarnations of God's presence, blessing human life and history.

It works that way, notwithstanding the fact that there will always be that dizzy, ditsy kind of emotionalism under which, far from being possessed by God, one becomes a loose cannon. Because of that dippy kind of passion for passion's own sake, it can be very tempting to decide that the path to Godliness, goodness, and maturity is that of never letting ourselves get carried away about anything. NOT SO! Those who are careful to never let themselves get carried away, never go much of anywhere. Emotional quietude, tentativeness, diffidence, timorousness, knee-jerk moderateness and dispassion—far from being Christian virtues—are merely a way of drugging the very spirit of us, through which we become incarnations of God (if or when we do).

What, then, does this being "possessed by a God" look like in you and me? How do you let it happen?

It requires, for example, believing that you are (that I am) uniquely in precisely the right spot to make some vital difference—whether through speaking some truth, awakening some hope, restoring some lightness, bringing some warmth, or yet something else—AND that nothing will be more life-giving to you or me than discovering it and doing it.

It is to go ahead, then, and trust the fire that God ignites in your own soul. Knowing how God has been able to move and speak through the passions of people throughout history, it is to take seriously the possibility that your dreams, your vision, your grasp of the truth could well be the very word of God where you are working or caring or struggling right now.

It is living with a certainty that God always has higher hopes for you and for me than you or I have for ourselves, and that opening ourselves to everything that might mean is our true spiritual task.

It is to be confident and buoyant because you know that, contrary to the sad bleating of the doomsayers, the future is radically open—that there is no inevitability, except for people stupid enough to believe in inevitability.

It is to be determinedly lighthearted, not because everything is always okay. There is much that isn't. You are light-hearted, though, because of a faith that, in God's own way, God can and does ultimately bring all things to work together for good. That sets you and me free to relinquish control, to quit trying to manage everything for God, and to be excited rather than anxious about whatever may be coming toward us from the future.

Can this being "possessed by a god" be complicating? Yes, it usually is. Is it ever controversial? Often. Will allowing oneself to get carried away make life less predictable? Count on it!

But if we are to believe what, in hundreds of different ways, this Bible of ours tells us, to be possessed by a god— THE GOD—is still the only way in which one becomes truly alive!

"Spare–Tire" Religion
(Scripture: James 2:14-19)

Not often, but from time to time, a total stranger will make an appointment to see me for a reason that I find unsettling. After introducing himself or herself, the person will explain that this is a little uncomfortable, since he or she is not a part of any church and has never felt much need for, or interest in, religious matters. Now, though (he goes on), everything has gone wrong and matters are worsening by the day. He says that he has tried everything he can think of to get life back in order, but nothing helps. He is desperate. The bottom line (and the reason for making the appointment with me) goes something like this: *"So I've decided that maybe what I need is a religion."* It is said with all of the grim resignation with which a person might also say, *"I've had to face up to the fact that I am going to have to get glasses (or wear arch-supports, or dentures, or carry a cane, or use crutches, or buy a hearing-aid)."* All pride has been swallowed in the feeling that, now, there is so little to lose that it might even be worth this visit to a minister in hopes of hooking up with some divine help.

To me, it echoes that old story about the man who, while mountain climbing alone, lost his footing and slid to the very edge of a rock overhang. Only a tenuous handhold kept him from plunging hundreds of feet to his death. Quite unable to climb back, he hung there yelling for help, but to no avail. Finally, although not at all a religious person, he began to pray, *"O God, I know I may have ignored you. I know that I have not been a very moral person and that I haven't earned your help. But if you'll get me out of this, I promise henceforth to be devout, moral, generous, faithful, caring, and........"* At which point, he interrupted himself. He listened for a second and then said, *"Never mind, God. Scratch all that. I just* heard voices. A search party is on the way."

I don't find anything gratifying about any person driven in blind desperation to "try religion" as some kind of last resort. To the contrary, it is frightening to me because of that person's sheer vulnerability to quackery when he starts looking for a quick religious "fix" for his problems or pain. In addition to whatever else has gone wrong in his life, he may well now also become a victim of exploitation and manipulation by any of countless religious charlatans.

And it is not only worrisome. It is also depressing. It is depressing because it is one more reminder of the all-too-common "spare tire" impression of what faith is. Your car's spare tire, as you know, doesn't cost much to carry around with you. Other than a very occasional look at it, it is "out of mind" most of the time. It will be brought forth only for very short intervals and quickly put out of sight again. It is easily hidden underneath a lot of other baggage. Nevertheless, one feels better knowing that there is one, even if he doesn't know how to access it.

"Spare tire" religiousness, of course, does not bear the slightest resemblance to what faith is and what it has to do with a person's life. No, it is one of several common "trivializations" of the spiritual dimension of us and, unfortunately, is not the only one. I would like to try to sort out just that with you for a few moments: what we mean and what we do NOT mean when we speak of faith.

The most common confusion in this area is the confusion between faith and belief. While belief and faith are definitely related, they are by no means the same thing. One can be an avid believer and still be shallow, self-absorbed, and amoral. The writer, philosopher, and researcher, William James, after decades of studying human religious behavior said, *"People will believe anything and would believe everything, if they only could."* Yes! Put simply, "beliefs are a dime a dozen" and some people put them on and take them off as they might a sweater or a hat. The writer of the New Testament book of James says it well:

> *"So you say you believe in God, do you? That's nice, but the very demons in hell also believe in God."*
> (James 2:19)

So while one's beliefs definitely can express one's faith and spirituality, they can just as easily be no more than the shallowest, most random dabblings of thought. In fact, as you may have observed, it is sometimes those with the least intellectual integrity and/or the least depth for whom beliefs come most easily. *"Just tell me what to believe. I'll believe it, no problem: the tooth fairy, the number seven, the blarney stone, oat bran, a weather-predicting ground hog or wooly-bear caterpillar, channeling, fortune cookies, crystals, coins in the fountain, Jesus, God, Buddha, bio-rhythms, the ouija board."* Without even straining hard, some seem able to cram much or most of that and more into their bag of beliefs. Maybe the hope is that the more dogmas, doctrines, and theories a person can swallow, the more spiritual it indicates that she is. That is not true, and it is not faith. One's faith is seen in what he is moved to do and become, not in what he is able to browbeat himself into thinking.

Faith is also not a way of making an end run around what is real—is not the kind of wish-magic, for example, in which, by closing your eyes, gritting your teeth, and praying something as hard as you can, you might be able to suspend reality or reverse some law of the universe or cause to be true what is not true.

An image for that was the Roman Catholic Missionary who, many years ago, encountered a Hindu man one day. After spending an hour or so explaining the wonders of

Christianity and Catholicism to him, he persuaded the man to let him baptize him into the Catholic faith. The Hindu finally agreed. The Priest finished the rite of baptism saying, "*And now, O God, in word and in water you have transformed this man from a Hindu into a Catholic. So be it!*"

The next day—a Friday—he found his convert dining on some cooked rabbit. Since this was back when Catholics did not eat red meat on Fridays, he scolded the man, reminding him that even as a Catholic, fish was the only acceptable meat on this day. But the man replied, "*It's okay. As soon as I caught the rabbit, before killing it, I baptized it and prayed, 'And now, O God, by word and by water you have transformed this creature from a rabbit into a fish; and so be it!'*"

The convert obviously saw his new belief as providing him with a whole bag of religious tricks for altering reality. Obviously, faith has nothing to do with that sort of attempt to manipulate one's world (though some keep hoping that they can make it work that way).

Also, faith is not at all to be confused with "fatalism," with passivity, with the pious helplessness that sometimes masquerades as being devout. "*It was meant to be*" and "*Whatever will be will be*" and belief in predestination and in foregone conclusions, rather than proving one's faith, is more often only a pseudo-religious way of excusing and exempting oneself from having to care, from forming demanding intentions, from maintaining intelligent hopes, and from using one's personal power to affect what happens. The mother of that "I-just-leave-everything-up-to-God" sort of thing had to be the woman reported in the news a couple of years ago who, after a serious one-car accident, told officers that, once the car had begun to skid sideways, she had just thrown up her hands and said, "*God, You take the wheel.*" It is merely a dippy superstition that hopes that if I make myself totally helpless, defenseless, and devoid of will, then God is obligated to come to the rescue. That is fantasy, not faith.

But if, then, faith is not really a psychological spare tire or a shortcut means of avoiding trouble and pain, or an anesthetic, or a holy kind of magic, or a capsule of beliefs one must swallow in order to stay on God's good side, how should faith in God be thought of? What role does it play in life? What difference should it make in us or to us?

It is actually much closer to being the set of presuppositions with which you approach your living—that which keeps you caring, moved, excited, and hopeful. There are many analogies that hint at it. One tells of a piano in which five mice were born. There in the piano, they were, of course, surrounded by wonderful harmonies. Being scientific mice, they investigated their surroundings and soon observed that the remarkable sounds came when wires vibrated as they were struck by hammers. So it was all a happy accident and *"Wasn't it fortunate that it happened to work that way for them"*? But then one day, one of the five tripped and fell through an opening, landing outside the piano. As he recovered from the shock of the fall, he realized that he was looking at a person sitting on a bench, deliberately pushing keys that caused the hammers to strike the wires, resulting in the wonderful harmonies.

This changed everything! He hurried back to the inside of the piano with great excitement to tell his mouse brothers. They laughed and ridiculed his story; told him that it was completely preposterous. They suggested that whatever fall he had taken had damaged his mind. For after all, they had all seen the hammers striking the wires, hadn't they? Why would any mouse in his right mind complicate things by coming to believe that there was some larger presence, purpose, process, or intention behind the harmonies that swirled around them? It was much easier on them to believe that there was no meaning beyond what they had determined.

The story hints at what is the legitimate link between

faith and belief. It is not at all belief, in the sense of making up one's mind once and for all, just how everything is. No. This is a much more humble type of believing—a kind of trusting that there is always more going on than I know. This is a belief that, whether I understand it or not, there is a yet more profound process, a still larger intention at work in us and around us. In the case of Christians, it is "belief" in the sense of staying open to the possibility that the God of creation actually works, speaks, and acts through you and me, something like that which we saw lived and revealed in Jesus.

"Faith" like this, by the way, is not exclusive to Christians. Etty Hillesman, a Dutch Jewish woman was in her twenties when the Nazis began terrorizing the Jews of Holland. She managed to keep writing diaries and letters during those black days of hardship and persecution—letters that survived and that reverberate of the sense of calling and of purpose that kept her moving, growing, and inspired, despite the horrible circumstances of her living. In one passage she wrote:

> I only want to be true to that in me which seeks to fulfill its promise. . . . I think I have matured enough to assume my "destiny," to cease living an accidental life. . . . It is no longer a romantic dream or the thirst for adventure or for love—all of which can drive you to commit mad and irresponsible acts. No, it is a terrible, sacred, inner seriousness, difficult and, at the same time, inevitable.

As perhaps you could hear, that was not about some teeth-gritting belief that God just HAD TO soon reverse her circumstances, that divine vindication was on the way, or even that a glorious outcome to her suffering was assured her. What Etty Hillesman believed was that no matter what happened or how things appeared, as long as she was able to draw breath, with God's help, she would still have gifts to give, would have truth to stand for, and would herself be a creator of meaning.

That's where the difference gets made. Once again, faith has very little to do with whether or not someone can make himself believe in the doctrine of the trinity or in the virgin birth or in reported miracles or in someone's picture of heaven and hell.

Rather, you'll know that you are looking at it when you see someone living and giving and caring, NOT because it is working for him, but because he seems to know that *that* is what he was created for.

Faith is what is behind it when she spends and sacrifices and risks herself trusting that, whatever the outcome, God won't lose or waste or discard what she has given.

Faith—not merely a collection of beliefs—is quite likely what it is when his concern seems to us to be excessive, her dreams are impossible ones, his love appears to be wasted, if not trampled, or when she keeps on "keeping on" well beyond the normal dictates of her self-preservation instinct.

I read of an incident that took place in a Tennessee hospital that, for me, gets at it. A woman named Karen was pregnant with her second child. As part of preparing her three-year-old son, Michael, for the coming of his unborn baby sister, she encouraged him to sit by her and to sing to the unborn baby each night. He did this, night after night.

The pregnancy seemed a normal one, but there was serious trouble at the time of delivery. Michael's baby sister barely survived the birth and was rushed to a neonatal intensive care unit in Knoxville. There the infant girl continued to become weaker. The physicians began to prepare the parents for her probable death.

Though too young to understand all that was going on, Michael kept asking his parents to let him see his little sister. He said he had to sing to her. He was so passionate about it that, at the beginning of the second week, they finally dressed Michael in a far oversized scrub suit and took him into the ICU to see his sister. The medical personnel were upset and said that he would have to leave. Karen protested vehemently and dug in saying, *"He's not leaving until he sings to his sister."* They reluctantly relented, and Michael made his way to the bassinet and began to sing his same song:

> *You are my sunshine, my only sunshine.*
> *You make me happy when skies are gray.*
> *You'll never know, dear, how much I love you.*
> *Please don't take my sunshine away.*

The next day—the day on which they thought they would be making funeral arrangements—they were able to bring Michael's sister home. Her improvement was sudden and astounding. A news article called it the "miracle of a brother's song." Karen called it an act of God. The physician dubbed it miraculous.

Astonishing as was the outcome, though, don't become completely mesmerized by the unexpected recovery. It is Michael we should remember. Little Michael knew nothing of alternative possible outcomes. His song was not a religious one. All he knew (with or without proper theological beliefs) was that he had a song to sing—a gift that he believed he was there to give, no matter what anyone else thought.

Right there, in an exceedingly simple expression, is a strong hint of what faith looks like in a human being. You are a gift—you have gifts, and by God they are going to be given! I don't know what that might mean for each of the lives present here, but I hope we are working at it with all our hearts.

Not as Grim as Some Make It

There is an old story wherein a man driving across a high bridge notices a fellow on the outside of the pedestrian railing, perched on a girder. He is obviously poised to jump to his death. He stops his car and runs to where the jumper is, grabbing him just as he is about to take the plunge. *"Why would you do this?"* he asks the would-be suicide.

"Because there is no reason to go on living," the man replies. *"The world is sick. Life is a mess. I no longer have any hope."*

The rescuer protests, *"That just isn't true. We need to talk. I want you to tell me all about it."*

So the suicidal man does and, twenty minutes later, they BOTH jump off the bridge.

That story came back to me several days ago after hearing a radio preacher doing a Lenten sermon. The sermon was about how worthless and hopelessly sinful we human beings are. *"Even the best of our efforts and intentions,"* he said, *"are miserable and depraved in the eyes of God."* After many minutes of thus describing how despicable, vile, and damnable are every last one of us is by our very nature, he then went on to claim that it was only because of Jesus' torturous death (which he described in much gory detail) that God could even consider not damning every last one of us to an eternity of torture in hell. The hymn after his sermon continued the theme, at one point describing us as "worms" in the eyes of God.

I thought, *"If that sermon is the good news of the Christian Gospel, we can do nicely without it."* If one were to swallow his message, its effect could be as depressing as whatever was said by that bridge-jumper that caused his would-be rescuer to decide to jump to his death also.

It's not that the Bible does not take sin seriously. Throughout its pages, it portrays the cost and the ravages of selfishness, resentment, jealousy, egotism, cynicism, exploitation, callousness, ruthlessness, and violence realistically—clearly and unmistakably. Nor does the Bible whitewash the fact that, from time to time, we are likely to experience undeserved suffering, injustice, sadness, and conflict as a part of life.

None of that is there, though, to bully us or unnerve us to the point of thinking of ourselves and each other (as was portrayed in that radio sermon) as intrinsically defective—so appallingly so that the only good thing to be said about any of us is that, once upon a time, an outstanding man was tortured and killed in a particularly miserable way to soften God's smoldering rage toward us. I don't care how many preachers preach that stuff or how many "good old" hymns croon it—that is not God's word to us in the Christian Gospel.

A certain woman was overheard complimenting her church's new minister after his sermon: *"Oh Reverend Rupert, our congregation really didn't know how sinful we could be until you came to preach to us!"* Besides the inadvertent double meaning to her compliment, it isn't difficult to guess what was the central theme of his preaching, is it?

It is a familiar and longstanding distortion within the Christian Faith—one that has driven off a lot of thoughtful people. You may remember that remarkable poet and jurist, Oliver Wendell Holmes, having once said, *"I might have entered the ministry if the clergymen I knew had not sounded and acted so much like undertakers."* Similarly, Robert Louis Stevenson wrote in his diary (as if he had just experienced a miracle), *"I have been to church today, but I am not depressed!"*

Repeated encounter with gloomy religiousness that depicts God as more ill-tempered, more rancorous, more capricious, and more judgmental than the most unpleasant human beings we know, can be a real turn-off.

Happily, most of us have come to know God as VERY different from that vengeful, intimidating, menacing one.

Nonetheless, vestiges of it still can creep back in. Especially when we are most angry or self-hating, it can be tempting to think that maybe faith ought to be shame-based and predicated upon a foreboding, condemning God after all. NOT SO!

First is the matter of God and God's stance toward creation. It is true that in the most primitive stages of ancient Israel's belief, there are some ominous, even ugly portrayals of God. What those reveal is what belief was like back then, NOT what God is like. Such portrayals notwithstanding, especially in the New Testament, God is ultimately revealed in love—in good will. The opening story in the New Testament proclaims, *"Peace and good will to people of earth with whom God is pleased."* Later on it states that God is made known to us NOT to indict us or condemn us, but to lead us to a more abundant quality of life. Unless then, for some strange or neurotic reason, one prefers to think of God as relishing guilt and remorse, and as nourishing a major grudge because of a bit of disobedient behavior by some lady named Eve, there is no reason to see God as the vindictive divine curmudgeon that many have portrayed.

Second is the matter of the creation itself; that is, our world and life in it. If one reads carefully, the very first chapter of the very first book of our Bible is entirely about the fact that, not only did God create all of this which surrounds us and is us, but (as it says repeatedly) *"It is good." "It is good." "It is very good."* It is not the case, then, that earthly matters are automatically profane and only religious ones are holy. Sacredness is inextricably woven all through life and creation and history. Our calling is to celebrate it and to create with it, NOT detach from it and concentrate only on celestial matters (rather than earthly ones). One old gospel hymn says it about as badly as imaginable. It says,

> This world is not my home. I'm just a-passin' through.
> My treasures are laid out somewhere beyond the blue.
> The angels beckon me from heaven's open door
> And I can't be at home in this world anymore.

It is sad if the songwriter feels that way. For whatever might be there "*somewhere beyond the blue,*" as long as we are not there, the important truth for you and me is that God loves the world and has called you and me to love and care for it also.

The third matter is exceptionally important to have straight in our minds. It is about US—about you and me and what is and is not true of us. I touched on it earlier in talking about the radio preacher who proclaimed that God sees you and me as inherently worthless and defective and would never have forgiven us had not the slaughter of Jesus somehow calmed God down. If that distortion is still haunting you, feel free to dump it, too. It doesn't jibe with the God revealed in Jesus. If one stops to think about it, it doesn't even fit with what you and I have experienced directly in our lives of God's grace and love.

The writer of the Eighth Psalm obviously didn't buy it. He wrote,

> *When I look at your heavens, the work of your hands,*
> *The moon and the stars that you have established;*
> *What are we human beings that you consider us;*
> *Who are we that you so care for us.*
> *Yet you have made us only a little less than gods*
> *And crowned us with glory and dignity.*
> *You have given us dominion over your creation*
> *And put all things under our care.*
> Psalm 8:3-6

YES! That ancient psalmist is squarely on the track. Whatever our problems and weaknesses, we are not creation's abominable defect—so degraded and despoiled that our own creator can barely tolerate us. To the contrary, every indication is that we continue to be purposefully nurtured and loved and gifted. As one writer has described us:

> Each of us, made up of more than a trillion individual cells, all attempting to work together and maintain one another. Our bodies, communities with their own ventilation systems, sewage systems, communication systems, heating units, and a billion miles of inter-connecting streets and alleys.
> And not only our bodies as communities in themselves, but even more: communities in relationship with the earth and with all history. Our bodily fluids carry the same chemicals as the primeval seas. ... We carry these seas within ourselves. Our bones contain the same carbon as that which forms the rock of the oldest mountains. Our blood contains the sugar that once flowed in the sap of now fossilized trees. The nitrogen which binds our bones together is the same as that which binds the nitrates to the soil.
>
> —J.M. Nelson, *Between Two Gardens*

Do you get the picture? The truth about us is not "original sin," as some would have it. No! It is "original blessing" and ongoing hope and amazing support and constant love—even when we are far from at our best.

The other matter, though, that needs comment is that of sin. It IS a problem. I think we know that. We know how tempting it is, in our shallowest, most frightened, most angry, most selfish times to revert to a lower form of us; then to begin hurting, exploiting, cheapening, grasping and a lot more. We are, all of us, susceptible to ignoble, boorish and sometimes savage thoughts and actions. What is NOT true, though, is that we are helpless pawns caught in the middle of some kind of cosmic battle between God and good and the monstrous, demonic specters of evil. To imagine and believe it that way is a most unfortunate romanticizing of sin and evil. To portray evil as some kind of mystic, near-irresistible, cosmic force astride in the world, against which we human beings have almost no power, is both wrong and stupid. Seeing it that way is what empowers sin and evil. Meanwhile, when examined carefully, all sin is stupidity, banality, cheapening, narcissism, and the like. There is nothing remarkable or fascinating or glamorous or captivating about it. It gets most of its power from human ignorance, not from some dark reaches of some infernal nether-world. It is certainly no match for God or even for you and me, once we quit imagining it to have power equal to that of God.

Do you get the underlying message in all of this? It is that, notwithstanding the impression sometimes given, this Bible of ours—particularly the Gospel of Christ—reveals a creator God who is still actively, lovingly involved with creation and with you and me.

Faith, then, is a way of celebrating and responding to that, not some sweaty process of mindlessly jumping through religious hoops or browbeating ourselves into some set or other of canned beliefs.

Whatever our sins and failings, they are not beyond God's understanding or God's forgiveness. Though sin is an ongoing struggle, it is not the central truth about us. In no sense, whatsoever, is God our adversary.

Most simply (and this IS good news): God is far better, more understanding, more benevolent, and more enthusiastic about us than seems to be thought by a lot of those who claim to know the most about God.

So, while it is certainly good to be patient, charitable, and understanding with those around you who are burdened with the guilt, pessimism, anxiety, and peevishness that comes with certain grim kinds of religious belief, do keep in mind the scene where the man stopped on that bridge to listen to the jumper. Just because that suicidal person was so convinced of the truth of his unfortunate outlook that he was ready to die of it, didn't make it right for the other fellow to jump in with him.

Outgrowing Innocence

Genesis 3:22-24

> *The Lord God said, "The man and woman are becoming like one of us, knowing good and evil. ... So God sent them out of the Garden of Eden, henceforth to till the ground from which they were taken. At the east of the Garden of Eden, God placed the cherubim and a sword that flamed as it turned, guarding the way to the tree.*

That is the finish to the Bible's account of the beginnings of our human adventure. It had all begun for the man and woman in a blissful paradise. There they know nothing of conflict or worry or confusion or guilt. In that natural, innocent state (somewhat like the animals with whom they shared the earth), their basic needs were met, life was simple, and all seemed harmonious.

But all too soon that blissful innocence ends. Their encounter with the world and with each other, their curiosity, their envy, and their inclination to explore the limits, changes everything. So very shortly, they know too much to still be able to live in the primitive simplicity of paradise. Because they eat from the tree of knowledge, they now know, for example, that at some point they will die. That meant worrying about time. They also discover that their choices could have powerful consequences. That introduces concern, caution, and ambivalence. Similarly jarring is the realization that their impulses and appetites can be as much a problem as a joy. Yet more perplexing is learning that having others around has its complications. As important as were those lessons, learning them changes everything. Once they know all of that, there is no way to go back to NOT knowing it. The way back is forever barred. There is no getting that pleasant little genie of simplicity and innocence back into its bottle.

The spin that the writers of the book of Genesis put on

this exile from paradise is, that it is a punishment for misbehavior. For those who want to extrude a simple moral from every story, that is one way it can be read. But there are deeper layers of truth and of self-understanding to be found in it. Try to feel what it would have been like for a primordial couple like that.

Imagine, if you can, Adam and Eve, one evening years later, after a long day of work, of worry, of choosing, and of trying to understand their post-Eden world, as they reminisce about their former paradise.

"Eve, do you still remember how beautiful it all was back there in Eden?" asks Adam.

"How could anyone forget?" she replies. *"It makes me cry when I think about it. How we could let life get so complicated, I'll never understand. If only we could go back to the way it was and to the way we were!"*

Adam says, *"Yes, our needs were simpler back there. And we were content. I don't remember ever worrying or being afraid or confused. Do you think it was our ambition that complicated and ruined everything?"*

"Maybe," Eve answers. *"One thing is certain: it was very different between you and me in those early days. We were so excited about each other at first, so blissful together, so grateful, so intrigued with every difference and similarity, so anxious to know each other's every thought and quirk."*

"You don't have to remind me," says Adam, *"but it certainly came to a screeching halt when you helped yourself to the tree of knowledge. I'll never understand why you gave in to that temptation. What made you think we needed to know anything more than what we already knew?"*

"C'mon, Adam," Eve replies. *"We've been over this*

a thousand times. I've never tried to deny what I did. But don't you dare pretend that you weren't delighted to participate. You gobbled it up too, with no hesitation or persuasion. I'll tell you what hurts most when I remember. It's how you then tried to put all of the blame on me. Until that day, I worshipped the ground you walked on. I don't think I'll ever get over discovering that you could be like that."

"Well, you should have known better than to think I was perfect," Adam replies. "You were going to have to discover sometime that I was no more so than you are. It was just as well that you found that out early on."

"I suppose," she muses, "but I do so wish that there was some way we could get back to the way we were; to where there were not so many doubts, not so much to worry about, and to where everything could again be pristine and mysterious and believable and trustable.

"I think about that too," says Adam, "but apparently it is not allowed to work that way. Now we know what we know. We've experienced what we've experienced. We're never going to be allowed back into that sweet little Eden. And who knows, maybe in some hard-to-understand way, that's for the best. C'mon, lets rinse out our fig leaves and go to bed. Tomorrow is going to be another long day."

It is a fairly common form of nostalgia—this longing for some fondly-remembered Garden of Eden. Whether from Adam and Eve or us, reflections and rememberance of simpler times, of previous contentment, and of lighthearted innocence are tempting memories. It may have been a point in life when we recall feeling as if we had all the time and energy in the world. Perhaps it was when trust came much more easily, or when good and evil were unmixed and obvious, or when all our ideals were still intact. Perhaps it was when optimism came naturally, or when love was all bliss and no pain, or when everything seemed under control, or when there was little or nothing to make us angry or guilty.

It is with that picture in mind that, woefully or peevishly, we are inclined to ask, *"How come we have landed outside of Eden? Whose fault is it that it is not like it was anymore?"* If it could be like that once, why not again?" It's the feeling that, *"There has to be some way of getting 'the way it was' back again."*

With all due respect to the book of Genesis, that paradise with which the story begins—that innocent, uncomplicated state to which Adam and Eve were not allowed ever to return—was actually unreal and unlivable When they ate from that tree of knowledge, thus biting into curiosity, imagination, adventure, self-determination, and much more, it burned the bridge back to their simple and innocent paradise. Their lives (as would be true also of subsequent human beings) were irreversibly changed.

It DOES work that way. One cannot broaden his experiences and still enjoy the simplicity of being inexperienced. One can never really be completely open and still control what "gets to him" and affects him. Just by coming to know more, one gets more responsibility and accountability. In the exercising of one's freedom, mistakes and failures will be there with which one then has to be live. One cannot care deeply and love fully without some ache and grief being a part of it. So, yes, the more one experiences, explores, learns, loves, and grows, the farther out of reach lies whatever guileless, easy-believing, undoubting, uncritical innocence he may have once enjoyed. When, from time to time, life feels insufferably complicated, difficult, and uncertain, a person may feel that he would gladly exchange almost all that he knows—every experience that ever forced growth from him and any dreams that tug at him—to be back in some earlier intellectual or spiritual stage of his development that he recalls as simple and blissful.

What the Genesis story fails to say, though, is that to have remained in the Garden of Eden, would have been to stay forever childish, insular, shallow, simple-minded, and withdrawn; in short, "pre-human" in all important ways.

But even recognizing that, those times do come of thinking that life would be improved by getting back to where we didn't know so much, felt less, and understood less, don't they?

Part of an article I clipped from a newspaper some time ago found the writer homesick, for example, for when:

- a marriage was likely to outlast all three of the toasters the couple received as wedding gifts;
- a drug problem was trying to get a prescription filled on a Sunday;
- paperback novels had more passion on the cover than in the contents;
- the only person you'd find in a store at 3:00 a.m., was a burglar;
- a whole family could go to the movies for what it now costs for a box of popcorn; and
- "Crack" was what kids tried not to step on in the sidewalk, because it might break their mothers' backs.

We hear much the same existential homesickness expressed from time to time for the "old-time religion." For example: for the pre-television era; for that time when mothers didn't work outside of the home; for before there was "rock music"; for back when there weren't so many people of other religions and races and ethnic backgrounds; for when we had more spankings and hangings—any of the scores of earlier conditions or stages that now seem as if they held the real key to our lost serenity and simplicity.

Allowing one's memories to imagine blissful and uncomplicated past times is by no means a grave sin. But if we do it, the art is keeping our wits about us enough to realize that, first, it never was the paradise that we remember it as being. No, for some reason our minds are programmed to screen out most or all memories of the irritants and confusions of the past. Adam and Eve, for example, are very unlikely to remember the mosquitoes and black flies that tormented them in Eden, or to recall their several bouts with poison ivy and poison oak, or to recall how often they were nauseated because they didn't know what roots and berries they could and could not safely eat, or to recall how hurt Adam was when Eve refused to come near him for days after he tried to pet that skunk. Whether we are remembering a stage of life, a set of circumstances or an early stage of a relationship, this much is certain: it was not anything nearly as sublime as our selective memories portray it.

Second, even if there were some paradise-like conditions or once-upon-a-times allowed us, living there would be a step backward—a serious regression. C.S. Lewis once wrote: *"To live in a fully predictable world is not to be human."* That's right! Our minds and souls grow as we contend with our experiences, as we struggle with our fears, and as we are forced to rework and recreate what we thought we knew. Our very dignity, our purpose, and our grandeur as human beings has heavily to do with our learning to improvise and adapt, our coming to be comfortable with ambiguity and mystery and with all those times we had to be reborn and reinvented, even if somewhat against our wills. Seldom will any of that feel like any Garden of Eden, but it is where and how we were created to be.

Third, and most important, is keeping before us the fact that our calling is to somehow make holy our present set of surroundings and circumstances, including the current tangled predicament, the complicated relationship that isn't what it used to be, the infuriating political or social dilemma, and the stage of life at which we find ourselves.

That, in case you've forgotten, is what we saw Jesus doing. In his time, too, many suffered from a powerful, intoxicating nostalgia for the glorious way it was in the days of Solomon or Elijah or Moses. But you won't find a shred of it coming from him. No, instead he waded on into the crazy anomalies and inconsistencies of religion, into that badly fragmented social order, into the epidemic depression and smoldering despair of the people; and by speaking out here, by touching and caring over there, by being reassuring at yet another place, and by being, over all, drawn by hope rather than anchored in memory, he created a sacred time in our history to which we still look back for understanding and inspiration. It was, as it were, the new "Garden of Eden"—different in every way from the one in Genesis.

You get the idea, don't you? We don't need to "get back" to anything. When you find that the way back is not there to some more secure condition of your life, don't grieve. It's a healthy sign. Life with God is lived forward—never backward; lived by people who have taught themselves to be invigorated by today's complexity, inspired by its mystery, renewed by its struggle, and intrigued with the future's very uncertainty.

In fact, just for the record, people like that find the very thought of vegetating in some "comfy" Garden-of-Eden-like paradise, terribly boring!

Endemic Evil

Genesis 1:24-31 (portions)
> God said, "Let the earth bring forth living creatures of every kind."
> ... And it was so. ... And God saw that it was good.
> Then God said, "Let us make humankind in our image, according to
> our likeness; and let them have dominion over the fish of the sea, the birds
> of the air, the cattle, the wild animals, and over every creeping thing that
> goes upon the earth.
> So God created humankind in his image. ... Male and female, he cre-
> ated them. God blessed them and said, "Be fruitful and multiply and fill
> the earth and subdue it; and have dominion over the fish of the sea, over
> the birds of the air, and over every living thing that moves upon the earth.
> ... And it was so. God saw everything that he had created and, indeed, it
> was very good.

So, things seemed to have gotten off to a good start. It appeared to be a great creation with infinite variety and enormous possibilities. But as good as it all looked, it was only a couple of chapters later that we began to see some dark spots in the picture. First, there is that story of those first humans, despite the incredible array of options open to them, who immediately overstepped the boundaries of their authority. Not willing to accept any limits, they did the one thing that was forbidden. Then, hot on the heels of that comes the first murder: a brother killing his younger brother.

Those human failings would not have been all of it ei-ther. Though it doesn't say so, one can safely assume, for example, that before long a springtime flash flood caused someone's drowning, and a cold front moving into Eden spawned a killer tornado on a July afternoon. Then, possi-bly, it was an earth tremor triggering an avalanche that caused suffering and chaos for humans and animals alike. Or maybe it was a young mother stricken by a massive stroke, or a young man killed in a fall when a branch broke while he was picking coconuts at the top of a palm.

That was (and remains) the other side of the life and creation that sounded so good in those first couple of chapters in the Bible. And it would not have been too long before someone—reflecting in shock, grief, or anger—demanded to know, "Why?" Why had a presumed-to-be "good" God allowed life and creation to be laced with trouble and evil?

Though some of it was, not all the fault was of human beings. Sometimes evil (in the sense of violence, destruction, tragedy, abominable occurrences, unspeakable torment) was just there in the way things went: in those terrible combinations of circumstance, in cruel ironies not of anyone's making, and in crazy and random forms of unjust suffering.

Call it by other names if it makes you feel better, but isn't it "evil" that causes a drought to lay waste to an African country and bring mass starvation, or viruses that suddenly attack and destroy someone's health, or blood clots that form and get to where they close down a brain or a heart. How about when a hurricane or tidal wave drowns scores of people, or when too little or too much of some brain chemical wipes out the person and leaves the body walking around, or when cells go mad and become malignancies? Why in the world is all of that mixed right in there with the gorgeous flowers that bloom and the geniuses that are born and the symphonies that get written and the sunsets that dazzle and the heroes that inspire? But it is! Moreover, that often-infuriating mix is that in which you and I are called to live and to unfold meaning and to find purpose.

A lot of human energy, imagination, and ingenuity have been used trying to explain it. Some still blame it on the first man and woman, claiming that it would all be different had they not helped themselves to the forbidden fruit. Others insist on seeing it as punishment for current sins—

believing that for every suffering, every tragedy, and every cataclysm there must be a transgression somewhere back along the line. Yet others blame it on an all-powerful devil astride in the world, gratuitously causing trouble in order to make God look bad.

More modern thought has preferred to blame evil upon bad heredity, for example, or bad conditioning, or environmental irresponsibility, or repressed anger, or bad nutrition, or cultural jealousies, or the wrong toilet training, or stress, or other more scientific-sounding explanations.

All such speculation and would-be explanation doesn't really change much, though, does it? We still end up having to contend with and to suffer from the dark side of living in our world. Regardless of our cosmology or theology, the only important question is what we choose to do in the face of the fact of evil. Our answer to that (not our theories about evil) ends up making all the difference in what becomes of us.

One common human response that does NOT work, for example, is to throw up one's hands in the face of it, to "shrug," or to adapt and adjust to it. That can be tempting. Faced, as we often are, with the prevalence of injustice, with strident arrogance, with distortions of truth, with instances of love being betrayed, with blatant selfishness being rewarded, why should we continue to care? Why wear myself out or impoverish myself trying to stand against it or bring off some minor victory in regard to it?

One could hear some of this in the play *The Lion In Winter*, when, because Queen Eleanor was enraged at her son, Prince Richard, she called him an "unnatural animal" for having plotted to kill his own father, King Henry II. Richard's patronizing reply to being called "unnatural" is, *"Unnatural, Mummy? Unnatural? You tell me, what's nature's way? If poisoned mushrooms grow, and babies come with crooked* backs, if goiters thrive, and dogs go mad, and wives kill husbands, what's 'unnatural,' Mummy?"

Precisely. That is one all-too-common response to the dark side to life and the world: "*It's the way things are put together. It's not my fault. I'm only human. So don't you dare ask me to be compassionate in a world that is as merciless as this one can be. Don't expect me to be idealistic or generous when self-interest and self-preservation seem to be built right into your and my chromosomes. Don't talk to me about being Godly when God is allowing terrible things to go on. What earthly reason can there be for me to worry about wrongdoing in a world in which evil is endemic?"*

That's the familiar, pragmatic, expedient, supposedly practical response to the fact of evil: "*God has allowed it to be, so I'm off the hook. It's not my job.*"

Something else that happens to some in the face of evil is that they become permanent abject victims of it. A minister related that as being the case for most of his own life. When he was six years old, his mother (an immature, distraught young woman) had left him at an orphanage. It was his most lucid, searing memory of his life: that of standing on the steps of the orphanage administration building, watching as his tearful mother waved good-bye through the back window of a taxi. He said that, for a few seconds, he stood paralyzed with confusion, anger, and rejection. Then he squirmed free from the woman gripping his arm and ran after the taxi, shouting at the top of his lungs, "*Mommy, I hate you, I hate you. I'll never forgive you for leaving me.*"

The orphanage experience notwithstanding, the coming years did not go badly. In fact, he was reasonably successful at almost everything he did. Briefly, he was a professional ice-skater. Then he became a CPA. Later, he owned his own business. Nevertheless, there was always a nagging, driving unsettledness about him. He did reestablish contact with his mother and had some very occasional, very strained conversations with her. They always left him undone, agitated, and angry all over again.

In early middle age, he decided to enroll in seminary and become a minister. The seminary he attended required students to undergo a semester of clinical experiences geared toward self-understanding. The sessions were unnerving for him because they kept revealing a very angry side to him, lurking just below the surface.

Finally, just before his ordination, one evening he made the long-distance call to his mother. As soon as he identified himself, he said, *"Mom, I love you and I forgive you."* It turned into a long, tearful conversation. After hanging up, he said to a colleague, *"It's over! For forty years I've been chasing that same taxi, demanding an explanation, demanding to know, 'why?' It turns out that I didn't need an explanation. There wasn't one that could have helped. I needed to forgive. Thank God, it's over!"*

That image of chasing that same taxi for forty years is, to me, a powerful one. People do that in regard to destructive times in their lives. It is, in effect, to chase the illusion that there are helpful, healing answers to questions like, *"How could he?"; "What kind of a God would allow....?"; "What did I do to deserve.....?"; "Where is the justice in this?"; "When is this going to be made up to me?"; "Where is the appreciation?"* Not so. Though it feels as if getting such an answer would be healing, it isn't. The chase (as the man discovered after four decades) is absolutely futile.

One other unworkable response to finding that we are more-or-less stuck with some abominations and injustices and blatant wrongs in life, is to try to make a life out of staying enraged over it. This is a tough one to talk about because the line can be very thin between resisting evil or working to overcome it, versus being fixated—obsessed with blaming, with retribution, and with retaliation. We have all seen that malignant ferocity in someone, haven't we? It's the hating of evil so much that it warps and distorts someone's spirit to the point that the person then becomes a source of evil. One of the most insidious things about evil is the way it does just that: distorts and destroys good people by sucking them into (as they will describe it) "fighting fire with fire," into hating what is evil so much that they lose track of all that is good.

So a lot is at stake in this matter. That dark side to our good world is very real and is ongoing. And again, what we make of it does make a tremendous difference in what becomes of us.

One requisite, then, is obvious: don't get stuck in trying to explain it. Though some turn it into that, "explaining" is not what faith is about. When it came to evil, Jesus' whole concern seemed to have to do with choosing our response to it. In the language of the story about the man whose mother abandoned him, our Christian calling is never that of using our ingenuity and energy to chase that taxi. However awful it was, the injustice, the destruction, or the abominable must not be allowed to make victims of us by preoccupying and obsessing us.

Evil, the scripture says, is "overcome by good." That is, it is not affected at all by our frustration, by our complaining, by our scolding, by our accusing, or even by our outrage. It is overcome by concrete, positive, buoyant instances of good. It happens with the seemingly small "yes's" and "no's." What are those?

We say "no" to evil at one of its insidious levels simply by saying "no" to our own self-pity, and "no" to cynicism, and "no" to revenge.

We do so by letting ourselves go ahead and care about the problem or issue or mess, despite smooth-but-negative voices claiming that only a bleeding-heart-fool would keep caring in a world so riddled with users, losers, and manipulators.

We say "no" to evil by refusing to accept truisms, party lines, over-simplifications, propaganda, cliches, and all of the other ways that lies are marketed as quick-and-easy truth.

Yet another way of saying "no" to evil is flatly refusing to believe in inevitability, refusing to believe that we are helpless because the stars predestine our lives, or refusing to believe that one voice, one act, one gesture would be futile against the powers and trends that seem to control the world.

We say "no" to evil by persistently loving people and using things rather than loving things and using people, no matter how many others run it the other way.

Evil suffers defeat whenever we are able to forgive one more time than we retaliate, in each instance in which we stick our necks out one more time than we play it safe, and whenever we remain open just a tad longer than we had to or were expected to.

It doesn't take a genius or some rare kind of saint or major moral heroics to defeat evil. Whatever the hell of evil is, it is just NOT the irresistible, impregnable, all-powerful presence that has been portrayed by some misguided souls. Much of evil is only loosely organized stupidity. So it is a serious mistake to dignify it and empower it by thinking of it as some cosmic force with god-like, irresistible powers to trivialize, cheapen, and pervert us. It can do that to us only with our cooperation.

All that is required to overcome evil is for someone like you or me, with buoyancy and courage and vision, to keep saying, doing, and living the firm "yes's" that have to do with hope, mercy, generosity and empathy.

Once more, whatever the cause of the dark side of life in our world, the important question regarding it is not the why of it, but is, rather, what you and I permit it to make of us. And that (though in the heat of the struggle, it doesn't feel like it) is entirely up to each one of us.

Toxic Shame

Luke 8:43-48

In the crowd around Jesus was a woman who had suffered from hemorrhages for twelve years and no one had been able to cure her. She came up from behind and touched the very edge of Jesus' cloak. Immediately, her hemorrhage stopped. But Jesus said, "Who was it that just touched me?" All denied having done so. Peter said, "Master, people are all around you, pressing in upon you." But Jesus said, "Someone did touch me, for I felt that power had gone out from me." Seeing that she had been detected, the woman came forward trembling and fell at Jesus' feet. There, before all the people, she explained why she had touched him and how she had been instantly cured. Jesus said to her, "My daughter, your faith has cured you. You may go in peace."

In reading a book by Marcus Borg entitled, *Meeting Jesus Again For The First Time*, I was reminded once more of what a devastatingly powerful and pervasive thing was the "purity system"—the purity laws and beliefs that were a part of Hebrew life in the time of Jesus. "Purity" didn't refer only to physical cleanliness or what we might call moral purity. Whether one was considered pure or impure also had to do with a whole array of prejudices, superstitions, and biases built into their social system. Men, for example, by their very nature were considered to be more pure than women. Jews were believed to be born comparatively pure. Non-Jews—Samaritans, Ethiopians or Syrians, for example—by contrast, were seen as impure. People in some occupations—like shepherds, for example, or those who saw to the burial of the dead—were in jobs that made them impure persons. Anyone with physical defects or deficits or any kind of skin problems was considered defiled—impure. Women were thought to be particularly impure while menstruating and/or for several weeks following childbirth—doubly so if the baby born was a female. A woman was considered untouchable during such times. On and on went the stipulations and ramifications of this "purity system."

Worse yet, the distinction was completely blurred between this weird mix of social, congenital, or genetic "purity" and any purity that we might associate with holiness or goodness. One could be a saint in every important way, but, because of a birth defect or a defiling social status or certain illnesses, would be considered unfit and an outcast.

This played a major role in many of Jesus' encounters and healings, and had especially to do with this incident in which he was touched by a woman with a twelve-year vaginal hemorrhage. The hemorrhage itself would have been seen as defiling. But there was more. The woman was there in the crowd alone—an additional strike against her. Women never went out in public without their husbands, if they had husbands. Since she was alone, there was a good chance that she had been divorced by her husband, possibly because of her physical problem. It was very easy for a man to end a marriage and almost impossible for a woman to do so. Being divorced, if that was her status, made her still more an outcast in the purity system. Possibly for two reasons, then, in her own eyes and the eyes of others, she would have been seen as shameful.

It really was amazing that she did what she did: sneak in among the crowd and deliberately touch Jesus. That may sound like an inconsequential thing to you and me, but it wasn't. To knowingly defile by touching him, the most popular man in town that day, took unbelievable courage, faith, or desperation—or maybe all three. For if Jesus were a scrupulous believer, it would mean that, because of her defiling touch, he would have to go through elaborate re-purification rituals. So she took a big chance in trying to steal a healing.

The way Jesus reacted, one might have thought someone had just picked his pocket. He stopped cold and said,

"Who did that? I felt some power go out of me" or (as another translation has it) *"I felt some 'virtue' go out of me."*

For a few awful moments, the poor woman must have felt as if it had now turned out that she had traded a hemorrhage for a cardiac arrest. At the very least, she would likely be chased out of town and possibly beaten. So she did the only thing she could. She fell at his feet, throwing herself on his mercy.

It turned out, though, that Jesus' comment about her touch having robbed him of holiness or virtue, had been said by him with tongue in cheek. He didn't believe anything like that. In fact, throughout his ministry he had carried on a kind of guerrilla warfare against the purity system. He knew (as do we) that there was nothing "defiling" about this woman's predicament. So here, too, as he had done other times in encounters with persons considered to be impure, Jesus showed his open disdain, contempt, and rejection—NOT for the woman (as might have been expected)—but for the whole ponderous system. This was a set of beliefs by which people like this woman were encouraged to think that they were defiled, were unworthy, were a permanent source of discomfort and trouble to all around them, and were, in some inscrutable way, unforgivable social throwaways.

"Lady," he says, *"Get up from there and go in peace. It is your faith that has cured you."* And cured she was; healed, I suspect, not only of her physical problem, but maybe of that whole shame-based worldview that had crippled and contorted her life for more than a decade.

That ancient, cruel, purity system is long gone, and good riddance. But that doesn't mean that there are not still people around us and among us who suffer from a long-standing shame-habit as limiting as was hers.

"Toxic shame" I heard someone call this sort of thing.

"Toxic shame," I assume, is to distinguish it from the legitimate capacity for shame that is there when, for example, a morally sensitive, Godly person has violated his or her own ethics, cheapened something of value, given in to petty impulses, or has otherwise acted destructively. That can cause one to be ashamed, and there is nothing wrong with that. To the contrary, to be without the capacity to feel legitimate shame at such times is to be a sociopath.

That, though, was not the kind of shame that was squelching this woman and countless others like her. The shamefulness that she carried around with her—toxic shame—is that which somehow becomes built into a person's view of himself and his relation to his world, to other people, and even to God. There are any number of ways that this still happens to people. And not unlike the way the ancient purity system was supported by religion and public opinion of the time, toxic shame is sometimes still inflicted and/or encouraged by other people.

It should be admitted at the outset that, as it was true then, one's religion is still often a culprit. Even after all these centuries, there is a lot of shame-based religion around. Religious toxic shame comes with the teaching that the noblest of what you are and the best of what you ever might do are still utterly contemptible in the eyes of God. It comes with the belief that every last one of us is so thoroughly steeped in sin that we are deserving of the worst imaginable condemnation and punishment. According to that understanding, the only good thing a person dares to think about himself is that Jesus suffered and died a horrible death in order to get him off the hook with God regarding his depraved, congenital worthlessness. It is not difficult to see, is it, how believing that way can load one up with a lifetime supply of toxic shame? Crippling as it is, it hangs on in religion because shame-based people are controllable, gullible, and easy to manipulate.

But there are other sources. Toxic shame can also have taken hold by some sin or stupidity or public embarrassment of oneself earlier in one's life. At the time, there may have been, briefly, good reason to feel ashamed of it. The problem is that it never ended. The legitimate shame was never replaced by penitence or forgiveness as it is meant to be. So in the mind of the person and, yes, perhaps in the minds of a few sickies around him, his wrong-doing permanently sums him up. What he did (or failed to do) back then is who he is. As he understands it, believes it, and feels it, the central truth about him is that shameful thing that he once did. So he lives much of his life feeling disapproved of, and unworthy, inappropriate.

There is also toxic shame, though, that is caught from remnants of old social taboos and mores, from one's sense of the real or imagined buffet of disapprovals that are probably out there somewhere in society, and from being haunted by the opinions of the more judgmental, self-righteous, merciless people one knows (maybe even from a parent who is like that).

For example, I hear reverberations of toxic shame in the voices, of strangers who call me and timidly ask me whether there is any chance that a minister here would perform a private little marriage ceremony for them, despite the fact that they were previously married and divorced. In some cases, these callers have been turned down by their own church and by a half-dozen other churches and ministers. "Defiled" is the message that they have gotten. The church has seemed to decree that their divorce has made them unfit and unworthy of even trying to approach, sacredly, a second marriage commitment. Having gotten the message that, because their first marriages failed, there is something intrinsically shabby about them, they are clearly ashamed even to ask if we might help.

Toxic shame is also often a problem of the poor. Notwithstanding the fact that there are those who use poverty to exploit the sympathy and generosity of others, there are at least as many or more who feel deeply disgraced and shameful when they end up with serious financial problems. The official word on it is, of course, that it need be no disgrace, no discredit, no dishonor to be poor. Nevertheless, because of the way people love to condemn the not-so-deserving poor they've heard about, to many the real message that gets through is that everyone thinks that their money problems indicate that they must have done something badly or that there is some lack of motivation or character; in short, that for them to be without adequate funds is something shameful. That's why they withdraw. They feel ashamed because they get the impression that their poverty makes almost everyone around them either angry or uncomfortable, and maybe it does.

One can often see toxic shame in parents when one or more of their children has gotten into serious trouble or has ended up with an obvious character defect. The grief and ache for a parent is bad enough, but for those who, for whatever reason, believe that they as parents are the principal cause of their children's problems, the toxic shame becomes horrible. Unfortunately, it is not all self-torture, either. The odds are that their shame will be added to by the arrogant comments and the insufferable smugness of certain other parents whose kids happened to turn out well, but who lack the humility to understand that it was mainly the grace of God—not flawless parenting—that made their children okay, so far.

Toxic shame in industrial quantities has so often become built into those who have had to face the fact, often in earliest puberty, that their sexual feelings and orientation are bewilderingly different from those of everyone else that they know. Any kind of "being different" can feel shameful in early adolescence, but when the youth discovers that the snide comments, cruel stereotypes, and blanket condemnation vented on homosexuality are all aimed at what he fears is true of him, he is set up for a shame-based life as torturous as anything that the ancient purity system imposed on people.

And there are dozens of other ways in which toxic shame becomes a way of life. He or she is permanently ashamed because of where or how or by whom he was raised; still ashamed because of a couple of nervous breakdowns about which everyone knew; ashamed even years later because her husband strayed; ashamed because of being a recovering alcoholic; ashamed of the education he did not get.

So he or she either slinks and cringes, or blusters. Those are the two unfortunate, but standard, ways people adapt to toxic shame. Both are unnecessary, wrong, and inappropriate. Again, notwithstanding acts and irresponsibilities and stupidities about which it is natural to be briefly ashamed, there are no shameful human beings. There are only sufferings, sins, failures, weaknesses, and struggles that all people go through and which, while it may bring one to feel unlovable, unworthy, defiled, and a burden to life for awhile, the shame was never intended by God to stay on.

There are two aspects of this, then, for us to reflect upon. The first is obviously that of any toxic shame that has a hold on our lives. Though there may be some other people who have worsened it, you and I still do have to take primary responsibility for allowing it to remain a part of us. No one can make us feel defiled or unworthy without our cooperation. Crucial to the story of this woman is that she apparently had just enough faith to have said to herself earlier that day, *"I was not meant to live cringing like this. I am not that bad a person. I* was created for more than this. *I am going to be out from under this stupid shame or die trying.*" And Jesus said, in effect, "*YES, lady! And that's the faith that has made you well.*" Precisely. Toxic shame is not of God. It is merely a very bad habit of thinking—one that you are allowed to drop at any time.

The other matter is when we are on the other side of it—in a position to be what Jesus was to this woman. It is not enough merely to feel sad that she is doing this to herself. No, quite often when healing from toxic shame happens, it happens through the victim's experience of the friendship, the acceptance, and the hope for him or her by one like you or me who simply does not believe in unforgivable mistakes, permanent unworthiness, innate spiritual defectiveness, or any other of the modern versions of defilement. Yes, often their best shot at being free of toxic shame is as they "catch" from you or me the fact that we do not believe that God has made any rejects or any hopeless cases. And as it dawns on them that this is true, they find the courage to accept or forgive themselves.

However, there is still a lot of toxic shame out there, which means that there are miracles that you and I can make happen—happen in ourselves and happen in others around us. Let's not miss a single opportunity.

Addicted to Blaming?

As part of the very first story about human beings in the Bible, we are told that the first man and the first woman were already passing the blame. When confronted with having done what was not permitted, Adam immediately blames Eve and Eve blames the serpent who lives next door there in Eden. One might safely infer that blaming has been around for awhile.

There is a medieval fable about a land that had three castles and was ruled by three brave knights. One spring, a terrible dragon entered that land and began destroying the crops, terrorizing the people, and creating general chaos. Finally, these three knights decided to get together and rid the land of the terrible dragon. Though understandably frightened and nervous, they set out one morning to look for this monster. They checked all of the places that they guessed that a dragon might hang out (singles bars, golf courses, bike trails, etc.), but they didn't find him. As the day wore on, they began arguing about which one of them should have prevented the dragon from getting into their land in the first place. They argued about which one had dragged his feet the most regarding the problem and about whose stupid ideas were most responsible for making that day's search a waste of time. They argued so fiercely and bitterly about who was to blame for these and other related matters that, by the day's end, they despised each other and abandoned their search for the dragon, thereby allowing the dragon to go on destroying their country.

Other than the dragon part, that fable doesn't strain credibility, does it? It is easy to imagine the three of them bringing events to just that end. Blaming gets to be almost endemic among us.

I was told recently that a computer has now been developed

that is so incredibly sophisticated and so nearly duplicates the process of human thought that, when it makes a mistake, it immediately blames another computer.

Skill at blaming (if skill is what it is) can often be seen at quite a young age. A mother, guessing the likely cause when she heard the family cat yowling in discomfort, shouted at her little boy, *"Stop pulling the cat's tail."* Without a second's hesitation, the little boy yelled back, *"I'm not pulling the cat's tail. I'm only holding it. The cat is doing the pulling."*

A little more sophisticated was little Freddie who arrived home late after school, carrying with him a note from his teacher to his parents, reporting that she had kept him after school because he had behaved badly that day. Freddie's mother asked him what the problem had been. He immediately blamed the teacher. He said, *"She's unfair. She punished me because I was the only one who knew the answer to a question she asked our class."* Thinking that *that* didn't sound like his teacher, the mother inquired, *"What was the question that she asked?"* Reluctantly, Freddie muttered, *"Oh, she asked who put the dead mouse in her desk drawer!"*

Whoever does it and for whatever reasons, our formulations and assignations of blame do create major confusion, distortion, mischief, and wasted energy in our shared life as human beings.

One could hear real impatience on the part of Jesus when his disciples were dabbling in it one day. Regarding a certain blind man, they asked, *"Who is to blame for this man's blindness, he or his parents?"* Jesus tells them that neither is to be blamed—that no blame is to be assigned for the man's disability. Nevertheless, they ask a similar question as to whose fault was the death of some people randomly killed by Pilate's soldiers. They seemed ready to blame the victims, assuming that, in some way or another, they had deserved what had happened to them. At another point, they showed an inclination to blame eighteen victims for their own deaths when a nearby tower suddenly collapsed, crushing them. Jesus' annoyance with their need to blame was palpable. *"Would you really blame those eighteen people for what happened to them,"* he asked, *"as if they were the worst eighteen people in the country?"*

Blaming is, however, a knee-jerk reaction for a lot of us human beings in the face of a tragedy, a fiasco, an unpleasant turn of events, a misfortune, a conflict, a failure, a twist of fate. Instead of moving on to the matter of what it will take to get through it, to overcome it, to correct what is awry, or to bring healing to it, there is a better than average chance that, first, we'll get stuck for quite awhile in blaming. We'll blame our leaders, blame society and the system, blame parents, blame schools; we'll blame technology, blame heredity, blame the liberals, blame the conservatives; blame foreigners, blame the victims, blame the media; in effect, blame Eve and she'll blame the serpent and the serpent will blame the whole lousy arrangement (which was, after all, not of the serpent's making, was it?). There is always a way to do it, isn't there? In fact, if you or I cannot come up with at least three or four persons or circumstances that will feel satisfying to blame for any trouble, mistake, or frustration in life, then either we must be short on imagination or we aren't listening to the multiple voices that are always out there coaching us in our blaming.

The problem is not that our blaming is all inaccurate. Much of the time, we assign blame with some degree of accuracy. No, the problem is that blaming, even when quite accurate, is an overwhelmingly stupid distraction and a massive waste of our time, our ingenuity, and our energy.

So why do we do it? What do we think that it accomplishes? What are we getting out of it?

Obviously, some of what blaming seems to accomplish is

the creation of a comforting "smoke screen." The more evil and stupidity that can be assigned to others, the more innocent and responsible we may feel. You know the feeling, don't you?

Well, at least I never did THAT!

I suppose I could have been more helpful, but let's face it, he and his meanness are the real fault here.

I'm not saying I made no mistakes, but the real blame for this goes way back before anything I did or failed to do.

Do you recognize any of that? It can, moreover, even be accurate and still not be healthy for you and me. Any absolution we give to ourselves through comparative blaming is a very dangerous, narcotic comfort.

There are other sources of it. Blame is also used as a means of controlling others—controlling wives, husbands, and children, in particular. Surely you have seen it or experienced it. Because almost anyone is more manageable and manipulatable when he feels guilty, blaming is used as the means of effectively keeping him that way. Convince a person that old craven errors of his, or longstanding weaknesses and failures of hers are, in subtle ways, the underlying cause for whatever went badly just now. In this way, you can keep the person in a perpetual state of trying "to make it up to you" for all of that for which he supposedly is to blame. True, to treat a person that way is cruel, insidious, and evil, but unfortunately it often works and becomes a subtle, but powerful, form of intimate violence.

Speaking of being victimized by blaming, perhaps the most ironic way that it happens is through the phenomenon of compulsive self-blame. Having been blamed for so much for so long sometimes a person will quit fighting it and become all too willing to accept all, or most, accusations as true. They come to believe that they, in some way or another, are culpable for almost anything that goes badly.

"I'm sorry–so sorry!" are the words and spirit with which they present themselves in life.

But just as common is the synthetic self-blame that is nothing but an act put on in order to forestall the criticism of others, when he IS, in fact, the one who caused the problem or made the mistake. Some skillfully exploit the fact that, if one is really hard on himself, beating himself up with blame for everything everywhere, then those around him may tend to feel sorry for him rather than expect accountability from him. By acting as if he is in terminal despair over his depravity and uselessness, he hopes to beat the blamers at their own game. He may, but it is only one more transparent ploy in the "blame game."

I suspect that the majority of blaming is done, however, because it feels so very responsible, without requiring any relevant responsibility. Identifying and blaming villains can be quite emotionally satisfying—much more so than facing, analyzing, and intervening in the problems themselves. For the shallow and the self-righteous, pointing a finger feels like a perfectly legitimate alternative to lending a hand.

Unfortunately, this is not limited to the personal sphere. Sometimes a person's entire world-view, his politics, and his belief system becomes "blame-based." There are, for example, a remarkable number of people who have no reservations about placing the total blame for poverty, hunger, and homelessness on the poor. They'll blame the exploited, the abused, or the oppressed for not being grateful that they aren't still worse off than they are. They'll sometimes unashamedly fault the person who calls attention to a problem as being the cause of the problem (or at least of worsening it by making it visible). What is so destructive about this is that, so fiercely do they come to believe in their collection of blamable villains, that concern, involvement, empathy, and most of the rest of what has to do with being humane seems to them to be no longer needed. Their world, though, of simple villains, single-source evils, easily identifiable culprits, and chronic conspiracies doesn't exist. It might simplify things if it worked the way habitual blamers think it does, but it doesn't. Whatever it is that is tempting us to point an accusing finger, is almost certainly more complex, more intermeshed, and more unfinished than we are convincing ourselves it is.

So as tempting as it is, as righteous as it can feel when we are doing it, or as passionate as our indignation may be, by far the majority of the time, our blaming is just another problem—no kind of solution whatsoever—even when we do it with some accuracy.

The final word on what has ultimately been wrong—as well as on what was ultimately right—the truth about whether something is a symptom or is actually a cause, the real verdict on whether she was a product of the evil or an actual source of it, the determination as to whether someone was a rabble-rouser or a source of much-needed truth—all that is in the hands of God.

Yes, you and I do know a little bit about certain derivations, motivations, causes, effects and consequences, but NONE of us is smart enough to move around in life assigning blame with the kind of certainty that is so common among us.

So, why waste our energies and our joy that way? God has better, more creative, and far more useful things for us to do with the minds, the abilities, and the time given us: things like healing, restoring, reconciling, and forgiving. Those are guaranteed to leave us far happier, more peaceful, and more at home in life than even our juiciest blamings. Since even those times when we blame somewhat accurately, it accomplishes nothing good. Why not let go of it?

Coasting
(Scripture: Matthew 13:44-48)

On a winter Friday night a few years ago, I spent seven hours with one of our local police officers, Todd Newberry, on patrol. It turned out to be an unforgettable evening for me. Some of it is as clear in my memory as if it were only last week. About mid-evening, we responded to a call to investigate a location where a corpse had just been found.

The address was that of a third-floor, one-room tenement apartment on the north side of Mansfield. The deceased person was a man and, as it would turn out, he had been dead for slightly more than a month. You can imagine the condition of the body. Complaints about the odor from others in the tenement had finally persuaded the landlord to open the apartment.

When the coroner arrived, his verdict was that the man had died as a result of bleeding to death from a major hemorrhage in his esophagus. He estimated that the man's death may have taken as much as an hour. That was believable. One could trace the course of his ordeal by the bloodstains. It began in front of the television set (which was still operating), had moved briefly to the kitchen area, then for a time to his bed (which consisted of only a mattress on the floor in the corner), and finally ended (but not quickly) in the bathroom. That was where he died, sitting on the floor.

The others in the tenement had no recollection of calls for help from him. None of them, moreover, seemed to know him—didn't even know his name, although he had lived there for years. We also discovered that he had two sisters living in Mansfield, but had called neither of them during this extremity. There was no indication that he had gone near his telephone or his door after the hemorrhage began. His sisters had little if any reaction when told of his death.

One of the sister's first response was to ask if there was any money in the apartment.

We were there for well over two hours before the body was removed. I used the time to try and piece together what I could about his life.

He was in his late sixties and a Korean War veteran. His possessions were very few. In addition to his mattress, there was a decrepit old easy-chair, a small table, a television set, and a VCR. There were stacks upon stacks of carefully labeled video recordings that he had made of telecasts of old movies—most of which appeared to be the kind that are aired during the hours between midnight and dawn. It was my guess that he had passed his days watching them over and over.

There was evidence of heavy alcohol use; the coroner indicated that an esophageal hemorrhage was consistent with long-term, very heavy drinking.

One wall of the room was mostly filled with framed certificates and documents from his time in the service, which had ended decades before. None of them pertained to anything dramatic. It was not even clear that he had actually been in the Korean fighting. The certificates had to do with marksmanship, short training courses he'd completed, and other minor service recognition. The few clothes he had were poor. His army uniform, however, was in a clear, heavy plastic bag in the front of his closet along with his uniform hat. The various medals, ribbons, and service bars were all pinned in place. So, between the framed certificates on the wall, a couple of pictures of him in uniform, and the careful preservation of that uniform, my impression was that the last, and perhaps only, time of his life that had held meaning for him had been his time in the army.

Again, on that night of his final ordeal, there was apparently no one he felt comfortable turning to for help, OR, maybe it didn't seem worth the trouble to try.

I watched the paper for a couple of weeks thereafter. There were no services for him; in fact, there was no mention whatsoever of his death. It felt to me as if his life had just become more and more constricted until, when there was nothing much left, he went away.

The memory of that man—not his death, so much as his life—has stayed with me since that night. He seemed (admittedly on brief, after-the-fact evidence) an all-too-vivid and lurid picture of what, through sheer inertia, can happen to a life—any life. If you haven't looked at the definition of "inertia" recently, inertia is "the tendency of something to remain at rest or to continue on in the same direction" and/ or "a disinclination to move or act".

Inertia does not exactly appear in the list of the seven deadly sins. "Slothfulness" which is on that list is somewhat related, but inertia is more complex. Unfortunately, it is possible to be very hardworking at what is, nonetheless, the constriction of one's life; to be quite energetic in what is, nevertheless, only the emptiest of repetition; and to be downright industrious in pursuing what is empty, inconsequential, and lifeless.

It isn't that anyone sets out to enervate, congeal, or stifle his own life. To the contrary, a person generally hopes that his or her life will have meaning, will make an important difference, and is relevant to the rest of life. No, when inertia overcomes a person's life, it does so insidiously. It happens through a whole collection of minor choices to just "go with the flow." It happens because of seemingly harmless procrastinations. It comes about through what feels, at the time, like a perfectly permissible strategy of dodging whatever is complicated, new, or potentially upsetting.

Inertia's net effect, though, is that of very slowly pulling in the walls of one's life, cutting oneself off from all sources of challenge and growth, and becoming addicted to repetition and sameness. Worst of all is that the settling into inertia is so subtle that the victim is oblivious to it. While he thinks he is merely de-complicating, protecting, and securing his life, he inadvertently starves his own spirit to death.

I read a summary of a study based on in-depth interviews with persons at who first had indicated, on a survey, that they felt that something might be missing in their lives and said that they had attempted change or renewal for themselves. When interviewed, however, it was awesome how entrenched the inertia turned out to be with most of them. True, a substantial number had gone through one or more rounds of finding and attaching themselves to some hot issue or special project, but what came out in the interviews was that, with only a few exceptions, they chose involvements and concerns that did not force any changes in their thinking, did not affect their style of living in any way, and would not have an impact upon their priorities. The causes and special involvements they had chosen were selected (perhaps sub-consciously) to create the illusion of movement, without there having to be any. Their inertia remained intact.

It had reverberations of a conversation reported by the father of a girl in her late teens. She said to him, with all the earnestness of that age, *"Dad, I need to be doing something where I am really needed. I've figured out that I am the kind of person who really needs to be needed."* Her father replied, *"I understand, Connie. But I should warn you that people who are really needed usually have to do a lot more than they ever expected or wanted to do; that people who are really needed often end up with unbelievable demands upon them."* Connie clouded over for a moment, but then replied, *"Well, I am going to find something where I will feel needed, without having to do anything."*

Connie is not alone in looking for that. The tragedy is that, at her age, she already shows an openness to an approach that, rather than giving meaning to her life and forcing her to remain alive and growing, will simply give the *illusion* of meaning and of being alive.

One does not, then, need to have it reach a point of huddling in a one-room tenement apartment, watching an endless stream of old "B" movies, anesthetizing oneself with alcohol, and waiting for physical death to finish the job in order to be a victim of this deadly inertia. Usually it happens long before that.

Inertia is very likely what it is when we start lopping off involvements, responsibilities, and activities without having the faintest idea why; that is, removing life's demands and replacing them with nothing.

It is certainly what is going on at the point where one feels that simply coasting on past experience, past learning, and past achievement is okay for someone of her age, his station in life, or her past accomplishments.

Inertia—again, the mindless and automatic continuing in the same direction, same way—is easy to see when viewed as: the way I did it last year, the way I always say it or think it or handle it, not only goes unquestioned, but, in some cases, is almost adhered to religiously.

The same tragic "pulling the walls of life in around himself" is what is happening when the highest priority anymore is his comfort, is the absence of any "rocking of his boat," and is that of creating buffers to keep him unaffected and untouched by whatever change is going on in the world.

Spiritual inertia is the disease in progress when life's interruptions, intrusions, and unplanned or inconvenient impingements are now taken as personal assaults, outrageous injustices, and violations of one's rights.

It is probably what is happening to me when, now, the

individual differences, eccentricities, and shortcomings of others irritate me to death, rather than intrigue or interest me.

You do see, don't you, where it is headed? When one reduces enough the number of ways in which he is engaged in the life around him; when he has finally rid himself of any and all soul-size demands; when he has found a way to keep anyone or anything from altering or interrupting his routine; when he has succeeded in making every day and every week about the same as the previous one; when drinking himself into mild oblivion seems better than having to face the extent to which he has ended the life of him—then we are looking squarely at his death. Never mind how much longer his heart keeps beating and he continues to walk and talk.

Meanwhile, it doesn't require all that much to overcome inertia. But one does have to understand that it is our daily—maybe hourly—responsibility. I do have to be certain that some form or other of newness is constantly flowing into my life. You really DO have to force yourself, probably each day, to do something that it would be easier to avoid. We dare not ever relax keeping our curiosity and imagination nourished and active. We dare not ever cease to be givers; that is, we become much like any inert, stagnant pond if things flow only to us and never from us.

So it's a life-and-death matter. It has very much to do with what Jesus described as our "seeking first The Kingdom of God." Do you recall what he said?

> The Kingdom of God is like a treasure which had been buried in a field. When someone discovers it there, in his joy he goes and sells everything he has and purchases that field.
> The Kingdom of God is also like a trader who is in search of the finest pearls. On finding one pearl of exceptional value, he sells all that he has in order to have it.

Then too, the Kingdom of God is like a net thrown into the sea which catches fish of every sort. When full, the net is drawn ashore and the fish are sorted, putting the good into baskets and discarding the bad.
Matthew 13: 44-48

Only you can determine what that means for you—what holding off of inertia will require from you, but it couldn't be of more importance. Similar to sharks, which can only get enough oxygen if they keep swimming at all times, spiritually, we must keep our spirits on the move, or WE die. We are growing, or we are shriveling. We will embrace our living with genuine hope, or we will sour. In some way or other we give, or we stagnate. There are no exceptions.

Inertia may seem like a comfortable, even well-deserved, option. It's not. In fact, in all the important ways, it'll kill you.

And Still a Dark Side of Us

In one of his letters, the Apostle Paul admitted to going through the kind of internal battle that is probably familiar to a lot of us. He wrote:

> *I don't understand my own actions. For I do not do the good that I want to do, but will do the very thing I hate. ... Though I intend to do what is right, I cannot seem to do it. Far from doing what is good, I do the very evil that I abhor because of the sin that dwells within.*
>
> Romans 7:15, 19-20

He's describing the struggle with the darker side of ourselves that is all too common, isn't he? Especially for good, well-intentioned people, it can get downright demoralizing at times. It is not that we don't deplore the cheapening, destroying, betraying, exploiting, grasping, hurting, and deceiving that are the result of sin. We do. But often we're still secretly fascinated by them and remarkably susceptible to them.

Maybe you recall hearing, years ago, about the store-front chapel that was part of a slum mission in South Chicago, where they had a large sign out in front that said, *"If you're weary of sin, then come on in."* But in lipstick, someone had written underneath it, *"If you're not weary of sin, call 424-2111 and ask for Pandora."*

There were probably responses to both messages. For again, while being appalled at sin's corruption, distortions, and degradations in life, there remains a certain secret ambivalence toward it. Wrongdoing turns out to be more entertaining to us than it's comfortable to admit. *"It's terrible, but...uh...tell me more."*

The patron saint of this sort of thing has to be the man who complained, with great indignation, that there was far too much sex and violence on the videos he rented.

It can be that transparent, can't it? One deplores the wrong intellectually while, in other ways, that he tries to hide from himself, he cooperates with it at the very same time. Logically, one wouldn't think that this could be true of reasonable, moral, intelligent beings.

Part of the problem is a certain amount of naiveté about the way sin comes packaged. Only rarely, for example, does it confront us as an obvious, monstrous, rotten, vile, demonic, disgusting, heinous enemy. No. Most of the time sin is what might be called an "intimate enemy." Rather than through demonic forces from without, it reaches us from the dark, unfaced side of our own psyches. Think about it. Few, if any, of us are typically tempted to commit moral outrages or blatantly evil deeds, are we? No. Where we get sucked in (when we do) is through subtle, secret, intriguing little temptations to look into how much we just might be smart enough to get by with, through ostensibly harmless ventures into trying to have-our-cake-and-eat-it-too, or in hardly-worth-mentioning bits of "taking advantage" of someone, by miniscule misuses of personal power. Most of it is barely perceptible, just short of innocent, and hardly the sort of thing to cause us to put up our moral guard. It's too private and inconsequential to really be "sin," isn't it?

But negligible, insignificant, and picayune as that sort of stuff may seem, it is where we human beings not only are most vulnerable to sin and evil, but are likely to defend and protect it. It's in those carefully disguised, seemingly private pockets of selfishness, arrogance, hostility, jealousy, and complacency. While I am (and you are) usually on guard against stridently wicked external forces, at the same time, I can be terribly naive and/or tolerant of my own secret shabby motives, greedy ambitions, destructive enthrallments, and smoldering resentments.

Not long ago, on the front of the newsletter, I quoted

someone making the point that what we sometimes call "necessary evils" are merely the evils that we like so much that we don't wish to be without them. That's right. And an amazing amount of ingenuity is devoted to just that: to retaining and whitewashing those workable, practical, delicious, or ego-satisfying kinds of sin. Sometimes we're not even subtle about doing so.

Henny Youngman, for example, advised, *"Now, if you're going to do something tonight which you might regret tomorrow morning, just sleep really late tomorrow morning."*

Almost as blatant was the man with a drinking problem, who had solemnly pledged to his parish priest that he would drink no more. In a fit of thirst, though, he stopped into his favorite corner bar and ordered a lemonade. Then, as the bartender began to fix it, he said, *"And could you add a slug of whiskey to it, but be careful not to tell me about it."*

Another was the client who said to his attorney, *"I know that what is right and wrong is perfectly clear in this matter, so I'm hiring you to cloud it up for me."*

Most blatant of all: maybe you remember the oft-quoted prayer of St. Augustine as he struggled with his weakness for illicit sexual involvements. He prayed, *"Oh Lord make me chaste, but not just yet."*

So, yes, we bring incredible inventiveness, ingenuity, and self-deception to the defense of our own "necessary evils" and pet sins.

One favorite method, for example, is that of coming up with offsetting virtues. My stinginess might feel less serious if I am also a gung-ho patriot. No matter how unrelated patriotism and stinginess may be, by accentuating my patriotism to myself and to others, it will seem to me to offset my pet sin of being a tightwad.

Or, maybe I am judgmental or perhaps a gossip or a cheat, *"but at least I don't smoke, drink, or gamble."* Or, "Okay, I'm *prejudiced—some might say bigoted—but I am as devoted a church-worker as you'll find in this community."* Jesus called this one, *"Straining at gnats while swallowing camels."* It is often what underlies a person being prudish. They concoct an impressive pile of minor, offsetting good works that they practice fiercely, thereby forming a smokescreen to cover more serious sins like self-centeredness or "exploitiveness" or "judgmentalism."

Another approach to protecting one's favorite sin is through comparisons. One can know that he is falling into this practice when he catches himself saying to himself, *"Maybe I'm not perfect, but at least I don't (do such-and-such like so-and-so)!"* It's a dead giveaway that there is something deep inside being protected that should NOT be protected—something that he is trying to avoid dealing with honestly. The fact is, that even the worst of us can probably compare ourselves favorably with someone somewhere. Morally, though, that is utterly beside the point. As we know in our better moments, what is right and wrong in our lives is not determined by taking an average of what goes on in the lives of others. Popular sin is not less serious than more uncommon sin.

Helplessness is another strategy by which we sometimes allow ourselves to hold onto sins and evils that are providing us with something we don't wish to give up.

I can't help it. Something comes over me.

What do you expect me to do? It is the way I am.

I haven't the slightest idea what makes me do it.

Some like to support that religiously with a belief in an omnipotent devil who sneaks around subverting us, tricking us, and manipulating us in irresistible ways. Comedian Flip Wilson frequently ridiculed this one beautifully with his *"the-devil-made-me-do-it"* explanations for his mischief. "I'm this helpless battleground on which cosmic forces of good and evil are slugging it out, so, poor me, I can't really help what I am like and what I do."

Similar is the strategy of ignorance—of posing as not being smart enough or even aware of sin. All one has to do is keep himself detached and buffered. I might not come face to face with how uncaring and hardhearted I have become, for example, if I am careful never to look at what life is like for some others. Or, by not allowing close relationships, she'll probably find it easier to deny how insensitive or uncompassionate she's let herself become. Or, if I limit my associations to people who share my same pet prejudices, it will make it much easier not to deal with my bigotry. The explanation is: *It cannot be sin, can it, if I don't know any better?"*

Now, it is true that there are some places in the world where a person could still grow up morally impaired or unable to distinguish right and wrong, but this is not one of them. It is not true that the bigot just happens to be that way, that the elitist, the greedy person, and the arrogant one has had no chance to know better. When it comes to good and evil, to right and wrong, to morality versus irresponsibility, we all know more than we sometimes let on, and what little we don't know, we could know, but are more comfortable *not* knowing.

What it comes down to is this. Of the deeply entrenched evils, the organized corruption, and horrible depravities that go on out there in the world, only occasionally do we, individually, get a crack at them. But well within our reach are the darker sides of our own selves, which is where sin in human life germinates, is consented to, and is nurtured. In other words, it is always wrong, naive, and hypocritical to think one can fight evil as something that is completely apart and detached from you and me. Looked at carefully, it never is.

It is not that we are all hopeless, utterly flawed, contemptible, worthless, and decadent sinners (as certain kinds of religious beliefs claim). Far from it.

For example, you and I are generous—maybe even sacrificial at times. That is true. But at the same time, we are never completely free from the impulse for stinginess and greediness. It is in there somewhere, so refusing to recognize that impulse only empowers it.

We intend to be kind, and we are most of the time. But I, at least, also have some mean streaks. Therefore, I set myself up for trouble when I try to hide that from myself and re-label it as "just teasing" or "just having fun" or "just being candid."

Honesty and openness are important values to all of us. But that doesn't mean that we are incapable of deciding that "just this time" it will be quicker and more expedient to be cunning, conniving, coercive, and deceptive. The person who refuses to see that part of his dark side spells trouble for himself and everyone around him.

You and I are acceptable persons—each a person of worth. Each of us is a life full of meaning and accomplishment and purpose. But when I refuse to recognize that I can be a real louse at times—not just a louse "in theory," but in practice—I am many times more likely to become a full-time louse.

This young man had it right. An application that he was filling out said, "List your personal strengths" He wrote, "*Sometimes I am trustworthy, loyal, helpful, friendly, courageous, kind, obedient, cheerful, thrifty, brave, clean, and reverent.*" When next it said, "List your weaknesses." He wrote: "*Sometimes I am NOT trustworthy, loyal, helpful, friendly, courteous, kind, obedient, cheerful, thrifty, brave, clean, and reverent.*"

Exactly! One isn't required to like looking at the dark

side—the sources of sin—but, by God, he'd better be acquainted with it! Otherwise, he hasn't a prayer at controlling it. It will be free to warp, distort, and corrupt him or her or me.

So, yes, sin has to be taken very seriously by every one of us. The reason for doing so is not in order to fill us with guilt, or to humiliate us so that we'll be more cowed, cautious, or manageable. Absolutely not!! It is only to keep us realistic about ourselves, so that we don't waste our ingenuity, waste our energy, and dissipate our credibility trying to deceive ourselves about what was really going on in our weakest moments, our worst behavior, our cheapest motives, and our most irresponsible decisions.

So, see those episodes of us for what they are and be honest about what made them possible. Know, even when it isn't showing just now, that this, too, is a part of us. Accept forgiveness for it, and then move on.

Though sometimes it may not feel that way, we CAN—with God's help—handle it AS LONG AS we don't empower it by pretending it isn't there.

Stationed in the Valley of the Shadow

Near the end of World War II, a returning soldier who, because of severe battlefield injuries, had been completely out of contact with his family during eight weeks of hospitalization, phoned them upon his arrival in Los Angeles. After telling them where he was, he asked his mother, *"Mom, would you be willing to entertain a partly blinded soldier who had his arm and leg blown off?"* His mother hesitated briefly and then said, *"Why, yes, of course you may bring him home! But we wouldn't need to make his visit more than a few days, would we?"* The son, unbeknownst to her, was himself the partly blinded soldier who had just lost his arm and leg. He hung up the phone and put a bullet through his head.

The writer who reported this incident went on to use that soldier's mother as an example of insensitivity, a lack of compassion, and the most brittle kind of shallowness. That mother may have been all that.

But didn't you find the son's behavior somewhat infuriating, too? It's not that his grave, permanent disabilities were not terrible and depressing ones for him to which he had to adjust. They were. Nor is it surprising that he was demoralized and angered by what had befallen him. He would need a lot of patience, understanding, and support. Knowing his mother as he did, he correctly guessed that she would be a reluctant or awkward source of that, so he tricked her into saying as much.

Notwithstanding, though, whatever were his mother's shortcomings, his carefully setting her up in that phone call to say what would then (following his suicide) haunt, hurt, and otherwise punish her for the rest of her life, was appalling. It was not to be shrugged off as excusable if one is hurt badly enough.

Yes, it is true that one who has not been in the throes of

such personal hurt, shock, and loss can not know what it might bring forth from him or her. None of us can say, with total certainty, that if it happened to us, we might not explore the depths of spite, self-pity, and destructiveness. We certainly have read enough news items about previously nice reliable people who, having been fired or jilted or exploited or humiliated, grabbed the nearest firearm with which to commit multiple murders and then their own suicide. It is difficult to estimate just where our own breaking-point is and what we might be like, if pushed well beyond it.

Nevertheless, when someone does totally disintegrate as a result of devastating tragedy or hurt, it has to have something to do with what he assumes is permissible. When people refuse even to begin to heal—make no effort to come back to life after some awful juncture—one of several likely barriers to healing is the impression that only rage, bitterness, self-pity, or blind despair are possible. It is the sense that, while one is "in the valley of the shadow," all the usual capacity for good intentions, good will, good motivations, self-control, and concern for others is suspended for the time being. If I'm really hurt, victimized, or grief-stricken, then any regression, disintegration, surliness, or indifference on my part are okay, natural, normal, and permitted. *"For who that has not 'been there' would dare be critical of my self-destructive ways just now? For the time being, I am absolved from the usual expectations and responsibilities of living."*

It is a reasonably safe stance, since seldom does anyone challenge it. Thus, if I go ahead and make sure that a few other people hurt too, for example, or if I act helpless in order to force others to have to take care of me and allow for me, or if I withdraw from all contact and responsibility, or if I start drinking heavily, or if, in yet some other way, I make my pain into a way of life, who can say for certain that, in my particular case, it is not necessary—that it's not the pain that's doing it while I am merely its abject victim.

Obviously, this is a very difficult matter to talk about, since there is at least the theoretical possibility that, very occasionally, someone does become emotionally and spiritually helpless. I suspect, though, that if the real truth about it be known, far more often people are no more out of control (at some level) than they choose to be; that is, when people remain permanently stuck in some kind of non-being, it is because they give themselves permission to do so.

I don't raise this, though, to encourage criticism and second-guessing of what others around us do or have done as a result of their pain. It is rather to examine where our own thinking and expectation is on the matter. As unpleasant as it is to be reminded of it, few, if any of us will get through life without some truly profound disillusionments, some tormenting hurts, or some disorienting griefs. And the impressions, the beliefs, and the assumptions that we hold right now as to what they are bound to do to us will have a lot to do with what becomes of us in those difficult and demoralizing low spots.

There are, then, several misconceptions of which we ought to rid ourselves right now, long before we are there.

What is probably the most serious of them has already been implied: that is, the assumption that, for the time being, for example, a hurting person need not expect himself to be a humane person, a responsible person, or a person capable of being anything but self-absorbed because of his pain. Assume that, and you will allow self-pity, cynicism, hostility, and even mercilessness to have a "field day" with you. This is probably what made it okay for that soldier to contrive to get his own mother to say those words which would haunt her for the rest of her days. The truth is, meanwhile, that, very much to the contrary, an astounding amount of what has been most creative and inspiring from human beings, has, in some way, been tied into their times of blinding grief, profound hurt, and deep frustration. That's because woven right into the midst of the worst that happens to us are always the threads of additional self-understanding or of new levels of empathy or of insight of a sort that happens in no other way. That is not a call for deliberate suffering, nor does it make us hurt any less. But being determined, even while you hurt, that you can and will unfold some way by which you will have been blessed through it is the difference between handling the experience versus being handled by it. Suffering doesn't ever have to end up being meaningless, except for a person who has made up his mind that there will be no meaning.

Closely related, in our very worst moments, is the impression that this is permanent, that there is no real life on the other side of it—at least no life of any true worth.

This is especially a problem for the young. As one lives a little longer and has moved in and out of some very low spots in life, he will usually develop some confidence that "it won't always feel like this." But when one is young and/ or is suffering a first profound hurt, it can feel "cosmic," feel "terminal," feel as if there could never be enough healing to match this hurt. The pain is seen, not as a part of the fabric of life, but as the defeat of all that is good about life. That has something to do with suicides, particularly among the young. If one sees this as the ultimate, clinching, "end-all" of hope and good, why not suicide?

So this impression is a deadly one, especially for those who have heretofore had a trouble-free life. It requires all available, day-at-a-time patience to keep believing that there will ever again be enough light to overcome this much darkness. There will. The trick is that of being there to see it.

Yet another wrong assumption that gets in the way of coming back to life, after some deep anguish or outrage is that in which one tells himself that while, yes, there are some people out there who come back fully healed, stronger, and deeper after some horrible experience, I'm not one of them. *"It is nice that they are that way. I am happy for them, but I'm not like that. I am one who can't get over things. What can I say? It's the way I am."* That sounds like humility, doesn't it. Actually, it is a soul-withering mixture of stubbornness and petulance.

I see some of it in myself every time the media interviews someone—a parent, for example, who has lost a child to a child killer. The person says of the killer, *"I really don't hate him any more. I don't want to see him executed. I hope that some day he can be helped."* I have found myself thinking, *"How can she be like that? Had I lost a child that way, I could never heal enough to be saying that."*

Not true. One can come back even from something like that. God has managed to pull off healings even more astounding than that. Seldom does it "just happen" though. More often than not, every step of the way you will have to fight off your own reluctance to let go of the understandable hate and of your wish for retribution. It will almost certainly feel much more natural, more appropriate, and more normal to remain a permanent hater or victim, or even a "hurter." If you do that, though, don't tell yourself that you have no choice—that it is the way God made you. That is a lie. When a person settles into living out his own spiritual and emotional deterioration, it is something he chooses.

I'll mention only one more quirk that sometimes blocks a person's rising above his hurt: it is an un-faced sense that he hasn't yet gotten all that is due him after what he has been through. Whether what he still wants is more sympathy, or yet more extra consideration, or additional attention, or maybe some groveling on the part of the one who did the hurting, or some other inappropriate benefit, it can be tempting to want just a little more of it before letting go. That, too, leaves some people stuck indefinitely. Yes, a part of her really does know that she needs to move beyond what happened, but not yet. Putting it off a day at a time, the decision to put it behind her is never made. None of the required explicit steps to act her way out of it are ever taken. Why? It's because, while being pitied or coddled or excused from life may not be the greatest, it is habit-forming and it can be a difficult habit to break. Face it, most healing costs us something: costs us, for example, the special consideration we were receiving for awhile, costs us our delicious resentment toward the perpetrator, costs us our permission slip to be less than we could be, or costs us yet something else. So, notwithstanding all good intentions to put it behind one, unfortunately, it may never feel as if this is quite the right time to do so—not while there is still a little more that I can milk from it.

Whatever it is that has hurt us, unraveled our morale, or outraged our sensibilities, part of what needs to be understood from a Christian standpoint is that, though it may not always be the kind of healing that we might be wishing for or demanding, God does have healing for those who can take it—for those who have the stomach for it.

That soldier, for example, would not likely grow a new leg and arm. Likewise, the injustice done to us may never be reversed. The clock will not be turned back to undo some rankling embarrassment. We won't be given back the time that we lost in illness or in having been involuntarily relegated to one of life's backwaters for awhile. Nothing really replaces the life of a loved one who was taken from us. God or the cosmos, or even the human beings who played a part in devastating us, may never come by with a suitable explanation or apology or vindication. If we are waiting for any or all of that before coming back to life, we had better count on never being a whole person again.

But for those who are willing to let down the barriers of self-pity, resentment, blaming, and withdrawal; those who are willing to declare, *"By God, the damage stops here!"*, there ARE ALWAYS forms of healing. Most often it comes quietly amidst small in-breakings of brief joy, for example, or tiny glimmers of new hope, or flashes of unexpected well-being, or unexpected insights into one's own worth. It comes as part of little "riskings" of forgiveness or out of timid experiments with new ways of being. And then, with some time, he or she realizes one day that she is no longer stuck in what happened; that, in ways she would not have thought possible, she has become a living example of God's ability to resurrect us from the dead.

This, then, is where it all comes out. We seldom have much, if any, choice as to whether, from time to time, we end up in that "valley of the shadow" of which the Psalm speaks. Remember, though, valleys are open-ended. We do get to choose whether we move on through them or stop to live there in the dark.

In fact, the dark valleys are somewhat like what has been said sometimes of certain troubled cities: "They're difficult enough just to have to visit. You certainly don't want to live there." The good news, as it has to do with life's bleak, miserable low episodes, is that WE DON'T HAVE TO LIVE THERE!

A Time of Judgment?

For whatever reason, a longstanding religious scenario in the imaginations of Christians has been that of an awesome, celestial courtroom where all of us have to appear after death. There, as some imagine it, we each stand before a heavenly magistrate who is armed with a giant ledger book (or perhaps, by now, a celestial computer with incredible memory). It is envisioned as the time and place in which we will be called to account for every screw-up, every falsehood, every nasty comment, every selfish act, every lapse in duty, every doubt, every four-letter word used, every dirty joke told, the holes in our church attendance, every six-pack or lottery ticket we purchased, and God only knows what all else. If, indeed, that is the set up, there could be a long line. One might want to die early and avoid the rush. For some of us (me included), just going over all of that negative material is going to take up a substantial part of eternity.

As a youth, I heard a lot of grim sermons at so-called "revivals" (as did some of you), threatening that kind of scenario. We were told that, at any moment—in the twinkling of an eye—one might go from mowing his lawn, balancing her checkbook, driving to the post office, or maybe even sitting on the john, to standing in God's awesome, dreaded judgment hall where, based on that detailed review of his life, one would get his housing assignment for all eternity. Fear of facing such a Day of Judgment was supposed to make people more obedient, cautious, and believing.

One evangelist who was trying to terrify his listeners that way, got an unexpected response. Near the climax of his sermon he leaned out from the pulpit, towering over the congregation and thundered: *"Every single member of this parish is going to die and then stand naked in the great tribunal of God!"* It appeared to be a sobering thought for everyone *except* for a man in the front pew who looked right back at him with a shrug and a big grin on his face. Guessing that the man had somehow missed the gravity of what he'd said, the preacher again leaned out over the pulpit and shouted still more loudly, *"I say to you that every single member of this church will one day die and then face the Lord's judgment!"* The man in the front row now smiled even more broadly, glanced at the worried looks on the faces of his fellow worshipers, and even giggled a bit in obvious self-satisfaction. The preacher was now irate and pointed directly at the man, demanding, *"Didn't you hear what I said about every member of this church having to stand in the judgment hall of God? What's so amusing to you about that?"* With a smug chuckle, the man replied, *"I'M not a member of this church!"* (So much for scaring hell out of THAT man.)

A "time of judgment" then, is another concept that many thoughtful Christians have understandably dropped from their thinking because of the chronic "distortings," "trivializings" and "misusings" of it. Portrayals of God as being that kind of resentful, grudge-holding, vengeful, ill-humored deity are much too absurd to dignify by giving them serious consideration.

And yet, there is a danger of throwing the baby out with the bath-water. Jesus definitely does, in any number of ways, speak of judgment. Whether in doing so, however, he is threatening us with an event on the other side of death is quite another matter. He uses this analogy, for example:

> *Either you will make the tree good and its fruit good or make it bad and its fruit bad. The tree is known by its fruit. ... The good person brings good things out of his store of good treasure while the evil person brings evil out of a store of evil treasure. At the time of judgement, you will be accountable for every thoughtless word.*
>
> Matthew 12:33, 35 & 36

If one chooses, I suppose, he could read that as Jesus describing a celestial courtroom on the other side of the grave. To me, though, it sounds much more "down to earth," much more immediate than that. The tree of which he speaks is judged now by its fruit, not in some "tree afterlife."

In other words, the "days of judgment" are upon us constantly in THIS life. We may try to ignore them, to pretend that they are not what they are, but over and over again we DO get the verdict on how we've been acting, on choices with which we are experimenting, and on forces and influences we have set in motion. God's judgment for you and me on what, for example, we've hoped to get by with and/or on directions we have been moving is very real and present.

Even so, one has to be careful how he understands that too. That is, this is not to be mistaken for that superstitiousness under which it is believed that there is a tit-for-tat payback from God for every little wrong; where God supposedly afflicts you with business problems because of your spotty church attendance, or zaps someone with a dread disease for having walked out on her husband, or sends a flock of tornadoes to get back at a community for the moral turpitude of its city administration. That, too, is a distorted picture of God's judgment.

But again, the fact that God's judgment is not vengeful, retaliatory, and implacable like that, does NOT mean that there is no verdict for you and me on, for example, irresponsible choices, distortions, sin, indolence, selfishness, mercilessness, and all the rest of the ways we end up cheapening our lives, or maybe the life around us.

No, what we do and choose and intend is apparently important enough to God that God stays in touch on such matters. That's because, put simply, we are each an ember— a holy flame—from an eternal fire *and*, more awesome yet, beings who are given the freedom and the power to keep that fire burning brightly or to let it go out. And it's on the matter of what is happening to that holy flame, that every day of each of our lives is a "day of judgment."

We already knew that, if we let ourselves think about it. For example, we know something about judgment for the person who hardens herself, makes herself impervious, emotionally inaccessible, and "hard-nosed." Will she be literally called to account and directly punished for having turned herself into that sort of creature—for her callousness and indifference to everything beyond her self-interest? Maybe not. But that doesn't mean that there is no "judgment" there for her. Judgment is there in the spiritual narcosis, in the loss of her emotional color, and in the way her soul relentlessly shrivels and withers away into insipidness. Given that, does there still need to be some kind of eternal torturing? One would think not. Being punished *for* sin, after already having been so contorted or destroyed *by* sin, would be redundant—would be "overkill."

There is a similar day of judgment when someone cheapens and trivializes all or most of the time given to him, desecrating the time of his life. What more "hell" does there need to be beyond the devastating realization (as Henry David Thoreau put it) that, as a person approaches the time of death, he realizes that he never really lived. That's judgment! To know that one has spent all of one's time, but can not recall what he spent it for; to have it dawn on him that, while he made a lot of money during his life, he made little or no real difference in life; to realize that, while there had been a fair amount of comfort and even some pleasures, there'd been very little real joy or fulfillment; these realizations are to arrive at a time of judgment—an unmistakable one. Even when the person is too far gone to fully recognize it himself, nonetheless, it is there.

What is it but judgment in the case of the harshly critical, condemning, belittling, blaming, nitpicking snob when she discovers that the price of having made her life like that has been ending up in her own terrible, self-created hell, in which there is no mercy for her, no slack, and no grace. It is to have trapped herself in an awful world, in which she now assumes that her own slightest error or weakness will be treated by everyone else with that same cold, remorseless pitilessness that she has dealt out to others.

There is a day of judgment for the tight-fisted, grasping, miserly person. Possibly without his even noticing, it has arrived when, while he now knows the price of almost everything, he no longer has a sense of the true value of much of anything. It's the day when the stuff that he thought he owned now turns out to own him. It is to be at that awful place where he has lost his ability to relate to any part of his world other than by price. Judgment doesn't get much more vivid than that.

Such times of judgment are there in countless other ways. A state of boredom is often a time of judgment. Isolation sometimes is, as well. Jealousy always is. Again, those conditions and others like them are the collisions with the fact that, one way or another, a person is abusing, starving, or ignoring that holy flame placed in each of us by God.

Fortunately, much of the time, instead of in judgment, God's Word reaches us in happier ways. We encounter God in love, in episodes of forgiveness, in healing, in experiences of God's Grace. But for every one of us, there are also these "Godly collisions" with tough reality, with painful truth, with unyielding limits, with important guilt, or with unpleasant verdicts on what we've done, been, and chosen. In their own way, they are every bit as important to recognize and learn from as are the positive, encouraging, inspiring, reassuring signs that become a part of our living.

Maybe what follows can serve as a closing image. Years

ago, someone wrote about watching on a spring afternoon, as a buzzard feasted on a dead animal out on the ice along the edge of the Niagara River. The piece of ice on which the buzzard sat suddenly broke loose from shore. The noise, as well as the splash and spray of the water, spooked the buzzard enough that, for a second or two, it flapped its wings, but then immediately settled again to its eating, as the ice flow now slowly moved downstream. There in the warm sunshine, it was a contented and complacent buzzard. After all, it could fly safely away anytime it chose. A number of minutes later, though, when the ice floe was pulled into the main current leading to the rapids just before Niagara Falls, the roar of the falls caught the bird's attention. It looked up and again began to flap its powerful wings. Nothing happened. Apparently, the water that had splashed onto the surface of the floe had frozen the buzzard's claws fast to the ice under the couple inches of slush. In futility, still flapping those huge wings and undoubtedly wondering where it had gone wrong, the stuck-fast bird went over the falls.

Was that divine punishment? Was it God getting even with the buzzard? No, of course not. Was it, in a primitive sort of way, a verdict on, and a time of judgment for, the bird's priorities? Or on its complacency? Or on its sense of entitlement to have what it wanted for as long as it wanted it or on some kind of "buzzardly" illusion of indestructibility? I guess it probably was.

Believe, if you wish, in that literal judgment hall where everyone will answer—one at a time—for the dumb things we've done that we shouldn't have (as well as that which we didn't do that we should have). Maybe so, but I strongly doubt it. But whatever you believe about that, you and I would do well to pay very close attention to the verdicts and judgments that are here for us right now, in the midst of our living. Without question, they, too, are a major part of

God's way with us, God's grace to us, God's word to us, and, yes, God's love for us, doing everything possible to keep us fully alive and human.

Beginnings and Endings

A father reported sitting down to read the paper in the same room where his six-year-old son was watching some kind of suspenseful adventure story on television. Apparently, the saga was at a point where the hero was in deep trouble and the gloating villain was closing in. Then he heard the boy saying earnestly under his breath, *"If you only knew…. If you only knew!"*

The reason was, it turned out, that the boy had seen the film before so he knew the outcome—he knew that help was on the way. But he was so caught up in the story and, at this point, was identifying so strongly with the predicament of the hero, that he longed to deliver the hero from his worry or stress by telling him what was going to happen—that there was going to be a good outcome.

Some have always hoped that religion could do that for them; that is, that Christian belief would give them a sneak peek at the last page—the closing scene of our whole human adventure.

That's what drives some people's fascination with the New Testament Book of Revelation and also with parts of the Book of Daniel in the Hebrew Bible. They are convinced that the strange symbols and numbers and images and metaphors of those books can be arranged, interpreted, and computed in a way that will reveal the year, maybe the day, and perhaps even the hour when God will intervene, Jesus will return, the true believers will be vindicated and glorified, and all things will come to the end. They, of course, having advance knowledge, will be prepared.

It can be a strong hunger—this longing for a glimpse of the "last page," so that we'll know what to believe, what to prioritize, and how to arrange our hopes. People continue to search for correlations between the Bible and current events, looking for anything that might be a hint or indicator that time is running out.

In fairness to them, even Jesus did speak quite often of endings, finishes, and finalities that need to be taken seriously. For example, back-to-back in the 24th and 25th chapters of Matthew, he presents four parables or analogies warning against being glib and complacent about the fact that time or opportunity or life itself can and will run out.

First, he talks about the ancient saga of Noah and speaks of the way the people of Noah's time were complacent, up until the rains actually began to fall and the door of the ark was sealed shut.

Next, he speaks of a householder who puts a servant in charge of the rest of the servants while he goes on a journey. When the journey takes longer than expected, the servant he'd put in charge becomes increasingly irresponsible and arrogant, abusing his position, as if what he did or didn't do made no difference. The servant forgets that this is a temporary arrangement which will run out at some point.

There is also the well-known story of the five wise and five foolish bridesmaids. There, too, the theme is that of the dangers of glibness—of living as though there were little or nothing at stake and no need for any sense of urgency.

The last of the four is the parable of the three men entrusted with varying amounts of gold to manage while their master is away. When time runs out on their stewardship, the tragic and foolish one of the three is the one who decided that it was okay to "sit it out" and "blow off" the opportunity.

Jesus talks about it other times too, but never describes it as foreknowledge, forecasting, or any other kind of fortune-telling about outcomes and endings. It is only to warn against the deadly kind of glibness by which, when things are going well for them, human beings sometimes lose track of how temporary are the gifts of time and meaning and opportunity. His point or warning is that, right in there among our blessings, god-sends, thrivings, and strokes of luck, are also all manner of uninvited chances and changes, and untimely or unreasonable finishes—doors that unexpectedly slam shut on us. Pretending that this is not so is to be out of touch with a crucial truth about the way it is with us.

In our more thoughtful moments, we understand this, maybe better than we wish we did. But when things are going okay, the dangerous assumption too easily sneaks in, to the effect that we really can count on things going just about as we expect, the assumption that we do have control over most outcomes, and, worst of all, the assumption that we are somewhat entitled to a fair share of time or stability or wish-fulfillment.

Do you see why his warning is important? The purpose or intention is not to frighten or threaten anyone. It is to make "holy" that which is uniquely in front of us—to bring us back to focus on the moment in which we stand right now. It is to remind us that, not only is the past over and out of our reach, but the future is unformed, not really under our control, and is not ours—at least, not yet. Practically speaking, the present is all that we have to work with. We very well may have a future, maybe a lot of it, but when we try to project ourselves into it before it is here, we almost always start to trample roughshod over the present. And that is always a very serious mistake.

One obvious symptom of it is seen in those afflicted with the illusion that there will always be plenty of opportunities to catch up, to make up, to straighten out, to renew (for example) starved, stagnant marriages, dormant friendships, or neglected relationships with children. Their nonchalance is NOT because they don't think those things are important. It just feels as if, since those options are "always available," they are not urgent. They cannot get their minds around the fact that love, for example, can turn out to have limits—that it dies of mal-nourishment, that relationships come to an end, that children grow away, and then go away.

The same craziness is evident in the comfortable impression that there will always be a later opportunity to make oneself into a much more humane, mellow, flexible lighter-hearted part of life. I have seen books that inadvertently support that illusion—the illusion that one can plan out his or her life in predictable stages. The idea seems to be that we are entitled, not only to a developmental and educational stage, but also to indulge ourselves in a fiercely competitive stage, followed then by a stage for pursuing social success and then, after yet a couple more such segments, finally to settle into a nice, contented, genial, sanguine golden stage. That is SO tragically misleading! Life does not submit itself to that kind of thing. Judging by their way of living, though, there are some who do believe that it is worth a try, that it is okay to postpone whole areas of their development. They put qualities like generosity or sympathy on the back burner untill later in life, and assume that personal depth, social concern, playfulness, and sensitivity can be evolved on down the line. Unfortunately, as in the imagery of some of those parables of Jesus, one way or another, the door does get slammed shut, leaving them on the outside wondering how it could happen. *"How could I have run out of time or have lost my ability to find joy or no longer know how to love or not be able to care much anymore or not have the close friends that I need at this stage?"*

It is the same bad assumption that tricks some people into postponing, a year at a time, the development of the poetic, the artistic, the ardent, the playful, the spiritual, or the tender side of them.

It is what will even allow some of us to accept, on a week-at-a-time or month-at-a-time basis, a sickening or destructive life situation, all the time believing that, while, yes, at some point I need to do something about this, there is no urgency—the option will always be there.

If, as was the wish of that little boy for his embattled television adventure hero, you and I were given a glimpse of the last page, it really would be most helpful. We might change some things if we were shown some alternative completions, given some indication of where the limits would turn out to be, or had it revealed to us which choices were more final than they had felt at the time.

Obviously, we're not given such foresight. Since we don't know, and can't know, the outcomes, the net effect is to add a lot of weight and urgency to "the now", the present moment.

To play or not to play with your seven-year-old this evening becomes much more serious when you realize that, "like a thief in the night," that day sneaks up when she is seventeen, instead of seven, and there is a finality about that which is irreversible. When they finally run up against it, some feel as if they have been robbed. Rightly so. They have been robbed, but the thief is that person themself.

The hard truth of these kinds of finalities changes the worth of such things as the music that I may or may not listen to, the sunsets that could be enjoyed (but can be shrugged off for now), the walks taken or maybe postponed, and any number of the other small, soul-restoring moments that are so easy to postpone, since they'll always be there, won't they?

It ups the ante on all of those acquaintances we have who would be so nice to turn into friends "if we are ever able to get around to it." Won't there always be plenty of opportunity for that?

The very matter of longstanding friendships is an even more vivid example. One sometimes hears people talk about how, though they have little or no contact, this or that friendship will "always be there." That's charming, but it's only more of the same unfortunate illusion that there are some things in our lives in which we are protected or exempted from changes or endings.

A haunting poem someone gave me years ago says,

> Around the corner I have a friend
> In this great city that has no end;
> Yet days go by and the weeks rush on
> And before I know it, a year is gone.
> And I never see my old friend's face
> For life is a swift and terrible race.
> He knows I like him just as well
> As in the days when I rang his bell
> And he rang mine. We were younger then
> And now we are busy, tired men;
> Tired with playing a foolish game.
> "Tomorrow," I say, "I will call on him
> Just to show I am thinking of him."
> But tomorrow comes and tomorrow goes
> And the distance between us grows and grows;
> Around the corner—yet miles away!
> "Here's a telegram, sir." Tim died today.
> And that's what we get and deserve in the end.
> Around the corner—a vanished friend.

That poem may seem overly heavy. But the reason it feels that way is that it flies squarely in the face of the kind of nonchalance that lets a person get by with not quite getting around to saying it, or offering it, or doing it because, again, there are so many weeks and months and opportunities yet ahead, aren't there?

And death is far from the only way that we run into this part of it. The matter is spread all over the Domestic Relations Court docket. People end up every bit as wide-eyed, shocked, and bewildered as that irresponsible head servant in Jesus' parable, when they are hit with the fact that their forever-and-ever marriage is actually ending; that there were, it turned out, absolute limits to how much what once was a love relationship could be starved or neglected or abused or ignored, before being irreversibly finished.

This even comes into play in regard to the environment, doesn't it? Apparently, there are still people out there who are militant in their denial that there are limits, endings, or final points beyond which reclaiming or renewing or reversing things will be forever out of reach. Taking comfort in how clean Lake Erie has become again or how much improved is the air above Pittsburgh or how wrong were early calculations on resource depletion or on global warming, they stubbornly insist there is no end to the health of our earth. That makes no sense at all, since the earth is finite just as is life and everything about it. But some illusions die hard.

It is well worth examining ourselves in this matter. Have any such self-destructive or mindless illusions sneaked in upon us, regarding our gift of life, our gift of time, the gift of meaning, the gift of health, the gifts of each other, and all the gifts of opportunity? To lose track of the fact that all those gifts have both beginnings and very real endings does terrible things to life. It makes people ungrateful and unappreciative. It leads to not taking seriously, the vital throbbing moment in which they are living. And it sets a person up for painful disillusionments and bitterness when reality catches up, as it always does.

Yes, it is likely that most of us won't experience shocking disruptions or interruptions of God's grace to us any time soon. But please don't lose track of the fact that *that* is what it is: God's grace to us—every last bit of it. It can't be stored up or locked in or protected. It has to be cherished and lived clear to the hilt today!

More Power to You?

Matthew 20:20-26

The mother of two of Jesus' disciples, James and John, came with them to Jesus. Bowing low, she asked a favor. "What is it that you wish?" Jesus inquired. She replied, "I want you to decree that in your kingdom my two sons will be the ones who sit, one at your right and the other at your left." Jesus turned to James and John and said, "You don't understand what is being asked. Are you ready to drink the cup that I must drink?" "We can," they both answered. Jesus said, "You shall indeed share that cup, but to sit at my right or left is not something that I can grant."

The other ten disciples heard of the request and were indignant with James and John. Jesus then said, "Rulers lord it over their subjects, and people in positions of authority make others bow to them. It must not be so with you. Among you, whoever wants to be great must be a servant, and whoever wants to be first will be as a slave to all."

I can almost hear the conversation that had gone on earlier, the last time James and John had stopped home to visit their mother. It wasn't the first time their mom had brought the subject up. She'd been talking about it ever since it became clear that they were not going to give up hanging around with Jesus to go out and get respectable positions in banking or shipping. So she raises it yet again: *"Well you could at least ASK him! You are both bright, loyal, deserving followers—exactly the kind of men that should be first in his kingdom. Jack, you'd make a wonderful chief executive officer for his kingdom, and, Jim, you'd be great as chief operating officer. That would leave Jesus free to do more of that which he does best."*

James and John have to admit that her suggestion has a certain appeal, but they wince at the thought of coming right out and asking. What if Jesus rips them up one side and down the other for their pushiness and lack of humility? Even if he doesn't, the other disciples will be merciless if they hear of it. So James makes an alternative suggestion: *"No, Mom, it will be far better if you are the one who asks him.*

He'll understand a mother making a request like this for her sons and so will the others. They all have mothers."

So their mother does it. And why not? Why shouldn't her boys be the ones in positions of power? They'd certainly be as good or better than Thomas or Philip or Andrew, or that loud-mouth, Peter.

True, in reading about it from this distance, it seems to be a brazen and presumptuous bit of power-grabbing. But I suspect that we understand it better than it may be comfortable to admit. The appetite for power is a major dynamic in our life together. Both for those who have power and those who don't, it can be a real preoccupation or obsession.

The headlines keep us quite aware of abuses of power, of those in positions of power who become merciless, insensitive, selfish, arrogant, corrupted, and even delusional. There are plenty of living illustrations of the truth of that cliche that says that "power corrupts and absolute power corrupts absolutely."

More subtle, though, and not nearly as well understood, is what can happen to people who have come to feel that they are powerless (or nearly so) and, thus, boil with resentment over their powerlessness.

One writer described a conversation with a young man who had really chafed against working for someone else and couldn't wait to get into business for himself. He finally did— a healthy sub-assembly operation. A couple of years later, when a friend inquired as to how it felt now to be in a position of power, he replied, *"I haven't the faintest idea, because I have no power. The police won't let me park in front of my own building. The tax people dictate how I have to keep my own books. My banker decides what my minimum bank balance will be and what chances I am allowed to take. Suppliers end up controlling productivity. The union tells me who can work and what work they may do."* He paused for a moment and then went on sullenly, *"To top it all off, I got married last year."*

There you have it—even from one we'd think wouldn't feel that way. But one doesn't have to listen long to hear echoes of people who feel dis-empowered. It is a major source of smoldering dissatisfaction, free-floating resentments, and of people viewing life as little more than a permanent competition for power.

One of the more ominous recent examples of people sickened by their sense of powerlessness has been the common-law militia groups springing up throughout our country. Those who study them tell us that they are made up of people who, for real or imagined reasons, feel stripped of the power to which they believe themselves entitled, so have set out to bootleg their own kind of power—whatever power there might be in violence, terror, and disruption.

Something similar is believed to fuel a certain amount of the fixation with guns in this country. For people who feel pushed aside, ignored, not taken seriously, and who generally feel shoved to the bottom of what they perceive as "the pecking order," guns represent power to them—the power of life and death. *"You may not respect me or listen to me or care about me, but what you may not know is that I have the hardware—the firepower—to make people take me seriously anytime I want to do so."*

Some studies indicate that the astounding sale of the larger, four-wheel-drive pickup trucks and utility vehicles has to do with the power needs of purchasers. They point out that the overwhelming majority of those vehicles are purposeless; that is, they never come close to being used in ways or places that require either the size or the off-road capabilities they offer. In such cases, what is apparently appealing about them is the feeling of dominance and the fantasy that, should I wish to, I could turn right off this pavement and drive through that ditch, over that fence, across that field, through yonder creek, and just about anywhere else I choose. Again, they never do it, but it feels empowering to know that they can if they wish.

There is strong conjecture that some of the battering of local schools in much of this country goes on because the schools are almost the last public entity over which people feel that they can exercise power. Though having no power over federal or state taxes, what they can do is vote down the local school levy. It may be the dynamic at another level, too; i.e., *"Though I didn't educate myself as well as I now know I should have, I do have some power to prevent the schools from having certain kinds of classes and certain books in their libraries that I don't understand and that make me feel obsolete."*

Over the years I have known a few churches that were badly torn up by people who felt powerless in every other theater of their lives, so used their church as the theater for acting out their power needs: blocking, leading factions, becoming tyrannical—anything and everything that passed for influence, authority, or control.

Do you see? Whether because of relationships, a work situation, social injustice, poverty, background, race, or yet something else, feelings of powerlessness easily breed erratic, troublesome, and strident behavior.

And yet, at its best, the wish for power is not a bad thing. In fact, it has a noble side to it. The wish to be effective in one's world, the desire to have one's life make a difference, the appetite for becoming some kind of light and inspiration to others, and the striving to understand and claim one's own dignity and unique worth are the profoundly good side of striving for power.

The problem comes in the misunderstanding of the nature and the source of personal power. Unfortunately, even after everything we've experienced in our human history, there is still an impression that power is conferred upon us from outside, rather than created within us. The mother of James and John believed that, if they were given those high positions, it would empower her boys. Jesus answered her by saying, *"This is not something that I can give to them;"* in effect, *"What you desire for them is a 'grace' that has to happen from within. I cannot bestow it."*

That IS the way it works with real personal power. One can acquire a position demanding obedience. She may achieve some kinds of dominance and control. He may become skilled at strategies of intimidation and/or in the use of force. But those are merely what people resort to who don't have the real thing. Real personal power and personal authority, meanwhile, are an inner quality—something that radiates through and from a person.

It is very difficult to describe, but every one of us has seen and experienced the real thing in people.

They are men or women, for example, who may have no position of authority, no special credentials, or even any particular expertise, and, yet, we always remember whether they were present that day or not. We find that, for some difficult-to-explain reason, what *they* think is important to *us*. When they speak, people listen—even those who don't agree with them. They "make sense" as we say, not because their logic is always flawless, but because there is something coherent about them as individuals.

Where does that kind of power come from? It is dangerous to generalize about it, but some part of it definitely has to do with the person having a "center" to his or her life; that is, a foundation of principles, values, and convictions that make sense of her. She is NOT "space for rent." When he speaks, you do not have the feeling that you are hearing merely echoes of the last person he talked to, the last article he read, or what she thinks (and hopes) will make everyone like her.

There is a profound confidence to the truly powerful person. It isn't confidence in the sense of bravado, but a confidence underneath that comes of believing that there is a larger process at work in life and the world, one which makes it unnecessary to scurry around, trying to control everything, pin down every outcome in advance, make up his mind about everything that goes on, have something to say on every subject, or always appear to be right.

Another component of personal power seems to be that of self-forgiveness. One who does not get stuck in the withering, exhausting work of having to disguise his every weakness, or does not have to justify or whitewash every mistake, one who does not have to carry the baggage of old guilts and remorse is an empowered person. That's because propping up those unreal ego-fantasies of total competence and illusions of near-perfection saps not only one's credibility, but his strength.

People of real power—the ones who have the kind of internal authority of which we are speaking—are also almost always "lovers"—lovers of people, lovers of the creation around them, and lovers of the whole throbbing, changing, demanding, mind-boggling experience of being alive. Why would it work that way? Because a person sees and understands infinitely more in whatever he or she loves. Whether it is loving people or time or the created order or yet other dimensions of our "aliveness," to love it and be enthusiastic about it is to become wise with regard to it. It is to be able to sense what is needed and, thereby, have the power to bring forth the best from whatever it is

If all this begins to sound a lot like a man named Jesus—that one who never held any official position of power, whose education was informal, whose supporters were "nobodies" from the margins of society, who never got out of the borders of what was his forlorn little country—this is no coincidence.

Part of what made him so astounding to those around him was that, with none of the trappings of office, no credentials, no organized support, without power plays, influence games, intimidation, or "one-upsmanship," there was, nevertheless, something so powerful and so authoritative about him, just in the way he lived and spoke, that people were in awe. They were at a loss to put into words what they had experienced. They told stories, came up with anecdotes, and invented theologies that they hoped would partly explain how his personal coherence and integrity, his composure and confidence, and his insight and spirituality always left them feeling that maybe they had seen, in him, what God might look like in human form.

And though not to that extent, that same quality of personal, internal power and authority is within the reach of every one of us. It comes with our discovering, and then trusting, the fact that it isn't how much we control, but how much we understand; that, instead of how imposing we are, it is all a matter of how authentic we are; that it unfolds from how much we appreciate, not how much we possess; that, instead of talent or charisma that sometimes get so much attention, empathy and perceptiveness are the real source of it.

That, in a nutshell, is the gist of it. No one is powerless, unless he chooses to be. But the only power worth discussing is that which comes exclusively from being credible, coherent, responsive centers of love, creation, hope, and healing. And, as we saw in Jesus, it is precisely what we were created to be: amazing, inventive, marvelously effective, powerful beings. Every one of us, if we choose to unfold it, has far more capacity to create and improvise and inspire and transform the life around us than we'll ever need.

Understanding God's Way With Us Through An Assortment of Ancient People

NOAH:
And Those Big Answers That Don't Work

The story of Noah and the great flood is one of the most well known. Not only does it appear in the Hebrew Bible, but it appeared in writings from long before the Book of Genesis. It is a disturbing story—actually quite violent, in its own way. It begins:

> When the Lord God saw that people had done much evil on earth, and that their thoughts and inclinations were always evil, he was sorry that he had made them and had placed them upon the earth. Deeply grieved at heart, the Lord said, "This race of people I will wipe from the face of the earth—man and beast, reptiles and birds. For I regret that I ever made them."
>
> Genesis 6:5-8

Only the man, Noah, had won the Lord's favor.

So the problem was a big one, needing a drastic solution. The story says that God decided that a gigantic flood ought to do it—flush everyone and everything away, including even the birds, beasts, and reptiles. Only a minimum number of breeding stock would be preserved—including Noah and his immediate family. They would provide for the re-population of the new and good time that was to follow.

Most know the story from there. Noah was instructed by God to build a cargo ship. It was an ugly monstrosity—an outrageous craft—especially since it was being built miles from the nearest water by a man without experience and without a boat trailer. There, in a neighborhood zoned only for single family residences, it began to take shape. If there were still any neighbors who were not irate because of the boat building, you can bet that they quickly became so when he began bringing in pairs of animals of every sort.

But Noah doggedly kept at it. After all, he was building

and working for a "new day," a time when the problems, and the people who caused them, would be gone, leaving only goodness and responsibility on earth.

Right on cue, the rain started to fall. Noah, his family, and his menagerie climbed aboard the ark. For six weeks, the rain poured down and the water rose steadily until the last of the irresponsible, the immoral, the irreverent, the troublemakers, and the corrupters had gone down for the third time, drowning beneath the storm water. Thus, the evil-doers finally reaped the consequences of their wickedness (notwithstanding the fact that the same deluge took a lot of babies and toddlers and puppies and bunnies and kitties along with them).

When the flood ended, Noah and his family came out, now to live happily ever after as good people in a world that had been cleansed of wrongdoing, viciousness, vice, and the whole catalog of other kinds of ungodliness. With such problems presumably solved once and for all, Noah and his family could start things over on the basis of sheer virtue and complete integrity.

But now jump ahead to the end of the story, where it says:

> *After he and his family left the Ark, Noah, who had been a farmer, planted vineyards. And he drank wine made from the vineyards and became drunk and lay naked inside his tent.*
>
> Genesis 9:20-22

It was a disappointing picture. Worse yet, a few verses later, he is heard cursing his sons. So, we are already getting the uneasy feeling that, as impressive and fitting an answer as the flood had seemed to be, maybe things are not going to go much differently after the flood than they did before it. Read still further and there is no longer any doubt that it is so.

So, the result of all that ark building, all that rain, and all of those choking deaths was little more than a lot of soggy real estate and a used ark rotting on high ground. All else is headed toward being about the same as it had been.

What is so frustrating is that it had seemed like such a good idea—a God-sized answer worthy of the problem. What could be more fitting, when so much was wrong? How could all of that cleansing roar and splash and foam have failed to be the answer to the sins, susceptibilities, and weaknesses?

But, if there ended up being a "moral" or message to the flood story, it was not really the one most people have sometimes thought: that when things get bad enough and God becomes sufficiently fed up, we might expect God to do something really big. No, if there is a moral to be seen or a lesson to be taken from this old story, it is to be found in that final ignominious picture of Noah, lying there naked, drunk, and cursing his own family members—that, and then the disappointing resurgence of human troublesomeness that was to follow. To state it bluntly, the real moral would be, that if you were serious about ridding the world of sin, selfishness, hurtfulness, and destructiveness, you wouldn't let Noah get on that ark. You'd have to drown him and his family, too—and also you and me and everyone else. The flood, comprehensive as it was, did not do what was expected of it. As a final footnote to the tale, the Bible writers' report that even God said, *"laying waste to the earth,"* as a way of getting at evil, would not ever be tried again.

Isn't it amazing to find that insight in such an ancient and primitive story? Way back then, someone understood how ineffectual are those tempting, massive, once-and-for-all, meat-cleaver solutions. It is particularly astonishing because, even now, thousands of years later, we still seem to have an appetite for the big, impersonal, sweeping answers to our human problems.

I know, for example, that despite the fact that I like to imagine myself as a reasonable, somewhat civilized being, when the evening news portrays massacres and gives detailed accounts of gratuitous torture and systematic rape as a means of terror, I become quite bloodthirsty. By the time I watch for only a few minutes, I long, not just for a solution to whichever mess this one is, but for a solution that is big enough and total enough to correspond to my rage. Most of the time, I do know better than that, as do all of us. We do know that wars of annihilation, vengeful retributions, or a flood of legislation, for that matter, never accomplish what it seemed they would. In our better moments, most of us know that, even when we are dead right about what is wrong or who is wrong, the "drown 'em," "smash it," "make-an-example-of-'em," "take no prisoners" answers have this infuriating way of complicating and exacerbating things, rather than solving anything. History reveals that we often suffer as much damage to the fabric of our life together from those big, blunt, simplistic, angry, indiscriminate, naive assaults upon evil, as we do from the evil itself. But there are times when it is tempting to forget all of that and call for one of the modern equivalents of the flood: obliterate the problem with saturation bombing or extending the death penalty or starving them 'till they shape up or isolating them or whatever. *"How shall we drown them? Let me count the ways."*

It is curious that, after thousands of years of contrary experience, we still seem to have an appetite for unrestrained or meat-ax approaches to even the most intricate problems and troubles.

Part of the reason for that is that many, if not most of us, still can be seduced by illusions and promises of simplicity: of quick fixes and simple answers.

A minister doing a children's sermon was hoping to drive home the point to the children that, when something went wrong at the heart of a person, the person needed to take it to God and have it made right. So he held up his watch and said, *"Suppose this watch started running too fast or ran too slowly or maybe would sometimes quit entirely. What should I do about it?"*

One little boy's hand shot up and he said, *"Sell the damn thing!"*

There you have it, the once-and-for-all, quick-and-simple solution: the perspective that we frequently get from children. Unfortunately, though, the hope tends to hang on, far beyond childhood, that even the most complex problems can usually be dealt with in some big, simple, and instant fashion.

One night, the Discovery Channel ran what it called the "German death films." They were the propaganda films used in Germany early in The Third Reich to convince the German people that the moral, humane, and realistic thing to do with persons who were chronically mentally ill or mentally arrested, was to give them a quiet, painless death—to "deliver" them, as they referred to it. Very smoothly and cleverly, the films simplified the whole issue in a way that apparently worked with many viewers at the time. The solution, as presented, was a "forthright" and "sensible" way to solve a social issue, an economic problem, a problem of suffering, and a public safety problem—all very simply and matter-of-factly. Like all such miracle cures for the most wrenching of our human predicaments, it was horrible quackery, but the seeming simplicity of it apparently had a lot of appeal. One doesn't have to listen long to some of our political figures to know that over-simplification is still a popular way of trying to manipulate us.

Something else that makes the big "non-answers" look valid is coming to believe that we are confronted by or dealing with depraved enemies. Identifying villains, culprits, and insidious threats or conspiracies is so much more satisfying, and even intoxicating, than is the hard work of trying to understand human weaknesses, errors, differences, and anomalies. Once the problem or trouble comes to be seen as caused by people who are walking embodiments of evil, corruption, and destruction, there is no longer any solution too harsh, any punishment that is inappropriate, any assault that is too drastic, or any generalization that is unfair.

The story circulated a few years ago in which an Asian fellow was standing at a bar, drinking a beer, when a drunk swaggered up to him and said, *"My name is Goldberg. I was part of the Pacific Fleet in World War II. THIS is for Pearl Harbor!"* Then, he slugged the Asian man in the face. The man protested.

"But, I'm Chinese! The Chinese had nothing to do with the bombing of Pearl Harbor."

But, the drunk said, *"Chinese, Japanese, Burmese—you're all the same as far as I'm concerned."*

A few minutes later, the Chinese fellow walked up behind the drunk and hit him on the back of the head with a beer bottle, causing him to fall to the floor. Then he said, *"Mr. Goldberg, that's for the sinking of the Titanic!"*

Goldberg protested, *"But, the Titanic was sunk by an iceberg!"* And the Chinese fellow said, *"Iceberg, Goldberg, Hamburg—you're all the same as far as I'm concerned."*

Once a person becomes intoxicated with blaming, and believes that he has a valid license to hate broadly, he becomes just about that absurd and dangerous.

The third thing that makes drastic action tempting is closely related. Retribution, reprisal, and punishment all easily masquerade as moral engagement. Worse yet, the grander and more absolute the punishment or retribution, the greater the illusion that a mighty blow is being struck for righteousness. For example, coming out in favor, of severe punishment for those whose lives are now a disaster, because of human selfishness, moral confusion, blind desperation, or more, is a wonderful way to help me forget how little I have been involved in trying to do something positive to get at the underlying sources and causes of the very thing that I cannot wait to punish, in as big a way as possible. Most of the time, when human beings are anxious to "haul out the big guns," it is at least partly to distract themselves from their own problems.

What it comes down to is something like this: at any point that you or I know exactly "what the whole problem is," and can see with utter clarity precisely how it can be handled once and for all, watch out! Don't you believe it! It is not that simple. If you proceed, thinking it is that simple, you will almost certainly end up being part of the pain, not part of the healing.

In fact, we must never envision evil—never fight evil— as if it were something totally outside of ourselves, as if it were completely unrelated or dissimilar to our own weaknesses or complicity or misunderstanding or temptations. For, just as it turned out at the end of that ancient flood story, the problems are inextricably part of being human. Along with our proper upset over some of those awful ruptures that people cause in the fabric of our life together, we had better understand that we all have more in common than we may think with the troublesome hungers, fears, aggressiveness, neuroses, or mistakes that led to the problems.

Once one becomes honest enough to recognize that, once he finds the grace to quit thinking in cliches, slogans, and truisms, and has enough of a sense of his own need for forgiveness to keep his own mercy intact, then—with God's help—he'll recognize the knee-jerk, meat-ax reactions to the intricate needs and problems of life for what they are: sources of more problems.

It is not what we want to hear when emotions are running high, when our sensibilities are jangled, and when we are running out of patience, but (not counting that story of the flood that failed) God's real work in our world has never been in the big stuff, the across-the-board solutions, massive divine interventions, or example-setting retributions. No, it has been the long, slow process (just like that which was lived by Jesus), taking one life at a time, one problem at a time, one mistake at a time, and patiently creating the healing or the hope or the recovery or the growth that was required.

If that is God's way, we would probably do well to let it be ours, also.

MOSES:
A Holy Midlife Crisis

Exodus 2:11-15

After Moses had grown up [in the courts of Pharaoh], one day he went out to where his Hebrew kinfolk were enduring their forced labor under their slave-masters. There he saw an Egyptian beating a Hebrew. No other Egyptian was watching, so Moses killed the slave-master and buried him in the sand.

The next day, he again went out to where his people toiled and saw two Hebrews fighting. He said to the one who was in the wrong, "Why would you strike a fellow Hebrew?" The man answered, "Who made you a lord and judge over us? Do you plan to kill me as you killed the Egyptian?" Then Moses was afraid. He thought, "Everyone knows about the slave-master."

When Pharaoh heard what Moses had done, he sought his death. But Moses, fleeing from Pharaoh, had left Egypt and settled in the land of Midian.

It was a bitter, disillusioning outcome for Moses that day. Only twenty-four hours earlier he had felt so good—even felt heroic—after having struck a blow, on behalf of his enslaved relatives, by killing one of their tormentors. Now, he finds out that it was neither admired nor appreciated. How could that be so?

If you remember the story of his early life, it was through an amazing turn of events that Moses, though Hebrew, had been raised amidst all of the luxury, protection, and opportunity of Pharaoh's household. Meanwhile, all of his fellow Hebrews, including his immediate family, were slaves. This split identity, as a Hebrew living an Egyptian lifestyle, troubled his conscience and integrity. To his credit, he didn't rationalize it away. He forced himself to go look at the slavery being endured by the Hebrews. That's when this happened. While out at the work site watching the way the Hebrews were treated, it suddenly felt as if the right moment had come for him to do something—to make a gesture that would show the Hebrews that he was not insensitive, nor was he unconcerned about their plight. So, he killed an abusive slave-master.

He must have felt a lot better about himself as he returned to the palace that night. At long last, he had gotten involved, had finally taken a stab (so to speak) at making a difference, had, today, seized the chance to do something heroic in front of his people. Expecting some enthusiastic approval or admiration—maybe even awe from his enslaved brethren—he could hardly wait to get back out there the next day. Why, maybe, if the situation was right, he would "waste" another slave-master or two. Becoming the equivalent of "Rambo" to the Hebrews was an exhilarating fantasy.

So that next day, with yesterday's intoxicating taste of moral heroism still fresh in his mouth, he happened upon two Hebrews fighting. He said, in effect, *"Now fellas, you are both Hebrews. You must stop this right now. It's just not good—not right."*

And they turn on him! Far from the admiration or awe that he thought would be there after he had risked his life and position for them, these ungrateful slaves, these unappreciative slobs ask him who he thinks he is, messing in their affairs. *"Maybe you'd like to settle our problem by killing one of us as you killed that Egyptian yesterday,"* one says to him.

Poor Moses is stunned, shattered, flabbergasted. His emerging image of himself is now a shambles. His brand new appetite for moral engagement evaporates on the spot. His budding courage wilts. Instead, he is confused, hurt, and frightened. So he runs. He throws a few things into a bag and, with no good-byes, manages to get a seat on the afternoon caravan headed for a land called Midian, a comfortably safe distance away from Egypt.

He feels badly burned, and not just by the sun. He thought that he had done something important regarding the issues of tyranny versus oppression, done something about all that degrading mistreatment and deprivation, done something about the obvious need for social justice in Egypt. Unbelievably, though, he had been rejected. Those despicable, undeserving, ungrateful Hebrews had not appreciated it. *"Well so much for moral engagement."*

Moses takes a job with a farming operation in Midian, marries, has a couple of kids, and sets out to forget the whole disillusioning affair. He would let someone else worry about the world's cruelties, inequities, and injustices. Having discovered how unresponsive people can be—even those who really need the help—henceforth, he'll stick tightly and strictly to his own self-interest.

I can imagine Moses, a decade or so later, at a wedding reception or golf tournament, running into an old Egyptian prep school acquaintance, who asks him, *"Moses, what are you doing way over here in Midian? I always thought that with all the concern you had for the Hebrew slaves, you might be the one who would do something about them."*

And with indignation, Moses explodes, *"Hey, I tried. God knows I tried. But I've been there and learned the hard way that there are some things that aren't meant to be, some things that cannot be changed. As far as I am concerned, those Hebrews are getting about what they deserve."*

The old school friend asks, *"Then you don't care about them any more?"*

And Moses says, *"Look, I tried caring. I risked my life and lost a cushy position in the palace. I'm telling you that my help was not at all appreciated. I was not even thanked by them! I feel as if I made a real fool of myself trying to help people who just aren't worth the trouble."*

I don't know that this conversation happened, but I can imagine feeling that way. In fact, there probably are not many of us who haven't, at some point, felt that the gift we gave or the sacrifice we made or the effort we put forth was ignored, or was met with a shrug and a yawn, or maybe was even abused. When that happens (or feels as if it has), it can be a major crisis in morale.

A different kind of example was Ed Spencer, a young man preparing for the ministry at Garrett Theological Seminary in Evanston, Illinois. It was September 8, 1860. He was awakened in the night by the shouts of others in the dorm, saying that there was a shipwreck close by, just off the shore from Winnetka. An excursion boat with 400 people on board had collided with a lumber freighter and was sinking.

Spencer pulled on his clothes and ran the three miles north to Winnetka. It was a stormy night and the lake was rough. The strong undertow had proven too much for most of the would-be rescuers. Spencer, though, was a strong swimmer and plunged into the chilly waters and began pulling people to shore. For six hours, he swam back and forth to the wreckage, battling huge waves, and sustaining cuts and bruises from the floating debris. By dawn, he was exhausted, having made fifteen trips and rescuing fifteen people. He was resting by a fire when someone said that two more people had been reported still afloat, clinging to wreckage. Despite his terrible exhaustion, Spencer plunged back into the lake, barely making it to the couple, but managing to get them back to shore. There he collapsed, unconscious, on the beach. Of the 98 people who survived the disaster, he had rescued seventeen.

Spencer, however, never recovered from that night. The exertion ruined his health. He was not able to go into the ministry and, instead, lived out his days as a semi-invalid.

Years later, as an elderly man, Spencer was interviewed

in Los Angeles. When asked what he remembered most vividly about the incident, he said, *"My dominant memory is that, of the seventeen people I rescued, not one of them ever thanked me."*

Such a lack of gratitude is, of course, abominable and inexcusable. But can you hear yet an additional dimension of tragedy there? It is in the fact that, even decades later, the central memory and meaning for Spencer of that astounding night of heroism was that he was not thanked. In addition to losing his health, his very sacrifice itself was emptied—was, for him, robbed of its meaning by the fact that no one expressed appreciation. The net effect was that, not only in terms of his health, but spiritually, Spencer ended up a victim of the shipwreck. He was embittered by the very good that he had done and by the exceptional gift he had given.

Reams can be written and scores of sermons can be preached about the boorish ungratefulness of some people—those like the seventeen who were rescued by Spencer. In no way, is that to be excused or explained away.

But, just now, I would like to reflect for a moment on Ed Spencer's problem. In the Sermon On the Mount, Jesus warns us against doing good in order to be admired, appreciated, and rewarded; he goes on to suggest that we try to do charitable acts secretly; he says that the left hand should not even know what the right hand is doing. This is not to commend some dippy kind of Christian coyness or a subtle, but clever, strategy for appearing humble. No, it is, in some sense, a vaccination against the tragedy of Ed Spencer. It has to do with the tough-to-swallow truth that, with some of the needs that are most urgent, with some of the people who are in the worst shape, with some of the issues that have most to do with God's work here among us, there probably won't be any admiration or appreciation whatsoever.

So, do you see? If I expect or demand that there be eventual vindication or gratitude for any good that I do, there is a good chance that I will end up bitter and disillusioned from time to time. Either that or I will have confined myself to only minor forms of good that are safe little back-scratching trade-offs. If one never serves or sacrifices or gives anything out where there is little or no appreciation or admiration, it can very well mean that he is never getting out there to where the real needs are.

We all love to be appreciated and validated and thanked when we have offered what we have to give. It is very pleasant when it happens, and there is nothing wrong with enjoying it. But it is intoxicating and addicting, isn't it? It is so much so that it sometimes does become decisive, as to whether a person involves himself and gives of himself at all. As Jesus went on to say of such giving, *"They already have their reward."* In effect, there is nothing particularly Godly about giving or serving because of the acclaim, approval, and commendation that it gets you.

Worse yet, though, is that this "appreciation trap" sets a person up for precisely the kind of bitterness, disillusionment, and demoralization suffered by Moses, by Ed Spencer, and by countless others, some of whom you and I know personally.

> *Nobody thanked me!*
> *They took it and were irritated because there wasn't more.*
> *He wasn't even nice to me, even though I was the only one trying to help.*
> *See if I ever give to anything again, after the way they misused my contribution.*
> *She obviously couldn't care less how much I have sacrificed for her.*

The experiences that are behind statements like this can be very hard on the morale, for even the best of persons, but in the cases of the shallowest, they can permanently sicken the person, as they did with Ed Spencer and with Moses for forty years, until his "burning bush experience."

The goal here is not that of browbeating oneself into not enjoying gratitude and appreciation, when gratitude does happen to be there. But, this Christ-like kind of personal gracefulness, that is not dependent on the appreciation of others to keep us going, is extremely important for our own spiritual health and well-being (as well as for our morale).

It means giving, for example, NOT because it is a duty or because it sets a good example, but giving because you have come to see yourself as a channel of the resources and blessings that God has made available to you. It is giving because you are able to give.

It is learning to love, not because loving always eventually comes wonderfully back to a person. Sometimes it doesn't. No, grow to the point where you love simply because you are, in the most profound sense, a lover.

Don't sacrifice for someone, or for some good, out of some illusion that there is something magical or mystical about sacrificing that always gets good results and earns eternal gratitude. That is not so. No, if you sacrifice, whether for your kids, for a friend, for a cause, or for some truth, do it because it is what you have decided you want to do with some part of the life and opportunity that is on loan to you.

Most simply, whether it is time or resources, or talent, or personal influence, or forgiveness, or any of the other gifts with which God has entrusted us, to become a Godly person in the manner of Jesus is to be one who is growing out of "sticky-fingered" giving and "sticky-fingered" serving. It is to be working constantly and deliberately at dropping the subtle inclination to always estimate the public relations value of what we do, or to be carefully trading favors with others, or to be merely exchanging obligations, or to apply ourselves only in ways that, if the facts be known, are in our self-interest.

It doesn't come naturally, or even easily, but it can be done. We are capable of it. Among other things, it means not taking lightly the talents, resources, and opportunities we have. It means nourishing our sense of awe and gratitude for what has been entrusted to us. It means using all of that: giving it, applying it and then to LETTING GO. Don't get stuck waiting for reciprocation, appreciation, or admiration. If it comes along, wonderful. But when it lurks in our minds as our entitlement, we are setting ourselves up for trouble.

Pushing ourselves toward living with that kind of grace actually makes living and giving much simpler, more spontaneous, and free of a lot of unnecessary and avoidable frustration. Best of all, once free from that "what's-in-it-for-me" mentality, a person discovers how much fun it really is to be functioning as the very touch, the action, and the presence of God.

MOSES:
Getting Barefooted on Holy Ground

Moses' involvement in the exodus of the Hebrews from Egypt was not at all Moses' idea. It made no sense. He was past retirement age, was married, had kids, and was quite content with running his father-in-law's livestock operation. (By now, he was a member of Kiwanis, had joined the Chamber of Commerce there in Midian, and had become a registered Republican.)

As to the unfortunate enslavement of his fellow Hebrews in Egypt, he'd "been there, done that." In fact, though he didn't like to talk about it, forty years before, when he lived in Egypt, he'd actually killed an Egyptian whom he saw mercilessly beating a Hebrew. Running from that murder had landed him here in Midian.

But he'd matured a lot since then. He'd accepted the fact that though slavery was demeaning and unjust, it was very important to Egypt's economy; it was built into their society and system. He'd accepted the fact that life isn't always fair. He'd long since faced the fact that he couldn't solve everyone's problems. He'd come to terms with the fact that there is not much point in beating one's head against a brick wall of entrenched evil, no matter how much one disapproves.

So, anymore, he seldom gave much thought to what might be going on back in Egypt. That, for him, was now long ago and far away.

Then, one day when he was checking out a bush that seemed to have caught fire on a nearby mountain, the fire turned into a jarring, unsettling conversation with God— one having to do with Hebrew slavery. Though Moses had pushed it from his mind, God, it seems, had not. Interestingly, God's first words to him were, *"Moses, take off your shoes. You're on holy ground now."*

Since when does the God of all life and creation worry about whether someone happens to still have on his hiking boots or sneakers? Besides, the place didn't look at all holy. It consisted of dusty rock outcroppings, scrub vegetation, scrawny trees, and an occasional gopher hole. "Holy ground," had you asked Moses, might be the lawn and gardens around the local synagogue.

That though, was NOT what this was about. The holy ground to which God was calling Moses' attention was holy ground to which Moses had given little thought for some time now: the holy ground that pertained to human oppression, injustice, exploitation, and inhumanity. Moses was dimly aware that such things were still part of the social and political landscape, but such unpleasantness had long since been out of sight and out of mind. Besides, everyone knew that holiness had principally to do with praying, reading scripture, and attending Friday night services.

But when God set out to restore Moses' soul and conscience, the first instructions were, *"Take off your shoes, Moses—your socks, too. Get rid of anything that insulates you from feeling the holy ground. Right from the soles of your feet, you need to feel directly, once more, the oppression and exploitation of your Hebrew brothers and sisters, and know it as a sacred issue."*

It may sound like a trivial or off-the-wall bit of instruction, but it actually carried a powerful message. For losing track of which matters in life are really the holy ones is certainly a common struggle for even the best of people. At least I know that, what bothers me most, when I am bothered best, is how much there is that no longer bothers me, but should. For example, I do care that many people around the world go hungry, are being massacred, are dying for lack of elementary medical care, and are being terrorized. And, yes, it concerns me (as it probably does almost all of us) when I hear those statistics showing how rapidly is widening the gap between the "haves" and the "have-nots." I don't like it that such problems are still so prevalent in our world.

But, something like Moses (after his four decades of living comfortably in the bucolic simplicity of Midian), a practical kind of detachment creeps in. I, at least, can read news stories of terrible atrocities and tragedies, and feel appropriately disturbed as I read, but then, shortly, be just as upset in reading, across the page, another article warning that my retirement income might be adversely affected by projected fluctuations in the economy. The problem is, you see, that if one tramples rough shod upon holy ground long enough, one loses all sense of its sacredness.

Writer and Biblical scholar, Walter Brueggemann, tells of a time when he was in the sixth grade and a twin-engine plane crashed in a field near where he lived. He and his friends ran to the spot to watch the ambulance crew. Wearing rubber gloves, they removed the mangled remains of the passengers from the hole that the plane had carved into the cornfield. He recalls what his feelings were, looking at these remains of what had only moments before been living people. He says, though, that his most powerful image from that day is *"that of watching a woman standing next to me, holding a baby, and nonchalantly eating an apple."* Brueggemann says he still remembers his incredulity at that, wondering, *"How can she do that, …now, …here?"* He goes on to say that, only when he was older, did he understand that a person could be able to be so detached—have so lost the sense of what is awesome, sacred, or hallowed that he could chomp away on an apple in the midst of a scene like that.

Can that happen to good people? Unfortunately, yes. The prophet Jeremiah spoke of it when he said, of some of his contemporaries,

"They are never embarrassed. They feel no shame, for they have forgotten how to blush."

Jeremiah 8:12

Forgetting how to blush may be one good way of describing this. It is to have found a way to make peace with appalling facts; to learn how to deflect the impact upon us of troubling injustices, subtle exploitation, and camouflaged corruption. It is to keep the mind gorged with enough small concerns and parochial issues that those off-in-the-distance atrocities and outrages are kept pushed to the outer margins of concern.

Again, it isn't that one is exactly approving of the "cheapenings," compromises, "exploitings," decadence, and "corruptings." No. It is more like a kind of "resignation." It is to have decided that, as important as it is to keep some form of conscience alive in such a tough, complicated, troubled world, it is best to train one's conscience to stick to matters of personal behavior, and clear-and-simple issues of right and wrong. That's okay, as far as it goes. The problem is, though, that the REAL "holy ground" is almost always in rough, uncomfortable, complicated territory.

So again, God's first instruction was, to this sophisticated, well adapted, tough-minded, moderately skeptical Moses: *"Moses, before anything else, I want you barefooted—want your nerve-endings again exposed to 'the feel' of what real holy ground is."*

It's a marvelous image for then or for now! Until a person gets back to where he can feel how bruising and cutting—even crippling—are ALL instances of oppression anywhere; until every under-nourished child, every death that happens for lack of elementary medical care that could have been given, but wasn't, every family forced into homelessness or into being refugees becomes a desecration of holy ground, until empathy is recovered, a person is suffering from a serious, soul shrinking "out-of-touchness."

So whatever the emotional and spiritual equivalent is of "shoes" that make us able to stride around obliviously, they need to be taken off, in order to feel the holy ground.

A plot of one of John Katzenbach's novels (*In The Heat Of The Summer*) has to do with a returned veteran of Viet Nam who becomes a serial killer. He commits totally random murders in a metropolitan area. In his broken mental state, brought on by his horrendous experiences in Southeast Asia, he becomes enraged and then obsessed upon finding Americans dispassionately, nonchalantly watching the horrors of the Viet Nam war on television. It is that general, cavalier, easy acceptance of that war's horrors by the American public that pushes him over the edge. After committing a number of random murders, he phones a newspaper reporter to explain. He says:

> You ask why I am doing this. I'll tell you what this is. It is theater. It is a play. It is a chance for everyone here in this well-lighted city to know a little of nighttime emptiness—of nightmare. ... I watched on television as the world over there exploded. ... I thought then of all the horrors. I saw on the TV screen the faces, the fears. "No one knows," I thought. "No one really understands. It's become another television show, a newspaper headline, a grainy, gray photograph in the paper." And I decided then that I would bring my own horror to them; to all the complacent ones, the ones who sent me there uselessly. THAT'S what this is all about.

His psychosis notwithstanding, and as twisted as was his mind, he sensed, with deadly clarity, what a terrible thing it is for people, in effect, to have forgotten how to blush; that is, to have made peace with distortions, "cheapenings," and perversion of good.

Maybe it should be said this way: the "peace of mind" for which human beings search and about which Christians sing, while usually a very good thing, like most of what is good, can have a dark side. At its worst, it is a peace that passes God's understanding, leaves God incredulous and open-mouthed because it is such a cheap, inappropriate peace.

The peace that passes God's understanding might be, for example, our knowing (but being able to live with) the fact that almost one-and-a-third billion of our world's people live in dehumanizing poverty, without access to the most basic health care or even safe water; that 34,000 children die each DAY of hunger and of completely preventable disease; that the *forty-billion dollars* per year that would provide basic education, health care, and clean water for all people in developing countries is the same amount of money spent on golf every year. When it gets so that it's no longer "holy ground" for me—when it ricochets harmlessly off my soul like hailstones off a tin roof—then the thick shoes on my soul need to be taken off.

If, as a citizen of our world, I no longer blush at the fact that worldwide, an average of a little over $400.00 is spent annually per child on education, while the average annual expenditure per soldier is over $20,000.00, then I'd better be asking myself if I still know what a sacred issue means.

If, moreover, whenever I become conscious of some such disproportion, or of some bleeding injustice, or some blatant inhumanity or some crying need, there immediately comes a comforting recorded message in my mind, saying things like,

"You mustn't let this distract you, because there are more urgent things for you to be thinking about."

"True, this is unfortunate, but inevitable—this is the way life is and always has been."

"There is undoubtedly a very good explanation for this mess. Just trust those who have the whole picture and who know best."

"Anything you'd be tempted to do or give or try would

be such a tiny drop in the bucket that it would be totally irrelevant."

If it's gotten like that, then some shoes need to come off. You or I have lost touch with what is holy ground.

There is much, of course, to be enjoyed, celebrated, and appreciated and about which to be hopeful in our life and world. And we should do so. But never at the cost of smothering the deepest, most holy capacities God has created in us: our empathy, our concern, our acute sense of justice, and our overall ability, each in our own way, to love the hell out of the world.

So, let the holy ground get to you. BLUSH, for God's sake! Give in to some holy embarrassment. Become really uncomfortable. Make a scene. Get carried away! Do it, not only for the sake of the needs and problems. Do it also because living and moving and acting on the holy ground is all that keeps our souls alive.

MOSES:
Not Even a Gold Watch

Deuteronomy 34:1-6

Moses then went up from the plains of Moab to Mount Nebo, which is across the river from Jericho. There the Lord showed him the whole land [of Canaan]. The Lord said to him "There is the land which I promised to Abraham, to Issac, and to Jacob—promised that I would give it to their descendants. I have let you see it with your eyes, but you shall not cross over into it." So it was that there in the land of Moab, Moses, the servant of the Lord, who had led Israel out of Egypt, died. He was buried in a valley in Moab ... but to this day no one knows his burial place.

If it had to turn out that way for Moses, maybe it would have been better if the Bible had just skipped over telling us about it. Moses' personal story just did not end in the satisfying way that might automatically inspire you and me to keep hoping, persisting and working indefinitely at noble, but long term, ventures.

Many years before, Moses had walked away from a well-settled, pleasant life with a wife and family in Midian, and had dedicated the next forty years to this "promised land project." On the flimsy basis of a conversation with a burning bush, he allowed his life to be disrupted and turned upside down. It had involved him in confrontations with the Pharaoh of Egypt. It had required an infuriatingly difficult selling-job to convince the very people that he was supposed to be helping and liberating. When, finally, the exodus did get under way, it was a nightmare—nerve-wracking, confusing, stressful, and, at points, coming close to being a disaster. When finally they were safely out of Egypt, the headaches continued, owing to the fact that the people were ex-slaves—inexperienced, unstable, impulsive, and skittish. For most of four decades, they subsisted in a wilderness within sight of their promised land, but were afraid to go farther.

Moses continued to work in every way he could to keep up their morale. But it had been an uphill pull.

So now, finally, they are to enter Canaan, their promised land. They are on the threshold of seeing the dream fulfilled that Moses had worked so hard to keep alive in them.

That is when Moses gets the message that he is not going to be making the trip! No, there will be no promised land for Moses. What DID he get for all that effort and dedication? Arthritic joints, we suppose, probably an ulcer or two, undoubtedly a bunch of skin cancers from all the exposure to the sun, deteriorated hearing, fallen arches, insomnia, and who knows what else. Yes, that, and this one tantalizing, distant glimpse of the place where he had hoped to arrive, but now never would. As far as we know, there wasn't even a testimonial feast, where he was given a gold sundial in recognition of his several decades of faithful service.

That hardly seems like the way it ought to work out for someone so involved with God, does it? When a person has (as we say) paid his dues, has taken the risks, has done all the homework, and has been that dedicated, he deserves more than an unmarked grave in the wilderness, doesn't he? Putting myself in Moses' place, I think I would have found it more than just disappointing. It would have felt embarrassing. Wouldn't you feel as if you had made a fool of yourself, trying so hard and investing so much of yourself (especially compared to all the other people who got by just fine doing and being very little)? It is not the way it is supposed to be.

I suspect, though, that the Bible writers were careful to include this last part of Moses' story because this experience, in which a person never makes it to the promised land, is something that can and does happen. The most reasonable, legitimate "fulfillments," completions, intelligently-formed hopes, and well-deserved "vindications" sometimes are denied to us for no good reason whatsoever. Maybe Moses handled it well. It doesn't say. But for many to whom it happens, it brings a crisis of morale, of hope, and of faith.

It is expressed poignantly in a song by one of the characters in the musical, *Les Miserables*. Fantine, the single-parent mother of Cosette, sings,

> I dreamed a dream in days gone by
> When hope was high and life worth living.
> I dreamed that love would never die,
> I dreamed that God would be forgiving.
> Then I was young and unafraid
> And dreams were made and used and wasted.
> There was no ransom to be paid,
> No song unsung, no wine un-tasted.
> But the tigers come at night
> With their voices soft as thunder
> As they tear your hope apart,
> As they turn your dream to shame.
> And still I dreamed he'd come to me;
> That we would live the years together.
> But there are dreams that cannot be,
> And there are storms we cannot weather.
> I had a dream my life would be
> So different from this hell I'm living,
> So different now from what it seemed.
> Now life has killed the dream I dreamed.

Hers is just one of all kinds of examples where people are deprived of the "promised land" that had kept them going; the outcome that, by all that seems fair and just, should have been there.

We're not talking here about temporary frustrations and passing disappointments. No, this is where it feels as if the very meaning of one's life has been snatched away at the last minute, where that golden time or eventual vindication that would have made sense of all the sacrifice, struggle, and unconditional trust, just isn't there to do so.

It smacks a little of something portrayed in an old, but

famous, cartoon from *The New Yorker*. It is the one that shows a man in a dark passage with a look of utter despair on his face. The caption says, *"Discovering that the light at the end of the tunnel is only New Jersey."*

It is also reminiscent of the man who went to a fortune-teller and was told, *"In your future, I see a period of poverty, of tribulation, of terrible struggling, and of repeated failures happening for you up through the age of forty-five."*

The man asked, *"And what happens once I am forty-five?"*

Glancing again into the crystal ball, the fortune-teller replied, *"Oh, after that you get used to it!"*

Still another writer, obviously chafing against the way life so often fails to deliver the "fulfillments," "vindications," and pleasant resolution that would make sense and that would seem appropriate, suggested that maybe somehow it got turned around. He said that the way it ought to be is that, you die first and get that out of the way, then live for fifteen years in a nursing home until you are kicked out for being too young. You are given a gold watch and then you go to work. You work for thirty-five years until you are young, enthusiastic, and energetic enough to quit. You go to college, you play, you party until you are ready for high school. You do high school, then grade school, and then become a carefree child. You have fun and have no responsibilities. You then become a baby and go back into the womb, where you spend your last nine months floating, and finally you finish as a loving gleam in someone's eye.

Those are only some other echoes of this "elusive promised land" phenomenon that is there for a substantial number of us.

A most obvious place that we sometimes see it is when someone has worked, saved, planned and dreamed of a much deserved, fulfilling retirement, then it is shot down by a health problem, an untimely death, or a severe financial setback. Most of us have heard about, or know first hand, someone who was felled by a fatal heart attack the weekend following their retirement.

Moses' experience has also been there for the person who, through loyalty and service to the company that employed him, had seen every indication that a career would culminate in a top leadership position and lead to well-earned financial security. It was so close that he could taste it, when the promised land suddenly disappeared because the company was sold and, subsequently, closed by the purchaser.

All too often, it turns out to be the experience of parents who have invested every shred of their ingenuity, great quantities of patience, decades of concern, and much of their resources on their dream for their children. But then, not infrequently, it turns out that those children completely shrug off those dreams and hopes. Not only are they uninterested, sometimes they'll seem either ungrateful for, or oblivious to, how much of the very souls of their parents were tied up in those hopes for them.

Marriage can serve up an experience of it. For reasons that are sometimes beyond understanding, the most dedicated, selfless, well-intentioned, committed husband and wife—instead of finding their way into a promised land of close companionship, profound enjoyment of each other, and the blissful oneness of which poems are written—they never get out of the wilderness of marital mediocrity (maybe even ending up terminating the marriage after spending twenty years in a marital wilderness). Despite genuinely working at it, the relationship never comes together in the way they had both imagined that it was bound to.

The way it happened to Moses is still around, too. A noble dream, a selfless cause, a high ideal, a driving sense of purpose turns out to bless everyone, except the one who sweat all the blood over it. How can that be? If one is certain that he or she is really called to something, and he is truly sacrificial, and she is of noble intent, and they give 110%—can the promised land of vindication or appreciation or accomplishment not be there? Yes. Such wrenching disappointments are reasonably common.

When it turns out that way, the incredulity, the disorientation, and the blind frustration can be awesome for awhile. He or she often goes on a desperate search for an explanation—any explanation. *"Was the dream defective?"* he wonders.

Maybe some stone was left unturned?

Could it be that I am being punished for some reason of which I'm not even aware?

Maybe it isn't too late if I hurry up and do thus-and-so, or if I throw more money at it, or if I just make myself believe still more blindly, more fiercely.

In the absence of a credible explanation, there on the edge of the unreachable promised land, quite often a person beats up on himself with fragments of stupid old cliches like,

People who don't reach their goals just haven't tried hard enough.

Good losers are nevertheless losers.

If I had only had more faith or if only I had prayed harder, it wouldn't have turned out like this.

Not so! No! The difficult fact is that the most authentic, legitimate, appropriate promised lands sometimes will not be reached, for no other reason than the complexity of life, the randomness of events, the limits of time, and the interaction of circumstances that are part of being human in our world. Just as you and I, for no particular reason, are fortunate enough to not always be punished when we deserve to be, we also are sometimes stopped short of the well-earned "fulfillments" that would have made sense. When it seems to go against us, living with that requires as much faith and grace as a human being can muster.

It often means going back to understand, in a different way, the life you've already lived. (It certainly must have required that of Moses.) It is to discover, perhaps, that it was the journey that was the main event, not the arrival.

It will probably require the raw faith to know and believe that the absence of the right outcome (or worse yet, the presence of a downright lousy outcome) does not undo or diminish the quality or the meaning of that which was given and created and set in motion by you or me along the way.

Third, instead of giving in at such times, to the petulant, but powerful, temptation to believe that God is uncaring or unjust or incompetent or non-existent, what is desperately needed is the trust that, in God's own way, that which you have offered and through which you have struggled is already being used by God to create the meaning and the good that ultimately will have made sense of your life.

That doesn't take away all the frustration and pain that can be there in the face of a denied promised land. It can, though, lead us away from hanging around in the graveyard of old hopes, when those particular hopes are no more. It also frees us to know that we are not failures, even though something that was very important to us did not work out. And if we are open to it, it may even lead us to a new vision or understanding of what our lives have meant and what they can still mean.

Those "promised lands" in life are nice, and some people are lucky enough to arrive in them and live there for awhile. But as we saw with Moses, with Jesus, and with countless others, they are not ultimately what gives meaning or significance to our lives. No, what our lives turn out to have meant, and what turns out to have been their real worth, is left up to God, and we can be grateful that it is.

JOSEPH:
Good Things from the Dungeon

The story of Joseph, as told in the Book of Genesis, is far too long to print here. You may remember it, though, if for no other reason than having seen Andrew Lloyd Weber's delightful musical, *Joseph and His Many Colored Dreamcoat*, a story which is loosely based upon it.

Very briefly, the story is this: Joseph's father, Jacob, had two wives. Joseph was the son of the favorite wife. Unfortunately, Jacob was not at all insightful in matters of child-raising. Not only does he show favoritism toward Joseph, but does it blatantly at the expense of the morale of Joe's brothers. He dresses Joseph beautifully in designer clothes, while his eleven brothers have to make do with cheap jeans, T-shirts that don't have anything written on them, and sneaker brands that no one has ever heard of, all purchased at Odd Lots .

To aggravate that situation, Joseph doesn't have any better sense than to flaunt it—to rub his brothers' noses in the fact that he is treated far better by their father than are they. What, though, can the brothers do about it, except grit their teeth and put up with it? Then it gets worse. Joseph begins having dreams in which his whole family is bowing to him, worshipping him, and deferring to him. Instead of keeping such dreams of personal grandeur to himself, with much relish, he describes them to the family at breakfast. To his brothers, it is so nauseating that they can barely keep from vomiting up their Wheaties. That is the way it was through Joe's childhood and youth. He was growing up to be a handsome, well-dressed, self-confident, narcissistic, spoiled, obnoxious young man.

His brothers, somewhat understandably, feel that what their family needs most is a "Josephectomy." It is an operation that they will perform the first opportunity they get. Their chance comes when Joe is sent by their father to check on them, as they are out working in a pasture some distance away. Now they finally have him alone, out of Daddy's sight and Daddy's protection. Their plan is to kill him. As it turns out, a caravan comes along just then, so instead of killing him, they turn a profit on him by selling him as a slave to these traders headed for Egypt. They hold on, though, to the new sport-coat he'd been dumb enough to wear out to the pasture. They shred it and smear it with blood. Then taking it to their father, they tell him that Joe must have been the victim of a gang of local animals and they are sooo sorry. Jacob believes it.

Meanwhile, hands tied, stumbling along at the end of a rope behind the rear end of a camel, Joseph, the pampered, protected, overgrown brat, is starting to realize that, as wonderful and adorable as he had come to believe himself to be, he's been hated and despised by the overwhelming majority of his own family. Moreover, what he has assumed was a perfectly okay way for him to be, has suddenly cost him his security, his comfort, his future, and his freedom. He is on his way to a career as a slave in a foreign country.

Ahhh, but maybe all is not lost. He is still bright, very handsome and healthy. Maybe THAT will rescue him. And his attractiveness probably does help land him a position as a household slave—something like a butler—for a prominent Egyptian official. It seems like a nice break, but shortly he has reason to regret it. Because he is attractive, his owner's wife falls for him and tries to seduce him. When Joseph is uncooperative, she becomes angry and tells her husband that it was the other way around, that Joseph had tried to sexually assault her. Not surprisingly, that lands Joseph in prison. As a slave, he was lucky not to have been executed. He has had two close brushes with death in the same year.

Now reduced to being that nameless Hebrew kid in cell #3 of this Egyptian dungeon, with no hope of ever being released, he is hitting bottom. Everything Joe had believed to be true of himself is now in ashes: his status, his destiny, his self-confidence, and his family heritage. It is a perilous moment. It could easily have been the end of him. Sometimes, when people suddenly find out how different the real truth is about themselves, from what they now discover to be a terribly inflated impression of themselves, they don't survive. Joseph might have hanged himself in his cell, for example, or might have withdrawn into terminal self-pity and self-hate, withering away to nothing. It also wouldn't have been surprising to see him eat himself up with resentment and hate—hate for the brothers who had done this to him, resentment of his father who had bungled his upbringing, or a consuming rage at the injustice of being imprisoned for a sexual assault that he did not commit.

In his case, it does not turn out that way. For all that is not exemplary about Joseph, there turns out to be just enough to him to be reborn. The Bible doesn't enlarge on how it came about. It simply says (somewhat cryptically), *"God was with Joseph."* Whatever that consists of, shortly, this formerly spoiled, previously self-enthralled, so-recently-insensitive young man has begun to earn the respect and trust of his fellow inmates and his jailer. He gains respect to such an extent that, after a time (and mostly by coincidence), word reaches Pharaoh that there is an exceedingly honest, wise, reputable, and intuitive man down in the dungeon, whose talents are badly needed by Pharaoh and by Egypt. When Pharaoh sends for him, Joseph walks out of that dungeon very different from the severely underdeveloped person who had entered it, a few years before.

Among other things, Joseph has learned a lot about what, hundreds of years later, will come to be called "grace." He now knows something about what is the difference between advantages and blessings. He knows a whole lot more about the fragile way in which all of us human beings are placed here on earth, and about how much our various situations are "on loan" to us. He now understands that all the protection, comfort, support, and even fairness to which he (and many others) had believed himself to be entitled, was a gift— not at all an entitlement. So now, humbled, repentant, graceful, and open, Joseph actually begins to become a great man.

This does not have to do merely with the fact that he had been made a top official of Egypt, though that does happen. (He becomes, in effect, Egypt's Secretary of the Interior.) That is nice. But where we see, unmistakably, the depth of the transformation that God has brought about in Joseph, is on that ironic day when, during a severe drought, the very brothers who had despised him, to the point of doing their best to destroy him, now appear before him. They come as foreigners, begging to purchase enough food to keep their families from starving.

Yes, here they are—the very ones who had sent him through a hell of slavery, humiliation, and imprisonment— now bowing and scraping before him. It is quite reminiscent of his adolescent dreams of years before, in which the dreams had his brothers doing just this. It is probably one of history's greatest delicious moments for possible retribution. Who will blame him if he now humiliates them, terrorizes them, makes them "eat crow," or does an *"I told you so!"* that will ring in their ears for the rest of their lives?

That isn't what happens. The brothers have not recognized him, but after a bit he identifies himself and, when he does, he bursts into tears, begging them not to be afraid or to blame themselves for what has happened. He assures them that God has brought it all together to work for good and that he is grateful, not vengeful. They are reconciled on the spot. Then, he brings the entire extended family to Egypt to be with him.

I hope that you can see that, though this story has sometimes been used as one of those trite, rags to riches success-stories, that is not what is here. The moral is not *"You can't keep a good man down."* or *"Believe in yourself and you can't lose."* or *"Success is all a matter of hard work, intelligence, and persistence."* For Joseph wasn't a particularly "good man" at the outset. "Believing in himself" was a lot of his problem through his early years, since that self he believed in was not a credible self. And though ingenuity and hard work are often important, they, too, are not the theme of this story.

No, the meat of this story is Joseph's transformation, by the sheer grace of God, from that pretentious, self-absorbed egotist of his early years into someone who, having been stripped in that dungeon of all his favorite illusions, did allow himself to be reformed by God into something quite different.

A substantial part of it had to have been forgiveness: God's forgiveness, letting go of the rage at his brothers who had done what they did to him, and his own forgiveness of himself for wasting so much of his life being boorish and shallow. Facing, rather than trying to duck, one's need for forgiveness does not come easily to people who have been unlucky enough to have spent their lives being indulged, accommodated, and humored.

With that, of course, had to come the painful act of ridding himself of his elitism. Elitism is an insidious illness of character that warps a person's entire way of looking at, and relating to his human surroundings. In this case, some of it can probably be blamed on his father, Jacob. But however it started in him, early on, Joseph blithely bought-in to the idea that some people are intrinsically a cut above needing to worry about, apologize for, put up with, or be subject to much or most of that with which more average human beings have to struggle. It is safe to guess that his first weeks in the dungeon as a vulnerable, foreign "nobody" unburdened him of his elitism.

Shedding his sense of entitlement must have been another large and shocking part of it. Few things are more misleading to us human beings than a belief in our own entitlement. It is when I come to assume that, because of where I was born, or because so much has fallen nicely into place for me, or because I have this talent or am intelligent or have had good upbringing or inherited an appetite for work, then I am automatically entitled to and deserving of a full share of benefits and blessings: good health, good luck, exceptional opportunity—all of it. *"It's the way it is supposed to be for one like me!"* Those for whom that belief is never seriously challenged are NOT the lucky ones (as Joseph discovered). Those who get by with the entitlement illusion, in which they see all blessings and grace that come their way as appropriate and deserved, are the deformed ones of us.

There undoubtedly was a whole lot more that was at work as God took this seriously badly-developed, shallow, vain person and reclothed him in the kind of humility, sensitivity, gracefulness, insight, and empathy that made of him the center of wisdom and compassion that he was in Egypt. As the Bible says, *"God was with him."* It is difficult to argue with that!

God was, and still is, right there in those most punishing episodes where—perhaps because of the embarrassing exposure of a heretofore hidden weakness, because of a dismal failure, because of having all your sources of security snatched away, or, maybe, because of having some of your basic life assumptions turn out to be inaccurate—it feels like a dead end. Actually, God is quite good at the "dead ends" with which we collide in life.

It doesn't happen, though, by God bailing us out and putting things "back to normal." No, look for it more as it was with Joseph. The old Joseph had gone as far as he was going to go. Now, a new one was needed—one who was unencumbered with the pretenses, ego-fantasies, and self-delusions that closed down the old Joseph. The birth-pangs can be hell—no doubt about it—but for those willing to hang in there, at the bottom of that bottom is where, over and over and over again, a new person is born.

Does that really happen? You can bet your life it does.

NAAMAN:
Surviving the Demands of His Ego

II Kings 5:1-14 *(portions in summary)*

Naaman was commander of the army of Aram. He was a valiant soldier, highly respected, well regarded by his king, but he had leprosy. In his house, serving his wife, was a young girl taken captive in Israel. She said to Naaman's wife, "If only your husband would visit the prophet in Samaria, his leprosy would be cured."

Naaman told the king what the slave-girl from Israel had said. The king said, "By all means, go. I will send a letter regarding this to the King of Israel." So Naaman went, taking with him 750 pounds of silver, 150 pounds of gold, and ten exquisite garments. The letter from the king said: "I am sending my servant Naaman to you so that you will cure him of his leprosy."

The letter upset the King of Israel. He was afraid and said, "Am I a god that I can do this thing? Obviously, the King of Aram is making this demand to pick a fight with Israel." When Elisha heard that the King of Israel was afraid, he sent word saying, "Send the man to me." So Naaman, with all his horses and chariots went to Elisha's house. Elisha did not come out, however, but sent a messenger to say to Naaman, "Go wash yourself seven times in the Jordan River and your flesh will become clean." At this, Naaman was furious. He went away saying, "He ought to have come out to me, then call upon his God and wave his hand over the leprosy, thereby to cure it. Any river of Damascus is better than bathing in the Jordan." But his servants said to him, "Had the prophet told you to do something great or difficult, you would have done it. Why, then, not this?" Finally, Naaman did go and dip himself seven times in the Jordan River, as Elisha had instructed, and his flesh was restored.

Naaman was one of his nation's truly outstanding men. He was competent, resourceful, respected, influential, cultured, and affluent. He was a real asset to his country. It was, then, a shock, not only to him, but to everyone else, when it turned out that he had the crummy, lingering, repugnant disease, leprosy. *"Why would this happen to a great man like Naaman, of all people?"*

As one would expect, though, from a "can-do" person

like Naaman, he is going to fight this thing. Having been told that there might be some help for him over in Israel (one of those off-shore clinics, said to achieve remarkable healing of all kinds), he decides to go there. Resourceful person that he is, he leaves no stone unturned. He makes certain that his visit will be taken very seriously, by working through the highest of diplomatic channels; that is, by having his king write a letter to the King of Israel. Because he is the sort who always pays his way, he takes with him 6000 shekels of gold, ten talents of silver, and other gifts —about a million-and-a-quarter of our dollars. It's is a lot of cash to be carrying while out of the country, and far more than health care usually cost back in those times. Naaman, though, is not bargain hunting. He is willing to pay any amount to any foreign specialist in order to get the best of treatment.

That is why he is so totally unprepared for, and so incredulous at, the way he is treated in Israel. At his audience with Israel's king, the king is nervous, sweaty, and obviously anxious to be rid of him. That is not at all reassuring. The king makes a referral to Elisha.

When he arrives there, Naaman is not impressed with the facility. Elisha's place is not the exotic cave of a mystic hermit, nor the temple of a successful priest, nor an up-to-date medical facility. It is just an average dwelling: two-story frame house, vinyl siding, one-chariot garage, and no patio. It is not at all what one might expect of an international health expert. Nevertheless, Naaman and his entourage pull up and park along the street. He takes a few additional moments, "psyching" himself up for whatever this Elisha person might put him through.

He is just climbing out of his chariot to go to the door, when the ultimate put-down happens. A common servant, for God's sake—not even Elisha himself—comes out and tells him (tells HIM, Naaman, the commander and chief of the armed forces of Aram—an army which had conquered this two-bit little country more than once) to go soak himself seven times in the Jordan River. That's it. That's all. The messenger goes back in the house and Naaman gets back into his chariot and drives off in a boiling rage.

But you can understand that, can't you? He has done everything precisely and astutely; he has pursued a cure with sincerity, with taste, with dignity, with decorum, not to mention his willingness to pay "big bucks" for it. And here, out on the street, he has been told by some house-boy, who works for a scruffy, flea-bitten, foreign religious practitioner, to go jump in an Israeli creek, not just once, but seven times. The insolence, presumptuousness, and the impertinence of it leave him seething with blind fury.

After all, a man like Naaman doesn't have to put up with being treated this way, and he won't. He's not sure he wouldn't rather die. He prepares to head home and would have done just that were it not for the intervention of a couple of his servants, who persuade him to rethink this matter.

And right here is where we need to pause to look carefully at Naaman—maybe even to try to put ourselves in his place.

If, in his rage, he now heads for home, it will not be because he knows whether or not the seven baths in the Jordan will be helpful. It will not be because he knows anything more than he did when he got up this morning, as to whether Elisha has helped other people. If he goes home, it will not have to do with ANYTHING other than his incredulity over Elisha's lack of class and Elisha's failure to treat him and his problem with the special deference and dignity that he believes someone of his station, his intelligence, and his sophistication is entitled. This is unmistakable when he blurts out, *"The very least he should have done is come out here himself and invoke the Lord his God, wave his hands over the leprous spot, and command the leprosy to be cleansed."*

You do hear what he is saying, don't you? *"I will not tolerate a solution, will not put up with a cure, am not open to a source of help that isn't a proper fit for someone of my dignity and repute."*

(A novel I read some time ago may have described the kind of physician Naaman was actually looking for. The physician was described as a specialist; that is, one who specialized in "the diseases of the wealthy.")

Happily, when his servant pointed out that, had Elisha required some extraordinary, painful, intricate ordeal (walk barefooted across hot coals or drink the blood of a possum or eat twenty pounds of broccoli at one sitting), Naaman would undoubtedly have done it. So why not this? Naaman relented, took the seven baths, and was cleansed. But it WAS a close call—TOO close!

As maybe you know, in that blinding, near-fatal quirk of his, Naaman has a lot of brothers and sisters. It is not that a person like that doesn't want to be rid of the problem or free from the predicament or out of the stress or through the trouble. Rather, it is the feeling that certain answers are beneath him or her, are too obvious, maybe are too simple, or are too hard on the ego.

One can sometimes see it unmistakably in letters in the "Dear Abby" columns. These are the ones in which a person definitely wants help, but it has to be help that dignifies his problem. They are of that ilk of letters where, had it been Naaman writing, the letter would have said,

> Dear Abby,
> I've got leprosy and it is terrible. It is humiliating, depressing, and incapacitating. I'd do anything to be rid of it. But please don't ask me to go wash in the Jordan River. Dr. Elisha has

already recommended that, and I just cannot do it. I hate the Jordan River. But please, please help me.
                        Desperately yours,
                        Naaman.

The right answer to that would be something like,

Dear Naaman,
Having made up your mind that you'll accept only the help you want, rather than the help you need, I recommend that you develop a real taste for leprosy, because leprosy is what you're going to be living with!
                        Abby

Now, it is not that there are always simple, obvious answers to every problem and trouble. There aren't. But frightfully common is the problem Naaman had with himself that day; that is, the person's ego gets squarely in the way of the very thing which he hopes for and prays for. *"Yes, I want a solution, but it needs to be a solution that keeps intact the dignity and exceptional quality of my problem. It must be a kind of help that won't embarrass me. It needs to be a diplomatic kind of assistance that won't raise the question of why I have waited so long to do something about the problem. Surely, somewhere there is a solution for a person like me that will change things, without requiring change from me."*

If you don't think this goes on, think again.

"I'm willing to try to put behind me what happened, but don't ask me to forgive her. That I won't do."

"I'm willing to be reasonable and to make certain compromises, but one thing I am NOT going to do is go to a counselor. NEVER is some third person going to be allowed to pry around in my personal matters."

"I know I have a bit of a drinking problem, but one thing I'm not going to do is go to Alcoholics Anonymous. AA is for a whole different kind of person than I am."

"Oh, I know that in some situations, the thing to do would be to admit that I made a mistake—that I was wrong. That's not an alternative. For one in my position to do so would cost me everyone's respect and confidence."

"Yes, I sincerely want the conflict between us to be over, and it will be over, but not 'till she meets my terms."

"I'll admit I'm very lonely, but I'd rather BE lonely than have to settle for friendships beneath my professional level or my social level or my educational level."

On and on it goes.

"Of course, I want to be loved, but love me for that about me which I consider lovable. I can't stand it when people get so close that they are seeing things about me that are none of their business."

AND, YES—*"Of course I don't want to have leprosy,"* says Naaman (and all of his brothers and sisters), *"but the cure needs to be appropriately complicated, it must leave my ego intact, it needs to fit my image, and it should somehow justify all of the fuss I've made."*

You do see the implication of all of this, don't you? Maybe one way to cut to the moral of the Naaman incident goes something like this: *"Don't bother to pray for help if you are not open to the full gamut of answers that might be out there, including not only seven baths in the Jordan, but also quitting the job, coming right out and asking someone for his or her help, letting go of the bad marriage, going ahead with the surgery, using up the money, reversing your position, or opening yourself to yet some other seemingly unthinkable alternative."*

Like Naaman, we are NOT too special or too competent—not any of us—to never have to immerse ourselves in the most common kinds of asking, repenting, searching, returning, forgiving, apologizing, praying, relinquishing, starting from scratch, reaching out, or whatever.

The truth is (very much as it was in Naaman's case) that much of the time, it is not that the HELP isn't there. All too often, it is blocked by one's own sophisticated stubbornness, demanding that the help or solution be one that fits our appetites, our ego, and our self-image.

In Naaman's case, and right down to the present, most of the time, there are plenty of sources of hope, of healing, and of truth, plus unused alternatives and no lack of personal power. But embarrassingly often, prayers go unanswered, deep needs go unmet, or we remain permanently stuck in some problem or dilemma, much as in this ancient story. It's because I'm holding out for the answers I WANT, rather than embracing the ones I NEED. And that is about as self-defeating as a person can get.

SAMSON:
A Fascinating Loose Cannon

Judges 16:19-31 *(in summary)*

Delilah then lulled Samson to sleep on her lap. When he was asleep, she summoned a Philistine who shaved the seven locks of Samson's hair. His strength then left him. He was awakened and seized by the Philistines. They gouged out his eyes and took him to Gaza where, in heavy bronze shackles, he was put to work grinding corn in the dungeon. But his hair had begun to grow again.

The Philistines gathered in a great temple for a celebration, and had Samson brought from the prison, that they might ridicule him. They tied him between the pillars of the temple where all could taunt him. Three thousand onlookers were watching from the temple roof.

But Samson called upon the Lord, praying, "Remember me, O God. Give me strength this one more time that I may be avenged upon the Philistines." Then he put his right arm around one of the central pillars supporting the roof and his left arm around the other. He leaned with all his might. It brought the collapse of the temple upon the leaders of the Philistines and all the others within it and on the roof. So those killed by Samson, as he died there, were more than he had killed during his life.

That's the finale to the story of Samson. His stormy, dramatic, chaotic, reckless life ends violently in a suicidal act, bringing his death and that of thousands of his enemies under one big pile of rubble. By the time one finishes reading about his adult life, doesn't it seem curious that he made it into the Bible? There's not much to admire about his handling of his choices and opportunities.

Briefly, to refresh your memory, Samson had a unique start in life. He was set apart at birth by his devout parents, to be what was called a "Nazarite"—one given a special form of strict and religiously devout upbringing. Being raised a Nazarite involved additional dietary laws, for example. Nazarites were not allowed to ever cut their hair. Alcohol was strictly forbidden to them. Various special rituals and sacrifices were prescribed for them. Samson's upbringing, then, was exceptional.

Meanwhile, he was also physically attractive, was extremely clever, and was phenomenally strong. He was a "Hebrew Rambo" if there ever was one.

It was, moreover, a time when Israel might welcome a "Rambo." The Philistines, a larger and more numerous people, were making life miserable with their bullying, their border skirmishes, and other provocations. As Samson reached adulthood as a Nazarite, it was hoped that he might be an answer to prayer. It was hoped that God had sent him to be their champion against the Philistines. And, who knows, maybe that was what God had in mind; but, on balance, Samson was not one of God's better projects.

One problem with his being effective as a deliverer from the Philistines, was that Samson was obsessed with Philistine women. He even chose one of them to marry—a most objectionable marriage by Hebrew standards. Unfortunately, there was no talking him out of it. Since he was a Nazarite (The most Venerable Reverend Dr. Samson), who were they to doubt his wisdom?

So the wedding drew near. In a playful mood, at the bachelor party, he makes a sizeable bet with some of his Philistine in-laws-to-be. The in-laws win the bet, but they do so only by dishonest means. Samson, not liking to lose and anxious to punish them for cheating, then slaughters thirty of them and pays the gambling debt with what he removes from their corpses. This is considered bad behavior, even for a bachelor party. Those thirty people had been on the guest list for the wedding, so killing them is looked upon as a serious breech of etiquette by his future in-laws. It upsets the bride's father enough that he cancels his daughter's marriage to Samson and, instead, gives his daughter to be the bride of a nice hometown Philistine boy she had dated in junior high.

Given Samson's emotional explosiveness, it was not a wise move by that father. In retaliation for the broken engagement and the cancelled wedding, Samson captures 300 foxes, tying them in pairs by their tails. Then, attaching lighted torches to each set of tails, he turns these 150 pairs of panicky, yowling, torch-dragging foxes loose in the grain fields of the Philistines. The crop failure is instant and dramatic. It leads, of course, to further reactions and counter-reactions. At one point, for example, Samson wipes out 1000 Philistines using only the jawbone of an ass (a demonstration of the destructive power of the jawbone of an ass wouldn't be seen again until 20th Century American politics).

Eventually, he moves on to another Philistine girlfriend, a retiring prostitute named Delilah, and you know how badly that turned out. Overall, while he was always entertaining to watch, there was little to admire about Samson.

If you have seen the old Hollywood film version of the Samson story, you know that the scriptwriters try to superimpose some order, meaning, and even nobility to the chaos and mindless impulsiveness with which Samson lived and died. He comes off in that film as an ancient "Dirty Harry" whose gratuitous violence is all righteous violence, always richly deserved by it its victims.

The fact is, though, that, notwithstanding whatever positive things there may have been about Samson, and despite the fact that our ancient Hebrew forebears loved to tell of his raucous behavior, he was, nevertheless, a tragic "loose cannon." He markedly worsened what were already seriously troubled relations with the Philistines, thereby keeping things unstable for Israel. Even if it could be shown that ridding the world of several thousand Philistines was a good idea, Samson didn't do it out of any sense of broader justice, national interests, or self-sacrificing patriotism. No, carefully considered, Samson's behavior was that of merely one more giant ego wrapped in muscle.

So why, then, were the stories of Samson's brawling behavior some of Israel's favorites? It is for the same reason that Americans romanticized Wild Bill Hickock, Jesse James, Billy the Kid, and several others in the whole "Wild West" myth. It is the same thing that is at work in the countless successful films about rogue police officers who, enraged over legal aberrations and over the red tape of justice, grant themselves permission to throw off all restraints of law and order, and pursue retributions and vengeance in the ways that feel good to them to do so.

With Samson, moreover, there was an additional, exacerbating component. He was ostensibly a Nazarite and assumed to be righteous and wise. He would not have been thought of as just another insolent, mindless, muscle-bound bar-fighter. No, as a Nazarite, he was one believed to be set apart by God—trained, nurtured, and raised in the practices and disciplines of righteousness. Samson didn't even drink! He could talk the talk of a man of God. So, as sometimes unfortunately happens, he came to believe (as did many others who were hungry for a hero) that whatever he did was right, by virtue of the fact that he, a Nazarite, did it. His rages weren't tantrums. No, they were signs of strong character. His wasn't just "getting even" with people. No, it was God's own retribution. If one thought that some of what he did and said seemed stupid and insensitive, what you must have failed to understand is that Nazarites had a special form of wisdom. Even his uncontrolled appetites (such as his penchant for Philistine women) were to be seen as his way of meeting the "special needs" that "special people" (such as he) have.

Does Samson begin to sound a little less ancient and a little more familiar to you?

There is just a bit of him in anyone and everyone who comes to feel that, because he or she (like Samson) has been brought up right, has worked hard, has survived some hard knocks, and/or has extraordinary abilities of one sort or another, certain allowances and permissions are due them. People fall for that, don't they? Something like Samson, that which in other people would be considered to be pushy or pompous, or selfish or contemptuous, or snobbish or audacious is considered to be more or less acceptable in the talented, brilliant, or useful. A person will sometimes exempt himself from the usual requirements of being humane, considerate, benevolent, or compassionate because of who he is and how important he believes he is. Worse yet, others will not only go along with it, but like those ancient people, they will be fascinated by it—even admire it. They'll see it as "having class" or "having style."

It is not difficult to come up with lurid examples of high-profile, modern Samsons. A few are corporate executives that become loose cannons. Religious figures have been among the more bizarre. There is no small number of political Samsons out there. There are some really grotesque media ones. And they DIDN'T start out that way. It happened, one might say, when they began believing their own press notices, and came to feel that, because they had been brought up right and/or had managed to make a number of right decisions and/or were well bred or well educated, their decisions and actions were now beyond question.

That's the way, without even realizing it, that one gets to be a "loose cannon" in life. He becomes totally blind to his own bigotry, for example, because he knows that one like him is inherently above any bigotry. She excuses her own rages and tantrums as necessary and appropriate because one like her wouldn't have common, childish emotional frenzies. It never occurs to him that he has become selfish—an ordinary, garden-variety tightwad. No, he is merely prudent in a way that lesser people fail to understand.

But you get the idea, don't you? Whether it is Samson being raised as a Nazarite, or someone else having received a superb education, favorable upbringing, and special advantages, or still someone else having achieved some well-earned notoriety, WATCH OUT! Some of what seems like the best that could happen for a person, nevertheless, gets contorted into mere elitism, arrogance, narcissism, and worse.

How would one know? We'll know that this Samson disorder is afflicting us when we secretly begin to think, for example:

"With all that I contribute and accomplish, I shouldn't have to be burdened and distracted with the details of living that are there for more ordinary people."

"At this point, I have earned the right to be a little bit self-indulgent, to say and do pretty much as I please without having to bother my conscience."

"Yes, the rules are important under all ordinary circumstances, but what I am doing—what I can accomplish—is even more important than any rule."

"People who work under the stresses, pressures, and tensions that I do have special needs and need special privileges as part of taking care of themselves."

"In the case of someone in my position, to apologize for minor slights or hurts is unnecessary, if not dangerous. It undermines authority and respect."

"At this point in my life, it's time for them to take care of ME—indulge me and humor me, if necessary."

"I'm not just your ordinary person. I am well connected, have influence, and resources. Anyone who fails to recognize that and treat me accordingly is going to be

made to be sorry."

Very few, if any, would ever say such things in so many words, but that doesn't mean that it isn't sometimes in there. And when it is there, it IS a disorder. Insidiously, it transforms what had been a good, solid, sensitive person into one of those haughty, overbearing, self-promoting, loose-cannons that keep making life such a mess for those around them.

Nothing one has achieved ever justifies it. Nothing excuses it. Nothing exempts it. It is no more than a horrible, evil, tragic view, mistaking what actually started out to be God's grace to you or me, for special "rights" or excuses or privilege that God never grants to anyone.

Again, some of the brightest, the most talented, the most blessed people have fallen into it. Don't let it happen to you. Our life together doesn't need any more " loose cannons."

BALAAM:
On Taking Instruction from an Ass

Numbers 22:21-35 *(portions in summary)*

God was angry with the prophet, Balaam, because Balaam was co-operating with the Moabites, who were enemies of Israel. So as Balaam came riding on his ass to meet the captains of Moab, the Lord sent an angel with a sword to stand in the road, barring his way. When Balaam's ass saw the angel standing there, she turned off into a field. Since Balaam could not see the angel, he beat the animal to get her back on the road. The angel then moved to where the road ran between two walled vineyards. Again, the ass saw the angel and, in fear, pushed herself against the wall, spraining Balaam's foot. He beat her again. The angel now appeared in a yet narrower place. Seeing it once more, the ass halted and now lay down under Balaam. Balaam was filled with rage and beat the poor beast mercilessly.

Then the Lord gave speech to the ass, and she said, "Why are you doing this? This is the third time you have beaten me."

Balaam replied, "You have been making a fool of me. If only I had a sword, I would have killed you by now."

The ass replied, "Am I not the same ass which you have ridden all these years? Have I ever done this before?" Balaam admitted, "No."

Then the Lord opened Balaam's eyes and he was able to see the angel standing in the road, with sword in hand.

The Angel said to Balaam, "I've been sent to bar your way. Three times your ass saw me and refused to carry you forward. Had she not done so, I would have killed you and spared her."

Balaam said, "I did not know that it was the Lord confronting me. I see now that I have done wrong. I will turn and go back."

But the angel said, "No, go to the Moabites, but say to them only what I tell you." Balaam went and now did as the angel ordered.

A talking donkey and an invisible, sword-toting angel stopping traffic may not be typical of our standard ways of thinking, but it is an intriguing story! In the Old Testament, whenever one comes upon what seems to be an off-the-wall anecdote or description, one does well to ask himself, *"What made this important enough to become a part of scripture? That is, beneath its strange surface, what light did it shed or truth did it reveal?"* Looked at carefully, there's always something.

Balaam's jarring, sobering turnaround brought back to me the story of a young mother who put her two very rambunctious children to bed. Having done so, she changed clothes. She pulled on a pair of her husband's much-too-large-for-her sweatpants that happened to be lying nearby and, for a top, threw on a ratty old duster. Then she washed her hair. While letting it dry, she began to apply to her face, some heavy cake-like, bluish-gray facial treatment. All the time, she could hear her two children getting wilder and noisier in their room. Exasperated with them, she finally threw a towel partly over her still-dripping hair and, with this mud-like stuff on her face, and enshrouded in the duster and sweatpants, she burst angrily into their darkened room, screaming at them, *"You two had better shape up right now, because if you don't, I'll make you regret it."*

The kids dived into bed, but as she stormed back out of the room, she heard the three-year-old, with trembling voice, ask his brother, *"Who was that?!"*

Something like the unsettling experience of that three-year-old, the story of Balaam and his ass also has to do with the peril of stubbornly, blindly pushing the limits and acting as if there either weren't any limits or, in your case, it was okay to ignore them.

Balaam, with a not-unfamiliar bravado, stubbornly proceeds on a course that is disloyal, self-serving, and just plain wrong. He is so arrogantly oblivious that he seems to be out of reach of such considerations. With wry Old Testament humor, we're told that a certified ass is more in touch with the problems and dangers of the course being pursued by Balaam, than is Balaam. But when that ass—a faithful beast which has carried him and served him for years—now won't go forward and won't perform as Balaam demands, Balaam throws a tantrum. He begins to abuse it, to beat upon it, and to consider destroying it. One could say that he makes an ass of himself before the message gets through to him that he is flirting with disaster.

Do you hear anything familiar in that? The more I ran the story back and forth across my mind, the more familiar Balaam seemed. For hasn't there crept into a lot of modern thinking, the belief that we have become clever enough and resourceful enough so that, by pushing hard enough, making enough noise, or throwing enough money at it, we really can do anything that we want to do? It is the "Balaam Syndrome" when there is no shortage of determination, but a woeful lack of wisdom; when there is plenty of ingenuity, but no grace; when competency is no problem, but egotism is a major problem. That's when the picture of Balaam, blindly beating his poor donkey, becomes disturbingly contemporary.

Let's reflect a bit on that. Were we to modernize the story, who might be the faithful beast—that is, Balaam's ass?

Couldn't it be anything from marriage and the family to law and order? From religion to government or the economy to education? That is, any of those parts of our shared life that once were so reliable that they could be taken for granted, but that now upset us because we can no longer make them do and be what we want of them.

Take, for example, that faithful beast which is our American Democracy. It has carried us along very well for a couple of centuries. Now, though, it seems, at times, to have become somewhat erratic, hasn't it? What this story asks is: *"Might there now be, in effect, an angel in the path barring our way?"* What if, for example, because of that rapidly widening gap between the rich and the poor in our society, or because of the widespread disdain for the kind of human virtue on which any democracy is predicated, or because we have quit aspiring to anything more than "bottom-line" expediency and pragmatism, we are being prevented from progressing any further? Were that so, to vent our frustration on our democratic system with yet another flurry of Draconian laws, with yet more restrictions, with blaming, accusations, isolationism, and other such abuses, would be as idiotic as Balaam venting his fury upon his donkey that morning. The ass, the story tells us, wasn't the problem. Balaam was: his insolent, reckless, self-absorbed belief that he ought to be able to do as much of anything, any time, as he pleased.

Or, how about what was once our exemplary public education system? Hasn't it begun to react a little like Balaam's ass? Our public school system has the gall to balk at accomplishing the miracles of socialization, remediation, rehabilitation, and maturation that we have assigned it along with, of course, education. If you are Balaam, you might assume that if you clobbered our schools with enough legislative mandates, slapped them around with a wide enough variety of educational fads, purged them with enough failed operating levies, flogged them with enough law suits, or threatened them with do-or-die testing programs, it would do the trick, get things back to the reliability we think we recall being there in the fifties. Maybe so, but there seem to be indications that the scoldings and the punishments are not working. I don't know just what that angel in the road has to say. Perhaps some things about messed up community priorities, maybe a few words about the need to invest at least as much in nurturing the minds of our children, as we in this nation spend on liquor or on pet care or on video rental. Possibly, the warning has to do with more of us needing to be a direct, front-line part of the educational process than once was needed of us back along the road. Who knows? But as Balaam discovered, more was needed of him than only his criticism, irritation, and willingness to punish.

There could be a version of the Balaam story going on in regard to our country's place in the world. It is always more comfortable to believe that when something goes sour, the real cause has arisen totally outside of ourselves. But almost as eerie as an invisible angel in Balaam's path, is the discovery that country after country in the world sees us as the self-absorbed bully on the block or, in some cases, as the "great Satan." Without doubt, much of that may be blatant propaganda and deliberate misinformation in those countries. But again, this ancient story suggests that there could be more to it. If indeed our effectiveness in world leadership seems erratic, Balaam's experience suggests looking within ourselves as well as without. Listening to those who so annoy us, who show contempt for us, or who are outright adversaries, is admittedly difficult, unpleasant, and even humbling. But so was Balaam's having to take moral instruction from an ass before he saw the full picture of what he was doing and where he was headed.

I suspect Balaam's story could apply to our frustration, despair, and rage over the way things seem headed with marriage and the family and/or with the environment and/or with the economy, and still more. The question raised is, *"Might it not be self-defeating, and even stupid, to assume (as did Balaam) that the problem is entirely 'out there,' in the ills of the institution, the entity, the system, or the structure? Might it rather be, at least partly, the unrealistic or selfish demands that we (and even I) have begun to make, the pressures we've been exerting, or the punishing binds in which we may be putting them?"*

One can make this story very personal, too. An all too common quirk of competent, high-achieving, hard-driving individuals is losing track of the fact that, all competence notwithstanding, we are still required to accept certain boundaries and limitations in life. You might remember hearing a reverse spin on a familiar old, "you-can-do-anything-you-really-want-to" poem. The revised, comical version says:

> They told him the job just couldn't be done.
> If he'd try, he would certainly rue it.
> He tackled that job that couldn't be done!
> Sure 'nough, he couldn't do it!

That happens! Particularly those who are used to getting their way, used to controlling, and used to winning, routinely become ugly—as did Balaam—when one of those pesky angels gets in their way. They begin punishing anyone, and maybe everyone, around them—lashing out in rage at the very things and people they still DO have going for them. If it doesn't come out as hostility, it may show itself as petulance or despondency or childishness. It is all the same. It is an arrogant demand that one way or another, things should adjust to me. *"I am too smart, too competent, too important to accept 'no' for an answer in life."*

Meanwhile, for all our abilities and competencies, LIFE IS LIMITATIONS. We have limited time, limited ability, limited perspective, and limited wisdom. We are also limited in such matters as not being able to turn hatred into something good, for example. Similarly, we are prevented from being jealous and content at the same time, no matter how determined we are. All ingenuity notwithstanding, no one has ever been able to turn greed into a virtue. Try as some have, no one manages to arrive at happiness without first learning to be grateful. On and on go those kinds of absolute limitations—angels barring the way.

So as fashionable as it currently is to blithely insist that one can do anything if he just puts his mind to it, that really isn't true. Yes, we have much freedom and we are often amazingly creative. But to refuse to accept the fact that, to exist is to work with limitations—that there are very real boundaries which we have to take seriously and gracefully—is ultimately to make fools of ourselves.

That's the Balaam story. The moral? It is that you and I shouldn't have to be lectured by an ass; that is, not have to be chided by a heart attack or scolded by a divorce or brought up short by a nervous break-down. Nor should we have to be assaulted by social chaos, have to have shattering truth delivered to us by an environmental crisis, or have an outright enemy deliver the truth we need to know about ourselves.

As Balaam discovered, to his chagrin, God has provided ways of enforcing life's limitations, when we make it necessary. But it shouldn't BE necessary—IF you and I have learned to live with humility, openness and grace, AND if we will bring that along with us to our shared life, as a society. Meanwhile, remember Balaam as a lurid picture of the alternative: becoming one of life's surly, hostile, blindly stubborn, stupid grouches, rather than the gift to life which we were created to be.

GIDEON:
Why in Heaven's Name Would God Choose Him?
(Scripture: Judges 6–8)

Consuming three chapters of the Old Testament Book of Judges is the story of Gideon. If you don't happen to have a strong suit in Old Testament characters, you might guess that Gideon was the Bronze Age fellow who went around putting scrolls of scripture on the bedside stands in ancient motel rooms, next to the phone books and room service menus. Not so.

Actually, what was most notable about Gideon was that he was so UN-exceptional. The scriptures go to a lot of trouble to make certain that we understand what an ordinary person he was.

Gideon lived in a time when many things were going badly for the Hebrews. They were being harassed and bullied by some large, rough people called "Midianites." These Midianites, being more numerous and more warlike, routinely helped themselves to Hebrew crops and whatever else they might want. The Hebrews hated it, but there didn't seem to be much they could do about it.

Gideon was, again, a very average citizen, a farmer who wanted no more than to survive by keeping a low profile and staying out of the way. When the story opens, he is trying to thresh wheat indoors for fear that if he did it outdoors, the Midianites would come and take the wheat away from him, the minute he had finished threshing it.

In the midst of his trying to make that work, an angel drops in for a chat. Gideon is just short of rude to the angel. He isn't particularly religious, so he has little enthusiasm for this divine visitation. The Angel tells him, though, that God has chosen him—Gideon—to chase the Midianites out of the country.

Gideon is incredulous. First, if there was a God, then removing Midianites would be God's job, wouldn't it? Second, he did not have a combative, valiant, courageous, or heroic bone in his body. (That's why he was doing his threshing in his garage, with the door down.) There was no way that he was the right person to go off eradicating Midianites. Third, as he saw it, any God who would allow the shabby things that the Hebrews had endured from the Midianites, certainly could not be depended upon for back-up in any project as dangerous as this would be.

The angel, however, refuses to leave. They argue and negotiate until, finally, Gideon reluctantly agrees that he'll run a few tests on God. If, in those tests, God demonstrates that God has become more reliable, MAYBE Gideon will reconsider. The tests he comes up with are trivial, unimaginative ones—ones which God easily passes. That, then, makes it "put-up-or-shut-up" time for Gideon. With far more misgivings than fervor, he agrees to work at it.

He is first told that he must destroy the altar to the Midianite god, Baal, down on the town square. The erecting of that altar had been particularly outrageous to the Hebrews, so tearing it down would be a powerful symbol that a new leader had emerged and that changes were finally on the way. Unfortunately, God forgot to tell Gideon WHEN to tear it down. Gideon sneaks over in the middle of the night and does it, hoping that it will be blamed on a local teen-age gang. As a courageous, symbolic act, his toppling of the altar earns about a D-minus. The Midianites, moreover, find out who did it and would have lynched Gideon had not his father somehow talked them out of it.

Though still reluctant, Gideon does now get down to business. He sends out an "occupant" mailing, announcing that he is putting an army together. Unbelievably, 32,000 men show up. Oddly enough, God tells him that 32,000 is too many. So Gideon announces that anyone with the slightest misgivings should go home. Twenty-two-thousand do so. God tells Gideon that 10,000 is still far too many and to make another cut. Gideon sends the 10,000 down to the river for a drink of water. Ninety-seven-hundred of them drink in a civilized manner, bringing handfuls of water to their mouths. The other 300 stick their faces into the river and lap up the water, the way an Irish Setter would. Those "Irish Setter-types" are the three hundred Gideon keeps. He sends 9,700 home. Now, with his 300 intelligence-challenged men, Gideon (their courage-challenged leader) is going to drive off a couple hundred thousand large, well-trained, well-armed Midianites, right?

But he does it! Bringing to it a zany kind of ingenuity, which was undoubtedly heavily inspired by his having no stomach for armed conflict, he approaches the problem with a freshness and imagination that catches the Midianites totally off guard.

The Midianites have camped in a huge valley. On a dark night, Gideon provides each of the three hundred men with a horn, and a torch tucked into a jug full of flammable oil. He stations them all around the rim of that valley full of Midianites. On a signal from him, they all break the jugs, torching the oil. Simultaneously, they blow their horns and yell and bellow, as if they'd lost their minds (something that probably came quite naturally to some of them).

Awakening from a sound, and probably drunken, sleep on a black night, the Midianites see fire and hear noise everywhere they look. Assuming that some huge army is already upon them, they grab their swords and begin swinging them blindly and wildly in the darkness, killing each other, and then finally running in sheer panic across the now blood-soaked, body-strewn ground. Gideon's 300 men pursue and dispatch the stragglers. The victory is total. Gideon, who himself tended to be a bit self-defeating, had come up with a way to cause the Midianites to defeat themselves. With their army in disarray, the Midianites leave the area for good, never understanding what had just happened.

Afterwards, there are some who think that Gideon might make a good king. He would have none of it. He only wants to get home to his wives and children, to finish his threshing, and to sleep in his own bed again.

Some have tried to make Gideon out to be some sort of late-bloomer, a man of hidden genius, a closet hero, a person of marvelous, but heretofore undiscovered, abilities. That, though, is not at all the way the scripture pictures him.

No! He is relentlessly, determinedly, resolutely ordinary. Like most of us, he worries along from day to day with a full complement of hang-ups, temptations, and doubts. He catches a couple of colds each year, is a bit heavier around the middle than he ought to be, teeters on the edge of hypertension, has a touch of arthritis in one shoulder, has lost a lot of hair, always seems a bit disheveled, knows a little bit about a number of things, but is not an expert or authority on any of them, feels disorganized and behind much of the time, doesn't like conflict or confrontation, and gets very nervous when he is put on the spot. Do you recognize him at all?

Thank God, this Gideon saga was included in the Bible; it was not left out to make room for stories of the flashier heroes, the ones with more charisma, or the ones with more obvious talent, the ones who were paragons of virtue and faith. For as stirring as are the stories of some such swashbuckling exploits, looked at carefully, far more of God's work gets accomplished by the Gideon-types than by the spiritual giants, like the Davids and Daniels and Joshuas. It IS true that the spiritual hot-shots get more attention. But right there is a problem. The impression on the part of many good people is, that the landscape of faith and Godliness is made up principally of those few exciting, extraordinary, sensational people and seldom, if ever, of the rest of us—also "Gideons" who have more reservations than certainties, who do not naturally gravitate toward leadership positions, who worry a lot, who embarrass easily, who can come up with a much longer list of our troublesome quirks and flaws than we can of any important talents, competencies, and strengths.

That's NOT the Bible's picture—not at all. Moreover, Gideon isn't the only example. UN-remarkable, doddering old Abraham blunders, through trial and error, a nation into being—the nation of Israel. At an age when he should have been shopping for retirement housing, Moses stutters, bluffs, and improvises his way through getting the Hebrews out of Egyptian slavery. Barely married, adolescent, inexperienced Mary of Nazareth picks and sorts her way through the motherhood of Jesus. An impetuous, hotheaded, undiplomatic young man named Saul from Tarsus, after first persecuting Christians, reverses himself, changes his name to Paul, and ends up being used by God to ignite faith throughout the known world of his time. And, yes—prosaic, doubtful, introverted Gideon chases the Midianites out of the country.

Surely, there is a message in all of that! The message is something to the effect that, apparently God isn't the least bit bashful about using that about you and me that we see as hopeless barriers to our ever being a source of light, or ever bringing about change, or ever confronting some evil, or ever embodying some new truth. God, you see, didn't use Gideon IN SPITE of the fact that Gideon hated conflict. It was BECAUSE of Gideon's allergy to combat that he, uniquely, would come up with a strategy infinitely more effective than any "blood and guts" army captain.

THAT'S the principle here. What it means is, that when confronted with some need or problem or challenge or opportunity, it is a cop-out to automatically excuse ourselves by saying, "*I could never do such-and-such. I'm not put together that way,*" or "*What this would require is thus-and-so and I certainly have none of that about me,*" or "*With so many others who have the natural ability for this, it would be wrong for me to take it on, instead of them,*" or "*I would just 'know' if this were appropriate for me and, right now, 'that feeling' isn't there.*" Many of us can probably remember excusing ourselves on that basis: that we are inherently lacking or ill-fitted or flawed.

According to this very strange story, some of those dodged challenges may have been very similar to that pushy, unreasonable angel that showed up in Gideon's garage that morning, and kept bugging him. The angel kept challenging his assumptions about himself and kept refusing to let him hide behind his comfortable "averageness."

God regularly does that. "*Go—just you—and take it on, all by yourself,*" or "*You say it. You be the one who blurts it out and brings it out into the open,*" or "*I don't care how old or tired or terrified you are, wade on into the middle of it in your own unique way,*" or "*Throw yourself in front of it. Say the resounding 'NO,'*" or "*Prepare yourself to play a role in this that seems completely unlike you.*" "*Yes, Gideon, YOU take on those Midianites (or the bigots or the corrupters or the snobs or the self-righteous). You have no idea how uniquely and remarkably you are equipped to do it.*"

That, in brief, is the Gideon story. It doesn't require much more spelling out, does it?

The moral? Though it may sound a little strange, how about this: "*Don't throw the angel out, even when you think he may have the wrong address. God usually knows what God is doing.*"

KING DAVID:
Facing Tough Reality

II Samuel 18:33–19:8 (portions)

When King David was told of the death of his son, Absalom, he was overcome with grief, and went up to the chamber above the gate, weeping as he went, "Oh my son, Absalom, my son, my son, Absalom! If only I had died, instead of you! Oh Absalom, my son, my son."

The army heard that their king was weeping and mourning for Absalom, as did their commander, Joab. Hearing this, they crept into the city, not as victors, but as men ashamed to be seen after a defeat. King David continued to weep loudly over the death of Absalom.

Then Joab went to the chamber where the king was, saying to him, "Today you have put to shame all your soldiers who have served you faithfully, and saved you and the kingdom from the army of your son. You seem to love those who destroy you and destroy those who love you. It is clear to all that you would be content, were Absalom still alive and all of your officers and soldiers dead.

Now, O King, go at once and give encouragement to your army. If you refuse, I swear by the Lord, that not a man will remain with you and the disaster will be worse than any you have suffered since your earliest days.

Then David rose and took his seat by the gate. Hearing that he was there, his soldiers came before him.

It was the lowest moment in the life of David. The death of one's son would be a tragedy for any parent, but this was yet worse. Absalom's death at the hands of David's soldiers was the finishing touch on a major mess that David had made of his life. Some of it could be traced back several years to his affair with the wife of one of his captains. If you recall that story, when the woman turned out to be pregnant by him, David arranged for the battlefield death of her husband, before the man could discover the pregnancy. Had he not eliminated her husband, there would have been open government scandal, probably including the public stoning of the woman. With her husband dead, David married her.

Many knew the story, but it never became completely public. Had it been now, *The Washington Post* might have chosen not to carry the story, but *The National Inquirer* definitely would have.

Absalom, David's teen-age son by his first wife, Michal, had been a spectator to the whole thing. His disillusionment over that adultery and murder, as well as over David's clumsy handling of some other family problems, caused a serious break between David and Absalom. No one was surprised, then, when as a young adult, Absalom became David's major family problem and, finally, a real enemy. He developed his own political and military following, and shortly expanded his personal hostility toward his father into national civil war. David had little stomach for armed conflict against his own son, so offered little or no leadership. Absalom, meanwhile, turned out to be an imaginative, passionate, charismatic leader. So effective was he that he managed to drive his father and his father's armies into the hills for awhile.

Only by blind luck, one of David's patrols stumbled upon Absalom alone in an inopportune moment. They immediately executed him, bringing this tragic civil war to an abrupt end.

With that history, can you put yourself in David's place as he gets the news? True, the war is over, but his own men have just executed his son—a son whom he, David, has caused to hate him so much that it divided and weakened the country of which he is king. Public confidence in him and respect for him is badly eroded. Because of recent ineptness and indecision, his effectiveness as king has never been lower. So David has made, quite literally, a royal mess of things. There is no longer any denying that. Everywhere he looks, there is something about which to feel regret or embarrassment.

Overwhelmed with grief, guilt, chagrin, and despair, it is the kind of moment when some might commit suicide. For the time being, though, he just sits there in the little room above the gate, loudly sobbing out for all to hear, his grief, his remorse, his self-pity, and his self-hatred.

Let's leave him there, carrying on like that for a few moments, while we examine what are his options at this point. Fortunately, not many of us are likely to hit bottom quite as hard as he did. But even when mistakes and messes not quite that sensational "come home to roost" for us, the options for responding are quite similar to what David's were, way back then.

David's first alternative—the most often chosen one these days—is to "externalize" everything. Instead of facing up to his role in the chain of events and in the way things had turned out, or allowing true remorse for what he had done and failed to do, one option was to blame it all on extenuating circumstances.

For example, wasn't the way Absalom turned out principally the fault of David's first wife, Michal, who had stubbornly refused to get over David's affair? Obviously, she had turned Absalom against his father, infecting him with her hate and negativity and, thereby, indirectly causing the civil war in which he died.

Also, while he now knew that it had been an error in judgment on his part to have gotten involved with that woman, it never would have become a destructive, nationwide rumor, had it not been for the media blowing it way out of proportion. The "media" back then would have been back-fence gossip, graffiti that appeared on the city wall, and prophets who were always yapping and carping at anyone in a leadership position. Couldn't it be said, then, that most of the real damage done was from people not minding their own business?

Then, too, there was that appalling matter of so many people being willing to support Absalom's rebellion. Why should he blame himself in that, either? He'd been more progressive and less tyrannical than any other king he knew—at least he had in his early years. No, it was the fickleness of the public that accounted for Absalom's success. Absalom's unfortunate popularity was because the people were gullible and unpatriotic.

As to those who criticized him for not having nipped the rebellion in the bud—especially since it was led by his own son—that, too, was unfair. This was a military matter, not an administrative one. The problem was that his commander, Joab, failed to act decisively.

Do you see how easy "externalizing" is—even when one is looking at a mess as glaring and profound as that confronting David? Now self-persuaded that he is a victim of circumstance, misunderstanding, and public abuse, he can resign his kingship with a clear conscience and buy a nice little place over on the Mediterranean. So, yes, "externalizing" is a popular and tempting option.

But, there are other options one can select, when in the depths of embarrassment, error, or failure. David has, in fact, chosen this next one, as he sits up there publicly wailing in grief and regret. With this option, the principle is, that if one is hard enough on himself, other people might go easier on him. David, for example, might be able to deflect the public anger or disgust toward him if he puts on a dramatic enough demonstration of despair and self-hate. You have probably noticed that, when confronted with, "*I am worthless,*" "*I am hopeless,*" "*I've ruined everything and never done anything right,*" "*I am helpless,*" "*I am an emotional disaster,*" "*Everything is all my fault,*" "*I ought to just get out of everyone's way and kill myself,*" there is a reasonably good chance that people will pity you, rather than being as appalled or upset with you as they were at first. If he (or one of us) does it well enough, soon someone will come around and say something like, *"David, you mustn't be so hard on yourself. Nobody's perfect. It was just one of those things. It could be a whole lot worse. Now, you just forget the whole thing."* True, having people pity you like that is tough on the ego, but easier to live with than their anger. The truth is, though, that those multilateral paroxysms of self-hatred and bitter self-recrimination are often really a diversionary tactic and not the least bit commendable, as a way of handling one's most guilty or regretful junctures. All the person is really doing is saying, in effect, *"If I can no longer be seen as the greatest person around, at least I can be the greatest sufferer around. I can do the most unforgettable 'mea culpa.'"*

David was doing just that and might have continued, had not Joab, his army commander, confronted him in it, pushing him to the third, and only genuine, alternative.

Joab went to see him, neither to moralize about what had gone on nor to commiserate with David. There was no cheap forgiveness or shallow comfort in what Joab said. What he told David, very loosely translated, was that, no matter what had been his role in bringing things to this tragic and miserable point, it was not all right to sit up here doing this public self-punishment. *"However badly you have handled some very important matters, David,"* he said, *"if you continue this petulant wallowing in it, it is going to get a whole lot worse. There is nothing humble, commendable, much less noble, about this orgy of petulance, guilt, and self-loathing. So, David, get up and wash your face, comb your hair, change clothes, and get back to acting like a king. For if you don't, the tragedy marches on."*

It was an extremely harsh speech to deliver to someone who was at the lowest point in his life and in a state of near-total demoralization. It is somewhat amazing that David didn't throw him out. To David's credit, he apparently recognized that what Joab was saying was exactly what he needed to hear.

That was so for several reasons. First, was the practical fact that, past errors and sins notwithstanding, there were still matters that needed David. There were people who depended upon him, warts and all. There were decisions required of him. There was healing and rebuilding to which he needed to attend. True, when a person has been brought to a point of feeling despised, hopeless, and worthless, such responsibilities may seem irrelevant and even untrue, but it is virtually always true. Whatever has brought him down and however terrible the mess, it never accounts for more than a very few percentage points of who the person is, in total, and what he has to offer. So, while it may be counter to all feelings and inclinations, the luxury of withdrawing to lick wounds and nurse regrets is not one to which we are entitled.

Second, is the simple fact that the refusal to heal, the refusal to forgive oneself, and/or to accept the forgiveness of others, rather than being the humility and penitence that the person hopes it portrays, is actually, at best, cowardly and more often than not, a subtle ego-trip. It is cowardly insofar as it is always a whole lot easier to be embarrassed to death than it is to come back to life. Cringing may be depressing, but it doesn't demand any of the courage that healing does.

When it is an ego-trip, it is driven by the feeling that "one like me should have been immune to whatever was the sin or mistake or weakness." "*I've always been superior to that.*" Now that it's happened ,though, "*You'll not have me to kick around anymore. I'm through. Just watch me. I'll stay out of everyone's way.*"

In an excerpt from *The Journals of Sylvia Plath*, she says,

"*I have this demon who wants me to run away screaming if I am going to be flawed or fallible. It wants me to think I am so good that I must either be perfect ... or nothing.*" What she describes there has absolutely nothing to do with humility, has nothing to do with repentance, and is an outright barrier to recovery. It is, as Plath says, a kind of "demon." It is another show of the same kind of engorged ego that may have caused the problem in the first place.

The third reason that David so needed to hear what Joab said to him that afternoon is the well-established principle that, when you or I cannot think our way or feel our way out of the pit of despair, then we have to act our way out of it. At such times, don't wait for it to "feel" right. It is unlikely to. Acting as if you have forgiven yourself when you haven't finished doing so, holding your head up high, looking others in the eyes again, smiling when it is the last thing you feel like doing, is all incredibly difficult. Often, though, it is the only way to recovery. "*David,*" Joab said, "*get out of here. Fix yourself up. Go down to that front gate yet this afternoon and start greeting the people.*" Though it was undoubtedly the most difficult thing he'd ever had to make himself do, David did, and the healing of the country, and of David, was underway.

You catch the underlying message, don't you? It is that this God of ours won't quit pursuing us, even when we have landed in the muck of our own well-earned guilt, regret, and unpleasant consequences. The God revealed in Jesus, is not served by guilty groveling, but by our recovery. God could not be less interested in our "mea culpas"—only in our "nevertheless." "*I told you so!*" is never the word of God to us. No! As God spoke through Joab to David, it is a message of permission and responsibility to accept forgiveness and come back to life—not sometime later, when it feels okay and the memory has faded—but right now!

Untangling the Daniel-Darius Incident

Daniel 6 (in summary)

The presidents and governors of the kingdom went before King Darius and said to him, "We, your presidents, governors, and other officers have all agreed that you should issue a decree we have prepared for you, which says this: 'Whoever, within the next thirty days, prays to anyone, whether god or man, other than you, O King Darius, shall be thrown into the lions' den.'" King Darius signed the document.

Daniel, one of the king's most trusted presidents, was told of the decree. Nevertheless, he continued, three times a day, kneeling to pray and give thanks to God as he had always done. Seeing this, the other presidents went to the king and said, "O King, Daniel disregards both you and the edict you have signed." Hearing this, Darius was deeply upset and was determined to save Daniel. For long hours, he searched for a way to preserve him. But the whole group of men returned, reminding him that no edict or decree was allowed to be altered or cancelled, once signed.

King Darius then ordered that Daniel be arrested and thrown into the lions' pit. He said to Daniel, "The God you have served so faithfully will have to save you."

The king was distressed and spent the night fasting. He did not sleep and, at the crack of dawn, went to the lions' pit. In anguished tone, he called, "Daniel, has your God been able to preserve you?" Daniel replied, "God shut the jaws of the lions. They have done me no harm.

The king was overjoyed. He ordered Daniel released and found him unscathed. Then King Darius ordered the arrest of Daniel's accusers and sentenced them to the lions' pit. They had not reached the floor of the pit before the lions had seized them.

For those fellows devoured by the cats, that was a disappointing ending, but the vindication of Daniel's integrity and faith was certainly a satisfying outcome.

There is, though, a subplot to this story well worth looking at. Maybe you already picked up on it. It has to do with King Darius' role in the incident. As you may have sensed, even though he was finagled into signing the edict which almost cost Daniel his life, Darius was not a villain. No, he was a hardworking head of state—the kingdom's chief executive officer just trying to do his job in a complicated time. All that he thought he was doing, that day when he signed that edict, was taking decisive steps to improve national unity and patriotism.

Because Persia had conquered so many surrounding areas, it was now a melting-pot—in fact, almost dangerously diverse in its ethnic and religious make-up. Given that dilemma, what could be wrong with a one-month religious and patriotic requirement, by which, at least symbolically, the nation would be "one" in focus and practice, all worshipping and paying homage in the same way.

It was not Darius' idea that he should be worshipped. That came from his cabinet members. It was they who (albeit for ulterior motives) suggested that he, as king, be worshipped during that month. That may sound crass to us, but in those times it was not uncommon for kings to proclaim themselves to be national gods. Darius had never previously done this and might not have done so now, without the insistence of people he respected and relied upon. They seemed convinced that it would be good for Persia. How could anything be wrong with a temporary exercise in uniformity? His Attorney General assured him that the only people who might end up in the lions' den would be a skuzzy handful of atheistic troublemakers and subversive foreigners. That didn't seem all bad, so he signed the legislation.

Ahhh, but wouldn't you know it? There was the case of Daniel. Daniel, though a Hebrew, was someone Darius respected, depended upon, admired for his integrity, trusted for his moral sensitivity, and had made a significant part of the country's leadership.

Darius was stunned, then, when a committee of clergy, prosecutors, and politicians were waiting for him, as he arrived at his office one morning, to report that Daniel was openly violating the edict. They warned Darius that if an example were not made of Daniel, it would be a real blow to law and order in the country.

Darius was trapped. Once signed, there was no credible way—even for a king—to rescind, disregard, or countermand a duly executed, official edict. NEVER had it occurred to him that Daniel, of all people, would be the first one sentenced to become cat food.

The rest of his cabinet officials, though, couldn't have been more pleased when the door to the lion's den closed with Daniel on the inside. Jealous and resentful of the high esteem in which the king had held Dan, they secretly relished seeing the king himself co-opted into ridding them of Dan's insufferable integrity.

Darius was now a basket-case. He couldn't sleep. He was too nauseous to eat, and was wracked with waves of blind remorse. How could this happen, when his intentions had been good? The legislation had seemed so sensible and practical when he consented to it. True, he'd enjoyed the thought of certain shrill, rebellious, disrespectful foreigners being fed to the lions, but never for a moment had he intended it for one like Daniel.

You do see how this could happen, don't you? Darius was certainly not the last "nice guy" to turn out to be a little too sleepy or complacent to recognize it when he was being used or manipulated by immoral or amoral persons or forces. How had they pulled it off? They merely presented him with a lurid scenario, replete with abstract dangers, surreptitious evil, and faceless villains. Then, when all of that had him provoked and indignant, they helpfully offered this quick and simple, "one size fits all" solution.

O King, we come here deeply concerned. Some of those people that we have brought inside the borders of our great nation show gross disrespect for the Persian way of life. They brazenly refuse to recognize your authority. They are unappreciative of your beneficence.

And God-only-knows what vulgar, barbarous, hideous, religious beliefs and practices they bring with them, to poison the minds of our Persian youth. O King, something needs to be done. This country needs a clear and high-minded focus, and you are the only one who can be it. That's why we recommend this thirty-day experiment in national unity. It only needs your signature. We'll handle it from there. We hope that we haven't waited too long.

You can see how that might have worked. If a person has allowed himself to become susceptible to pre-packaged snippets of reality; if he has become accustomed to basing truth mostly on emotionally satisfying (or emotionally upsetting) anecdotes and rumors; if he is in the habit of doing his thinking in cliches, generalizations, and "party lines;" and if, in order to get to "the principle of the thing," he is able to push from his mind any human cost to the easy answers being offered—he becomes as easy a mark as was King Darius.

If you have read George Bernard Shaw's *Saint Joan*, you might remember a powerful scene that touches on this. It has to do with the chaplain who was brought in to give the signal for the execution of reputed heretic, Joan of Arc. Initially, this chaplain is somewhat honored to be asked to do it. *"Light your fire, man. To the stake with her,"* he says. But when he witnesses the burning, and the spirit of Joan as she dies, he is dismayed and filled with regret. He rushes away to the Earl of Warwick pleading,

My lord, my lord; ... pray for my wretched, guilty soul. ... I meant no harm. I did not know what it would be like.

With his mind now seized and torn by what he had just witnessed, his words could well have been those of King Darius that night, many centuries before. He cries,

You don't know. You haven't seen! It is so easy when you don't really know. You madden yourself with words. ... It feels grand to throw oil on the flaming of your own temper. But when it is brought home to you, when you see the thing you have done, when it is blinding your eyes and stifling your nostrils and tearing your heart, then—then: O God take away this sight from me!"

The Earl of Warwick, quite unfazed, and even a bit irritated by the chaplain's regrets, tells him, *"If you have not the nerve to see these things, why do you not do as I do—just stay away?"*

This "how could I have been sucked into this abomination" shock that overwhelmed both that chaplain and King Darius has been there for a lot of people, hasn't it? In their heart of hearts, they were better, were deeper, were more sensitive, were more moral than they ended up appearing, from the way they naively cooperated, consented, colluded, advocated, or voted. Under ideal conditions, they really were thoughtful and principled people. But, unfortunately, being so, only under straightforward, obvious, ideal conditions, has never been enough. That's what Jesus meant when he told his followers that they must be as alert as serpents, while being as guileless as doves.

Even now, all that anyone has to do to co-opt the morally lethargic is invent for them a context in which it seems not only okay, but seems urgent to back-burner their usual sense of justice or their compassion or their ideals or their trust just long enough to get at what is being artfully portrayed as "this unprecedented, grave, evil threat now at hand."

I can tell Darius enough upsetting anecdotes about how foreigners are ruining Persia. I can inflame a contemporary Darius by telling him that, only last week, someone was seen driving a Mercedes when she picked up her welfare check. I can hit him with the suspected plans of blacks or gays or feminists or atheists to destroy the society. I might show him pictures of smirking criminals as they are set free on a technicality. Maybe I can convince him that his elderly mother is soon to have her benefits and health care snatched away. Perhaps I can appall him with statistics showing how many persons of foreign extraction hold sensitive government jobs. Done astutely, there is an excellent chance that I can get him to go along with whatever I wish him to. No matter how draconian, ill-conceived, inhumane, bigoted, or oppressive he would normally have recognized my proposals as being, he now sees them only against the backdrop of the lurid, frightening, maddening mental pictures that I, for my own purposes, have prepared for him, in order to short circuit his thinking, close down his good will, and, in general, morally disorient him. By the time King Darius discovers that he has been expertly used, the law is on the books, Daniel is on his way to the lions' den, the vote has been counted, "wrong" is in the driver's seat, and poor Darius doesn't know what hit him.

As you heard, in this Biblical incident, things didn't turn out as it appeared they would. When, after a sleepless night, Darius runs to the door of the lion's pit, hoping against hope for a miracle, he finds that Daniel is okay (other than the strong aroma one might expect from one who has spent the night in the cat box). Overjoyed, Darius takes this as a sign that it is time for him to become substantially more morally responsible. Though it supposedly couldn't be done, he cancels the remainder of the thirty-day edict and, moreover, gives those who engineered the incident an opportunity to test their faith in the lions' pit. The score was lions: 12, cabinet members: zero.

Unfortunately, that is somewhat misleading. Darius and all of us who may, at times, share some of his personal complacency and susceptibility, should not assume that God will usually step in to rescue us from the consequences when, as had Darius, we have been too morally sleepy or sloppy to exercise our own best and deepest instincts. By far, the majority of the time, the full human price is exacted when we have been finessed into shrugging off systemic wrongs, or when we've been duped into ruthless or brutal reactions to minimal problems, or when isolated incidents have cleverly been made to look to us like demonic, ominous trends, demanding bare-knuckle attack. No, God does not typically deliver us from the consequences of episodes in which we were conned into believing that, this time, it was okay to relinquish our moral prerogatives.

The good news is, though, that every one of us is perfectly capable of avoiding Darius' mistake here. All Darius (or anyone else) needs to know is that he is in immediate moral danger any time he is being encouraged, temporarily, to suspend compassion because of the urgency of this issue; or to not worry so much about justice, while attacking this extraordinary kind of villain; or not to be distracted with worries over what wrong might be perpetrated in certain exceptions; or to go along with the package or the policy, despite some of what is unfortunately included; or to believe that this matter is one of those rare instances that is totally black and white, leaving nothing further to think about. One doesn't need the brain of an Einstein to recognize any, or all of that as deadly. Whatever or whoever is doing the talking at such a point, is not befriending you. He, she, or it is trying to take you over.

That's quite likely what Darius finally understood by the time he crawled into the sack the night after the incident was over: that there are no shortcuts in this matter of each of us being a Godly, accountable center of principle, of truth, of influence, or of moral choice; in short, a center of the very work and presence of God. Those who try to make it seem otherwise are after our very souls.

Avoid them like the plague.

SHADRACH, MESHACH, and ABEDNEGO: Taking the Heat

Daniel 3 *(condensed)*

King Nebuchadnezzar made a 90-foot-tall golden image, nine feet in width. He summoned all officers and governors of the provinces to attend its dedication. A proclamation was made, saying, "Peoples and nations, you are commanded that when you hear the sound of the horns and the other music with them, you are to fall to the ground in worship before the King's golden image. Whoever refuses shall be thrown into a blazing furnace." Thus, when the music was heard, the people did prostrate themselves before that golden image.

Then some officials approached the king and said, "There are certain Jews, Shadrach, Meshach and Abednego, provincial administrators of yours, who ignore your command. They do not worship the image."

Enraged, Nebuchadnezzar had them arrested. He told them that if they were ready now, when next the music sounded, to prostrate themselves before the image, they would be released. But if they refused to worship, they would be thrown into the blazing furnace.

The three men replied, "We do not answer to you on such matters. If our God is disposed to deliver us, we will be delivered. But even if not, he is our God and we cannot bow to worship the golden image."

King Nebuchadnezzar was irate. He ordered that Shadrach, Meshach, and Abednego be bound and immediately thrown into the furnace. This was done.

But when he looked into the furnace, he became afraid. He asked his advisors, "Was it not three men that were thrown into the fire? Now I see four in there. They walk about in the flames, free and unharmed. The fourth looks like a god." Then the king shouted into the furnace door for the three to come out. When they did, not a hair was singed. Their clothes were untouched, and no odor of fire was on them.

Nebuchadnezzar then said, "Blessed be the god of Shadrach, Meshach, and Abednego. I hereby decree that anyone who speaks against the God of these men shall be torn to pieces, for no other God is like theirs."

With such a dramatic, gratifying ending to that story, it's very easy to miss what else is there for us.

True, there is that quick and obvious moral having to do with "sticking to one's guns," with standing up for what is right, and with remaining loyal and faithful to one's principles. Obviously, that is important.

When, however, one is embroiled in the midst of such dilemmas, unfortunately, it is almost never as clear-cut and uncomplicated as it may later seem, when the story is told after the happy outcome is known.

For example, to a casual Babylonian observer at the time, Shadrach, Meshach, and Abednego would almost certainly have seemed like no more than garden-variety dissidents, strident fanatics, and/or young men chafing against duly-established authority.

Nebuchadnezzar (who was, incidentally, a reasonably good king for the time) was only trying to bring about some much-needed national focus and unity. As a result of its very successful military conquests, Babylonia had brought quite a variety of peoples inside its borders. Most, if not all of them, brought with them their various religious beliefs and ideologies. Culturally then, the country was a potential "powder keg."

Instead of ignoring it, what Nebuchadnezzar did was try to bring about some bit of unanimity and some symbolic, intercultural conformity. He reasoned that a national shrine—this golden image approximately the height of an eight-story office building—might be just the thing to do the trick.

To his credit, it was not a statue of himself. Better yet, he never said that people could not keep their own private beliefs in the various faiths of their fathers, or that they couldn't continue to practice personal religious disciplines. No, he only added to whatever were their own religious practices, this one additional element: a uniform gesture of national devotion that all would hold in common, no matter what their race, creed, or ethnic background. When the horns blew and the music played, they must all bow down to the eight-story image, in which he hoped to combine elements of religion, patriotism, and multiculturalism.

It must have seemed like a perfect strategy, one with practical benefits and endless uses. If the stock market lost 400 points in one day, blow those horns, turn up the music, and, as they bowed, people might feel better for having done this faintly religious "thing." If high administration officials were found to be malfeasant or misfeasant in office, here again, make everyone bow together before the government symbol to help them forget about it. If some high-handed or heavy-handed government tactics become necessary, that too, would be a good time to use the gigantic golden image; use it to remind everyone of how much larger is the state and its interests than are the concerns, principles, and hopes of any individual person.

But even with the most clever and practical of ideas, there are always a few crazies who seem to have to try to foul it up. Shadrach, Meshach and Abednego claim that their integrity—their personal convictions about the God they worship—precludes bowing to the image.

What is a king to do? Just shrug it off because they seem sincere? Were he to do that, why would anyone take him seriously anymore? Trying to be patient and fair, he does give them one more chance. They still refuse. *"Well, the law is the law, even if it seems harsh and imperfect at times. If, on this simple requirement, these three men choose not only to throw away their lives, but to disregard all of the good things that they, in their government positions, might have subsequently accomplished, then so be it. They've made their bed. Let them lie in it."*

Do you begin to see what a tough call this was? Everyone else was tolerating it—most of them shrugging it off as one of those dumb, meaningless requirements that come along. Others smirked, joked, and giggled as they bowed, making it clear to themselves that they weren't taking it seriously—just being practical. Besides, any intelligent God would know that it meant nothing to them, and know their disdain for it. Wouldn't dying for it be pure stubbornness, futility, and waste?

For Shadrach, Meshach, and Abednego, though, apparently the issue was: where WERE the limits past which they would not go, in order to avoid unpleasantness? If not this golden image, where were the boundaries on their integrity? How many such minor, practical, expedient compromises could be made along the way, without ending up selling one's entire self in little pieces at a time? Or, another way of putting the question asks, *"Was it really okay to expect (as some people seem to) lightning to flash or bells to ring or a voice from heaven to be heard, telling them that now something 'really important' came up so that, this time, finally, they should stick their necks out?"* As well as it could be argued that bowing to this inanimate, amorphous "thing" was a silly, stupid, meaningless requirement, now that they were faced (however unfairly) with the choice, WAS it really inconsequential, neutral, and irrelevant in its effect upon them?

Somehow they arrived at the lonely conclusion that this was where the line needed to be drawn for them. They told Nebuchadnezzar to go ahead and do whatever he felt that he had to do—they weren't bowing. They went on to say that they served a God who was quite capable of delivering them, but that even if God chose not to, it would be okay with them. With that, they were tied up and thrown into the blazing inferno.

As you heard, according to the story, Shadrach, Meshach, and Abednego came through unscathed, without so much as a smoky odor to them. That was great for them, as it is anytime someone is vindicated who deliberately chooses to take the heat the way they did. Obviously, gratifying outcomes like that are good for morale.

But outcomes so nearly perfect as that are notable mainly as the exception. Godly or not, far more often, they would have ended up as three grease spots on the bottom of that furnace. Moreover, they were quite prepared to have it be that way, *as one had better be* when he puts himself on the line like that, embodying some moral principle, throwing himself in the way of a popular trend, or going to the wall on an issue of integrity. The nice way this story ended notwithstanding, one must never assume that, because the cause is just and right, God has the cavalry parked just over the next rise, ready to vindicate us. No, most of the time, one ends up having to take the full brunt of the heat, maybe not execution, but possibly isolation, rejection, ridicule, character assassination, vocational ruin, or worse.

But note this too. While the story does not promise happy outcomes for our acts of moral courage, there nevertheless IS a very important kind of encouragement. If you didn't pick up on it, it has to do with their in-the-furnace experience. When, as happened with Shadrach, Meshach, and Abednego, the heat is really put on one of us on some matter of principle, some outspokenness, an unpopular stance, or some embodying of an unpopular truth, then expect to discover a wonderful coolness in the middle of it. Maybe you remember it being so at some such juncture in your life. As hot as others sometimes try to make it when they are threatened, embarrassed, or challenged by someone's character and integrity, they seldom generate enough heat to stop those who, like Shadrach, Meshach, and Abednego respond, in effect, *"Do what you must. Kill me, impoverish me, reject me, isolate me, sue me. I do know where I stand and I know what I must be, and, by God, I'm going to be it."*

Notice that, in the story, when faced with that, it is Nebuchadnezzar who is all hot and bothered, throwing the tantrum, and ricocheting off the walls in rage, frustration, incredulity, and vengefulness simultaneously and, in contrast, his supposed victims are in control and are quite cool, both in and out of the furnace. Yes! In fact, they find that they can actually move around confidently in the middle of all of that heat—the worst torment that the King can devise. Keep that picture in mind.

The events of that story were not the last time that someone who was brutally under fire discovered an unanticipated, somewhat amazing kind of coolness—discovered, moreover, that he was a lot more durable and resilient than he had imagined he could be.

That is vitally important to know. For, most of the time, when people end up caving in to threats, pressures, grim foreboding, and intimidation, it is because they believe that they are inherently lacking in the fortitude or the faith or the innate heroism to do other than give in. It is not true, but there is no way to know that until, with the heat on, you have stood there and laughed, rather than cringed, before someone who is terrorizing you. Until you have gone ahead and spoken the truth that you had been warned must NOT be spoken (or else!), or until you have let your conscience proceed to suck you right into major disapproval, or until you have waded on into the mess, you won't know your strength. For whatever reason, the coolness isn't there until it's needed. Only when the heat is on does one typically discover that he has less to lose than he had thought, that there are fewer limitations and more miracles around him than he had dreamed, that the right words are there when they are needed, and (as it turned out with that fourth figure joining the three in the furnace) that it isn't as lonely and desolate as expected. As you've probably figured out, one of the words for this reality is "faith."

Again, don't get too cozy with all of this. Don't sentimentalize it. Shadrach, Meshach, and Abednego notwithstanding, many good, committed, selfless, courageous people do get hurt. There remains that crucifixion right at the core of our Christian Faith.

But if and when your or my turn comes, we'll pray that, rather than terrors and misgivings, it will be our vision of ourselves, as God's Word made flesh in the midst of the heat, that will move us. As is revealed over and over again in this Bible of ours, it is absolutely astounding what God awakens, accomplishes, creates, redeems, and heals through as little as one person, or maybe a handful of persons who are willing to take the heat.

JOB:
"It Isn't Supposed To Turn Out This Way"

You may recall one of Mark Twain's stories about a devoutly religious man who gave up everything to become a missionary to a tribe of cannibals. The man was determined that he would convert them to Christianity. When he arrived among them, the tribe received him politely, sensing his obvious sincerity and concern for them. They listened with great interest to everything that he had to say. *"Then,"* Twain says, *"they ate him."*

It wasn't supposed to turn out like that, was it?

The way such stories are supposed to go, is to have the cannibals become so touched by that missionary's sacrifice, so moved by his concern for them, so inspired by what he had to say, that they would all become Christians and, henceforth, wear loincloths and bras.

But no, Twain refuses to provide this missionary with the kind of deserved outcome that would seem to follow naturally upon sacrifice and sincere commitment.

Told that way, it is amusing. But when, in real life, the course of events unfolds like that, it can be both disorienting and demoralizing. Some time ago, there was a news story about a Brazilian man who entered one of his country's hospitals to have a bunion removed. Worried about the surgical pain, he requested a general anesthetic, rather than a local one. For some reason, the anesthetic triggered a heart attack and cardiac arrest. By opening his chest and massaging his heart, his physicians were able to restart it. The trauma of that procedure triggered, though, some subsequent terrible abdominal contractions that actually ruptured his stomach. As they rushed him back to surgery to deal with it, he fell off the gurney, breaking a leg and collarbone, and substantially worsening his overall condition. Now, with a breathing tube in his throat, a drainage tube in his stomach, a cast on his leg, his arm in a sling, and an impaired heart, his bunion was yet to be removed. Even granting, in retrospect, that some of his medical misfortune might have been avoided, the outcome was still unbelievably preposterous and unwarranted.

Another reported victim of such outrageous turns of events was the man who, upon retirement, moved from a large city to a small town, chiefly in order to escape the terrible traffic and congestion of the city. He had been living in that village for only a couple of days, when he was hit by a car while crossing a street, seriously injuring him. The car that hit him, moreover, was that of the local Welcome Wagon.

Probably most of us can think of other examples of undeserved, inappropriate, and outrageous outcomes. In addition to what they do to those to whom they happen, there is something unnerving and disorienting about them, even for observers. It flies directly in the face of the belief that God, life, and the world are supposed to be more orderly than that—ought to make more sense than that.

Just that, as you may recall, was the subject of the Old Testament parable of Job. Job was a responsible and noble person in every way. But for no reason that he can perceive or imagine, he comes to be afflicted with every kind of personal, social, and economic catastrophe. As good a man as he is, his children are all dead because of a tornado; his health is broken; he is bankrupt; most of his friends now avoid him; his wife thinks he is a wimp or worse, and his days are spent sitting alone at the city landfill, asking what kind of world this is, anyhow. He knows that he has done nothing to deserve this outcome—that his misfortune is not for lack of competence, diligence, devotion, or any reasonable formulation of justice.

For the next thirty-nine chapters, then, Job agonizes, objects, prays, struggles, argues, and, in general, searches for some kind of a perspective on this truly miserable way that things have worked out.

Particularly interesting, though, is the ending of the book. For it claims that after all the chaos, loss, and suffering in Job's life, everything turned out to be wonderful and he, in effect, lived happily ever after. The truth about that ending, though, is that it was not originally a part of the book. Scholars of Biblical literature discovered long ago that the language, the idiom, and the literary form of the final paragraphs are totally different than the writing that preceded them. So, do you see? It was some later writer who wrote:

> *Then all Job's brothers and sisters and all of his former friends returned and feasted with him in his house. They all consoled and comforted him for all of that which had happened to him.*
>
> *Furthermore, the Lord blessed the end of Job's life more than the beginning. He acquired fourteen thousand head of small cattle and six thousand camels. He had a thousand yoke of oxen and as many she-asses.*
>
> *He fathered seven more sons and three more daughters and there were no women in all the world so beautiful as Job's daughters. Job lived yet another hundred and forty years, dying at a very great age.*
>
> Portions of Job 42:11-17

That "Hollywood ending" was tacked on to the Book of Job because, we suppose, some well-meaning person or persons just could not bear to have a sacred story be without a proper, rewarding outcome. They apparently felt (as some still do) that in any real God-story, faithful and heroic suffering will be vindicated, patience must be rewarded, and good character has to win out. So, to get the universe back in order, they wrote in all of the replacement livestock, replacement sons and daughters, replacement assets, and even substantial extra length to his life.

I understand their wish to make the ending happy, don't

you? Notwithstanding some of the odd, crazy, inexplicable things that we have to admit sometimes happen to people, as quickly as I can I go right back to believing that, if I am thorough enough, determined enough, careful enough, or sufficiently knowledgeable, optimistic, or Godly enough, there is a system in place by which the outcomes will be the ones that I expect and the ones toward which I have striven. That is the way it is supposed to work!

Happily, much of the time it does. But the question that is asked by the Book of Job (without its false ending) is, *"Who are we; what becomes of us; what's left of us when we are assaulted (as was Job) by blind circumstances, capricious twists of events, coincidental tragedy or yet some other betrayal of our optimism, our confidence, our diligence, or elemental fairness?"* There are several common reactions when people are hit with outrageous, unwanted results.

For some people, such experiences become immediate and absolute proof that there is no God. For if there was a God, that God's job description would be that of maintaining order, dispensing rewards or punishments in a timely manner, and insuring "cause and effect." Flagrant injustice and disorder are seen as proof that, either there is no God or that, if there is, it is a god who is so detached or unknowing as to be completely irrelevant.

There are, of course, others who rationalize it by telling themselves that, if the victims were truly devout, God would not have let such things happen to them. Conversely, when such capricious, Job-like events DO befall them, they'd better be repentantly figuring out why, before they get punished some more.

The way still others explain it is that freakish, incoherent, arbitrary tragedies and sufferings are God's deliberate testing of our faith, AND that to let such experiences cause doubts or cause us to become unraveled or feel victimized or cause grief and depression is to flunk God's test. Obviously, such interpretations are not helpful. In fact, they add to a tragedy.

The truth is that the only thing proven by the unpleasant twists of fate, the occasional mind-boggling bad outcomes and the painful results following faithful and diligent efforts, is that life and history are much freer and far more random than we wish they were. Therefore, we must live with the fact that, much of the time, there is no real explanation, no appropriate blame to be fixed, and no comfortable interpretation at which to arrive. Picking at, dissecting, and constantly revisiting the strange and anomalous things that befall us is virtually always a waste of time. They are "just there." To survive them, one has to move through them and beyond them without being seduced into petulance, without cringing in fear, and without resorting to self-punishing recriminations. To do THAT takes a great deal of raw faith, trust, and hope.

A letter from a woman going through a divorce in midlife gives some feeling for what that might be like. The letter was sent, as a kind of newsletter, to her close friends and relatives. She wrote:

> It's happening to me—to "us"! It's the big seven-letter word against which we have struggled for 21 years; and I do mean struggled. Yes, "divorce." My children are about to join the ranks of the broken-home, single-parent statistics.
>
> I don 't like it, but I'm ready to say it's okay. I have been a long time reaching this point. I've denied it, clawed at it, wept over it, raged about it, and avoided it, but it kept coming back. It has lurked on the periphery for years. We tried Gestalt therapy, couples group therapy, Marriage Encounter, Family Service, private counseling, and prayer. But here it is and I have to face it. I've given it my best shot. So has he. Now the rest of life is waiting and we must get on with it. Life is not meant for waiting but for living.
>
> We kept telling ourselves that we could not give up no

matter what; that we had invested too much and that we were not the sort of persons who fail at something so terribly important. So we kept plunging in, on and on like swimmers in a lake without an opposite shore.

What we've been tolerating is the drowning of the spirits of what are two whole people. The ripping, tearing, and faking have been taking a terrible toll. A lot of beauty has been marred, but not irreparably so. We're not beyond healing. To come out of this as two whole people is the challenge now before us. It will be painful.

Yes, I am grieving and I am scared. You bet I am, but it is no longer a dread. Now I am finding it easier to face the unknown than to run from it. In fact, I am experiencing an inner serenity—sort of an "okay from On High." Life has not been ruined. It has been lived and mostly by my choices and intentions. So I'll stay with it, one day at a time.

Please try to understand and stay near and love me as I go.

That is a good example of someone wrestling her way through one of the inexplicable, undeserved, and seemingly intolerable outcomes of the sort that can happen to anyone. What is healthy and hopeful about her letter is in what WAS NOT in it. She is not stuck, for example, on the fact that, as hard as they had tried, they deserved success. She is not caught up in self blame and recriminations OR in trying to blame her husband. She has not made up her mind what the experience means; for example, that she must never risk marriage again. The frustrating outcome has not caused her to see the two decades preceding it as wasted. She is not raging at God for being uncaring or incompetent. Somehow, she has struggled her way to a solid kind of gracefulness, that is, of faith, resilience, and openness, because of which she is going to be okay.

Whether it is that woman or anyone else, for that to happen, there are some understandings about how it is with us here in life, that need to be firmly in place.

One is that, for all of the cause and effect that we can see, and for all of the order we do manage to put in place, life is not the tight system we fool ourselves into thinking it is. There is still a certain randomness, inscrutability, and stubborn uncertainty about the way events combine and life unfolds. To deny that and convince oneself that he has things figured out or "in place," in such a way as to be safe from being blindsided by unpleasant enigmas, is a cruel hoax one plays upon himself.

Second, spiritually and emotionally surviving such baffling times and incoherent experiences, has little or nothing at all to do with logically explaining them, or solving whatever is the mystery about them. Instead, it has entirely to do with your or my determination to create meaning from them.

What about the good, and even noble, outcomes toward which we work and invest the very best of ourselves? Even with those, the truth is that, as superb and appropriate as they may be, even the most Godly of them are always vulnerable and finite. Goodness gets no special "edge" or protection. To state it as simply as possible: sometimes the cannibals will go ahead and eat the wonderful missionary. So look for the meaning to be found in the journey, not only in the arrival.

Finally, where is God when it gets like this? Where is God when Job is sitting out, there depressed, demoralized, and isolated at the city landfill? God is sitting right there with him, suffering also. Usually it is discovered only later, looking back, but God always turns out to never have been more present and at work than in the very situations that argue God's absence.

Let's face it. As gratifying as those nice results can be, there will always be a lot of unintelligible, crazy, and just plain bad outcomes in life. Work for good results, then, but don't get your ego, your morale, or your faith tied to them. God's best work gets done along the way, in the mess, and quite apart from what seem to be the final results. That IS something you can depend upon.

MARTHA:
Bringing Her Back to Life

Luke 10:38-42

Jesus came to a village, where a friend named Martha invited him to her home. She had a sister, Mary, who seated herself at Jesus' feet and remained there listening to all that he said. Martha, however, was distracted by her many tasks. She finally said to Jesus, "Do you not care that my sister has left me to do all of the work? Tell her to come and help me." Jesus replied, "Martha, Martha, you are fretting and fussing about so much, while so little is really necessary. That which Mary has chosen is best and it shall not be taken from her."

It is a story that makes me squirm. Maybe some of you can hear it without any twinge of conscience, but I (and I suspect no small number of others) know exactly what made Martha tick. We've "been there, done that" and, therefore, know what was going on for this conscientious, thorough, hardworking woman.

That day was a special one for Martha—every bit as much so as it was for her sister, Mary. Jesus would spend time in their home and be there for a meal. Martha, therefore, was determined to handle it in such a way that, when it was over, she would not have to feel embarrassed or uncertain about how it had gone. She would not feel inept or inelegant about any aspect of it. That meant that there was much that needed her attention. As it often turns out, the harder she worked at her preparations, the more things occurred to her that really needed to be done. So, by the time Jesus arrived, Martha was moving very rapidly, finishing the hors d'oeuvres, trying to keep tabs on the meat, while polishing the silver, filling glasses, stuffing mushrooms, checking to see that guest towels were in place in the restroom, locking the dog in the basement, then back to check the meat again, breaking a fingernail as she tried to get a stubborn cork out of a wine bottle, brushing against a bowl that shattered on the floor, as she cut a corner too close in her haste.

It was demanding enough, without the growing undercurrent of anger she was feeling. The anger has to do with her sister, Mary, sitting in there with Jesus, not lifting a finger; Mary is oblivious, laid-back, and unconcerned about it all. We know how that feels, don't we? As the feeling grows, Martha begins slamming the cupboard doors and the drawers harder than is required to close them. She is now walking with a bit of a stomp. She is acting even more harried than she is feeling. Her sighs of frustration are quite audible—all in order to get through to Mary, blithely sitting there in the next room, unaware of the fact that there are important chores and amenities yet to be done.

It doesn't work. Ditzy Mary is quite unfazed, still relaxed, and nonchalant—just sitting there. Worse yet, Jesus is inadvertently aiding and abetting it. One might have expected more than that from him. Finally, Martha can no longer contain it. Mary's indifference to the unfinished tasks and details is so irresponsible and insensitive that it cannot be ignored any longer. Something will have to be said. In a way, Martha hates to do it; that is, she feels a little bad about setting Mary up to be reprimanded by Jesus, but how else is Mary ever going to change? So she stalks into the family room and tells them what she is feeling.

Jesus' response leaves Martha stunned. Instead of what she was so certain he would say to Mary, he tells Martha that SHE is the one who is not using her time well; that her frantic, frenetic, compulsive activity and busy-ness is unnecessary, unfortunate, and self-defeating.

That is all the scripture tells us about the incident. It doesn't strain the imagination to picture Martha going off to seclude herself and cry for a few minutes. At the very least, we can assume that, as the three of them sit down for the meal, it is a bit tense and awkward at first.

It is quite easy to be critical of Martha, out there slicing carrots and peeling potatoes in the kitchen, while Jesus is sitting right there in her family room. In fairness to us, even the most driven and compulsive of us might catch ourselves short of THAT.

And it is okay to raise some questions about Mary, too. We really don't know, for example, whether Mary's lack of help was entirely because she was so reverently attentive and awestruck in the presence of Jesus, or was it because she was just plain lazy? We don't know whether Mary's was the wisdom and urgency of "carpe diem"—to seize the day—or was she just seizing an excuse ("carpe cop-out" would be the Latin for that). Yes, Mary could easily have been the kind of person who always arrived late, knowing that Martha could be depended upon to arrive early. She may have let herself become quite indifferent, reckless, or careless, knowing that her sister was the sort who would always make things right and would cover for her. It is even possible that Mary actually exploited Martha's workaholic ways to her own selfish ends. There ARE such people and they are not uniformly paragons of sensitivity and spiritual receptivity.

But even if all that were true of Mary, it does not soften the tragic aspect of a Martha—of the Martha that lurks inside of me and probably some others. Even if she feels driven to it, in reaction to the real or imagined indolence, irresponsibility, and laziness of someone else, still, when Martha pushes and stomps and works and worries and obsesses her way into tight-lipped, self-defeating "joylessness," it is not justified. It is no more than a tragic self-punishment.

There is an ancient saying that says something to the effect that, when the devil sets out to destroy a person, he doesn't zero in on the person's obvious weaknesses or his habitual delinquencies or his troublesome appetites. Instead, the devil finds it easier to use our virtues to undo us. He is able to do this because, when we are doing that which has clear and unmistakable elements of good, we tend not to question anything about it or question the way we are applying ourselves to it.

The "Martha phenomenon" is an apt example of that. To care and work as she did, in order to make Jesus' time with them as perfect an occasion as humanly possible, WAS a kind of good. In and of itself, every one of her chores and preparations undoubtedly worked toward hospitality, excellence, or beauty. That being so, how could she go wrong pursuing it with every bit of her time, dedication, and energy?

Nevertheless, she blew it. Not because the things that Martha did were not nice. What was wrong was "pouring it on" with such a lack of proportion that she lost her way and ended up confused, irritated, isolated, feeling used, hurt, and unrecognized.

It doesn't seem fair that this could happen, does it? It is not the way it ought to turn out for someone who is as diligent, industrious, and responsible as was Martha that day. That's what's tough about this story. It seems to say that, even with the most obvious kinds of goodness, righteousness, devotion to duty, and hunger for excellence, it doesn't automatically mean that one is where he ought to be, is in touch with what is truly important, and/or is offering what is most needed of him. *"Martha, Martha!"* Jesus says. *"You are worried, fretting, and distracted about so many things, while so little is necessary. Mary has chosen a better way."*

Do you begin to recognize any of this? One place that, from time to time, I see it at work is at weddings. True, a wedding is not quite the same as having Jesus over for dinner, but it should be one of the inspiring times of real family joy and closeness—a celebration of love and of all the history and grace and hope that nurtures our lives. Quite often, it is just that. But almost as often, especially with the larger weddings, all or much of that is overshadowed by Martha's driving preoccupation with little issues of decorum, fretting over what could yet go awry, irritation over glitches in the schedule, grimly besieged by the most minor details until, on the day of the wedding, members of the wedding party show all of the grace, the "at-homeness," and the festivity of one undergoing a root-canal procedure. What ought to have been a time of deep celebration for the families and the couple has been sucked dry. Ironically, it has gotten that way out of concern, care, competence, and a wish to leave nothing undone that ought to be done.

Another possible, very different surfacing of it could exist. Dr. Todd Reiher, a writer, professor at Wartburg College in Iowa, and a licensed psychologist is worried about the extent to which this "Martha Phenomenon" has found its way into some very sincere efforts at being a good parent. One example he gives comes from his experience as a weekend guest of some friends. It was not that his hosts were anything like the ancient Martha, obsessing over having things "just so" for him. Far from it. He actually saw little of them, because their children were in gymnastic classes, dance classes, swimming lessons, tennis lessons, softball practice, soccer team, and so on. The parents were running themselves ragged throughout his visit, making certain that the children covered it all. In conversations with them, and with other parents like them, the writer became convinced that the highly scheduled, tightly packed lives of these children are a well-intentioned attempt to leave no stone unturned in parenting. However, the concern of the article is that, however well-motivated, what this creates is children who (not unlike the ancient Martha) grow up feeling uncomfortable unless something is constantly going on and is, demanded of them at all times. They don't know how to "kick back," relax, use time to think, or to wonder, or to imagine, or to get to know themselves, other than as bubbles in a stream of activities. Here, too, this is certainly not everyone's problem. There are plenty examples of parents who fail to bring any enrichment to their children's lives. But the possibility of falling off Martha's side of the bed in parenting should not be taken lightly.

And there are other ways that we become Martha—at least I do. As important as I believe Christian worship to be, it is all I can do to keep "the Martha" in me from making my Sunday mornings into orgies of graceless nervousness, worry, and distraction. I begin behaving like Martha as I enter the building early on Sunday morning: double-checking the heat, making certain the altar candles were replaced after yesterday's wedding, going back to see if I did unlock the elevator door or just thought so. Then there are the coffee, the lights, the tape recorder, the "small-talk" microphone to check, making certain for the third time that I still have all the pages of my sermon. Then: *"Where are the flowers?"* *"Did the Chapel orders of service get over there?"* *"Now what time is it?"* So after working myself into acting like Martha for an hour, I feel like Martha. It is anything but the kind of receptivity, calmness of spirit, and feelings of "at-homeness" that are conducive to worship. In my overheated state of mind, I could walk right past Jesus himself in the lower hallway and mistake him for a florist or a plumber.

What I have to make myself understand over and over again (and maybe in your own settings, some of you do, too) is that no one is doing this to me other than me. It is the Martha neurosis—the compelling, back-of-the-mind sense that, should she or I slow down, or relax the pressure, or not double- and triple-check everything, the earth might quit turning, the sun quit shining, time would be no more, and chaos would cover the earth. That is a stupid kind of self-importance!

Another hint of it comes from writer, Max Guenther, who tells this on himself.

> One blustery weekend I was strolling with my little boy on an Atlantic beach. We were sailing empty clamshells into the onshore wind and watching them curve back to us. I don't know why this was fun, but on that particular morning, sailing clamshells felt like the best of all possible things to do. But then after awhile, I looked at my watch. It was lunchtime. We left the beach reluctantly. Only after we sat down to eat did I wonder why I had stopped that game. What is so important about noon? Why must we be hypnotized by the clock?
>
> My boy and I went back to the beach after lunch, but the mood was gone. The clamshells and the wind did nothing for us now but blow sand in our eyes.

That is yet one more piece of the Martha phenomenon, isn't it? *"There just isn't time!"* our inner "Martha voice" says. In a way, she may be right about "not having time." For rather than a gift, time has become her chief adversary in life, driving her to try to cram more into it, to set a lot of deadlines—all supposedly in order to save some time for later. All it really does is take her away from the present to focus instead on whatever comes next, and then next after that. That is one of the most certain ways of being constantly absent from one's own life, thereby robbed of it.

Again, Jesus' words were shattering ones to a person as good, diligent, and well-meaning as was Martha (and all of her descendants): *"Martha, Martha, you fret and fuss over so many things, while so little is necessary. What Mary has chosen is the better way and it shall not be denied her."*

For those who contend with "a Martha" somewhere lurking within, don't shrug this story off. The urgency and the truth of it sits squarely in the middle of our priority setting.

It pertains to what we embrace and what all we let go of in our living. It touches directly upon the way we approach and nourish our relationships. It is very likely to be woven all through the way we come to both our work and our leisure.

There is much about Martha to admire, but if you turn your living over to her, she can cost you a lot of its joy, most of its spontaneity, all of its grace, and far too much of its meaning.

Obviously, that is NOT the life God intended for us.

About That Man Who Hung Around the Pool

John 5:2-9

At the Sheep Pool in Jerusalem, there is a building called "Bethesda" which has five porticos, around which were gathered crowds of disabled and ill persons—blind, lame, paralyzed. They were waiting for a stirring of the water in the pool. It was said that, when that happened, it was an angel disturbing the water. The next person to enter the water, it was believed, might be cured of any ailment from which he suffered.

One man had been there, because of his illness, for thirty-eight years. Jesus saw him lying there and knew that this had been his condition for a long time. He asked the man, "Do you want to be well again?" "Sir," the man answered, "I have no one to put me into the pool when the water is disturbed. While I am moving toward it, someone else always gets there ahead of me." Jesus said, "Get up. Pick up your sleeping-mat and walk." Finding himself cured, the man did pick up his mat and walk away.

Thirty-eight years—some fourteen-thousand days—that man had been lying there by that sheep pool, waiting to be the first one in after the next angelic disturbance of the water. Not once, though, in that whole time did he get there first when the waters stirred. No, someone always got there ahead of him. To have had a four-decade run of bad luck like that, boggles the mind.

Ah, but he's not bitter about it. Not he. He knows the way people are these days: pushy, unsympathetic, thinking only of themselves. He's adjusted to it, borne up bravely, and made the best of it.

During those thirty-eight years, he has, in fact, become something of an expert on the pool. After all, he is now seeing the grandchildren of some of the persons who came to be healed, in his early years at the pool, also come for healing. With all that pool experience, he can tell you the best locations for quick access. He knows which parts of the pool do best for psoriasis, which for hemorrhoids, which side of the pool for gout, which for bronchitis, and which for cellulite. So now, when people arrive, seeking help from the pool, he is the one to orient them. Only a couple of years ago, when the Jerusalem Journal did a feature story on the lore and history of the pool, they included several of his comments. Expert on the pool though he is, the fact remains that he never has become well himself. When the water stirs and bubbles, either he is too far from the edge, or he happens to be looking the other way, or he is having one of his dizzy spells and forgoes the chance, not wanting to risk drowning while being healed.

And yes, of course he overhears some of the talk about him: he hears certain people saying that he isn't really ill at all, while yet others have said that he doesn't want to be well. It hurts his feelings, but what can he say? One can't convince unsympathetic, insensitive, heartless people, can one?

So that is the way it is for him, year after year, until comes the day when that young man, Jesus, visits the pool. Pool-tourists were usually a pain. In his opinion, they were there to gawk at those not as fortunate as they. But he is always cordial to them. He's found that being pleasant makes such onlookers more sympathetic.

The problem with Jesus, though, is that, instead of allowing the conversation to stay with matters such as recent pool healings, crowding in the area, and how more food and shelter was needed around the pool, Jesus keeps zeroing in upon HIM, upon HIS life, HIS outlook, and how he sees HIS future. He doesn't like where this conversation seems headed. It makes him nervous and he does his best to derail it. But Jesus is persistent, and finally works it around to the very question that the man is desperately trying to avoid. Unlike others in the past, though, Jesus doesn't ask it accusingly or patronizingly, as a put-down. No, he asks it gently, as if he really wants to know the answer, and as if he might take it seriously, whatever it is. *"Do you want to be well?"* he asks.

When people had asked that before, it always sounded faintly contemptuous, like a judgment, a scolding, or even ridicule. That doesn't seem to be so with this Jesus. Maybe that is why, in spite of himself, he risks trusting Jesus enough so that all of the accumulation of loneliness, hurt, unhappiness, and resentment comes pouring out of him. With his voice now breaking, he says,

Jesus, this is all I've got: this pool, this mattress, these few square feet of space. I have no one. Not once has anyone cared enough about me to help me into the pool when those times come—not in all these 38 years. Let's face it, Jesus. Other than my sitting here like a bit of pool furniture, I am a human throwaway, a discard. I'll be the first to admit that being the permanent fixture at a sheep pool may not be much, but it is all that there is for me: this place, some random scraps of sympathy, some little bits of attention, and some very occasional, temporary illusions of friendship. So, Jesus, 'Do I want to be well?' I'm not sure I know. I'm not at all certain that there can be any other life for one like me anymore. I may be a joke around town, but it has reached a point with me where being a joke is better than being nothing at all.

If Jesus replies directly to what the man divulges, it is not recorded. At some point, what he does say to him is, *"C'mon, my friend. It's over! You don't need this pool any more. Now take my hand and stand up. I want you to roll up that mattress of yours and get away from here. Trust me. You'll be okay!"* (And the man was.)

But why make so much of this man's recovery? After all, wasn't he just one more hypochondriac? Similar to some others we've all known, he enjoyed being pitied. He wasn't really trying to change his life. His illness, after all, was his permission to not pull his weight in life.

Probably Jesus would not have argued with that diagnosis, or argued with a lot of the others that we attach to people having trouble with their lives.

She has an alcohol problem, but she won't face it. It's as simple as that.

He has withdrawn from everything and everybody, and only sleeps and watches TV. THAT'S his problem.

Of course she's lonely! She has become so negative, so ill-humored, so full of gripes and gossip that, even those who once were close to her, now find excuses for avoiding her. What else would you expect?

As selfish and wrapped up in himself as he has become, he soon won't have any friends left. But that's what you get when you're like he is.

Most of us are quite capable of accurately diagnosing what has become of someone when he or she has fallen into some such state of disintegration. Even from this distance, we're probably not far off in guessing that, in addition to any physical disability that this ancient man may have had, he was probably also a hypochondriac.

But such armchair diagnoses, even when perfectly accurate, accomplish little or nothing. Most of the time, they are done as a way of dismissing someone from further consideration—writing him or her off.

He's one of those.

There's nothing one can do with someone like that.

He likes being that way.

He'll never change.

It's his attitude.

Then, having so said, it feels okay to shift from caring to simply tolerating, right?

What we saw, though, in Jesus' encounter with this man, suggests that maybe that is NOT enough; not for a couple of reasons.

One reason is that, though it is uncomfortable to think so, there are subtle ways in which *we* may be part of the reason that a person remains stuck at that sheep pool, once he ends up there. Nevertheless, sometimes, without our having said a word, someone like that comes to believe that he is now getting powerful, depressing, humiliating messages from you and me.

Whether real or imagined, it makes little difference. He thinks he perceives in our tone of voice, our lack of eye-contact, our haste to get away, or our body-language, a verdict to the effect that he is obsolete, that he is now perceived as a walking problem, that no one expects anything of him anymore, that his real job is staying out of everyone's way, that he has outlived his usefulness, and that he is only taking up space. The message he believes he is getting is that he is not loved or enjoyed, but only pitied; that even if he does change, no one will take it seriously, that he is frozen forever in people's thoughts—locked into this miserable, irrevocable version of him.

When someone's morale is already low, when she's plagued with self doubts, or when her self-image is crumbling, then her fears and impression of what you and I might be thinking about her (even when it's entirely in her own head) feed upon themselves, cruelly and mercilessly. At that point, it only takes one or two boorish people to confirm her worst terrors. Convinced that she truly is being "talked down to," patronized, tiptoed around, avoided, or grimly tolerated in whatever is her problem, she'll very likely give up believing that there is any reason to even try to make anything different.

This is where we run squarely into the hard fact that, all talk about independence notwithstanding, we human beings are still formed in relationships. We are easily deformed in and by relationships. And if we are to be reformed or transformed, that too is all tied up in what is taking place in relationship to those around us.

It turns out then, that when you or I—even competently and accurately—diagnose and label someone as being "pitifully withdrawn" or "self-destructive" or "neurotic" or dysfunctional, there is a strong chance that we become a participant in it. Moreover, the same is often true for working up our indignation and irritation at them, enough to lecture them on what they ought to be feeling, or what everyone is saying, or on how senseless and self-defeating is their behavior. That is not always as courageous as it can feel when we are doing it. A loveless, graceless scolding only reinforces the worst fears of someone like that man at the pool. When I have finished unloading upon someone who is stuck, like he was, when I am finished "giving him a piece of my mind," I had better not expect him to be inspired. All I am likely to have done is confirm his worst fear, to the effect that, all he is good for anymore is awakening people's irritation and anger.

Meanwhile, most of the time the restoring of people's souls, their transformation, their return to life, happens as it did that afternoon, two-thousand years ago, by that pitiful, probably stagnant, livestock pool. It happens because someone causes a person to believe that she is invited back, that he is wanted back, and that there really is life on the other side of this place where he or she has become stuck.

There is, moreover, not a one of us who is not capable of offering that to another human being, not a one of us who is incapable of becoming, in effect, Jesus Christ to someone who has gotten cornered by his own anxiety, her guilt, her self-doubt, his bad habit, or his sickened outlook. It requires from you and me, determination and "intentionality." It means, first, dropping all of what we are certain are our most astute armchair impressions of what he or she is like—of how stubborn, or lazy, or selfish, or neurotic he is. Then, it requires becoming fully present to the person, being gently, but firmly, honest with her, and being truly hopeful for whomever it is. It requires being so expectant that he or she begins to feel invited back to life—begins to feel not "washed up" as a worthy human being, after all. But becoming that means of healing grace to someone will demand all of the patience, imagination, and ingenuity most of us can muster.

And, yes (if that's what you're thinking), it still may not always happen. For whatever reason, a few will still remain at the sheep pool and die there. That is sad when it is true. But the real tragedy is not that, out of stubbornness, so many remain at those miserable sheep pools of life. The real tragedy is in how seldom they are made to feel genuinely, lovingly, personally invited back to life. That is something that only you and I are capable of doing.

The Woman Who Was at the Well, But Not Well

John 4:4-10 *(condensed)*

Passing through Samaria, Jesus and the disciples arrived at noon at Jacob's Well, near a Samaritan village. Being weary, Jesus sat down by the well, while the disciples entered the town to buy food. A Samaritan woman came for water and Jesus said to her, "Give me a drink." The woman said, "You, a Jew, are asking a drink of me, a Samaritan, and a woman at that?" (Jews and Samaritans never shared the same utensils.) Jesus said, "If you knew what God has to give ... you would be asking for living water." "Sir," the woman said, "you have no bucket and the well is deep. How can you offer me 'living water'?" Jesus replied, "Those who drink this water will soon again thirst, but not so of the living water of which I speak, for it will be an inner spring, welling up eternally." "Then give me this living water," the woman said.

"Go home and bring back your husband," Jesus said. "I have no husband," she answered. "True," said Jesus, "for though you've had five husbands, the man with whom you now live is not your husband." "I can see that you are a prophet," the woman answered.

At that moment, the disciples returned and were shocked to find Jesus talking with this woman. But the woman put down her water jar and ran into the town, where she said to the people, "Come and meet this man who has told me everything about myself." The townspeople did come out and made their way to him.

There was a lot more to that encounter between Jesus and that woman than a casual reading of it might indicate. For example, it says that the woman was there at the well to get water at noon. During the torrid heat of noon was NOT when people typically did that. Normally, townswomen would have made the trip to the well hours before, at daybreak, chatting and socializing on the way out there and back. Only someone trying to avoid the other women of the town would have gone in the heat of the day, when chances were good that she'd be the only one there. It was the strategy of a social outcast. And in her time, a social outcast is the way she'd have been seen, after five marriages, and now living with a man, unmarried. That marital history and present living arrangement would have been considered most disreputable, shameful, and disgraceful. Also, this was Samaria and she was a Samaritan. Jews and Samaritans were sworn enemies and adversaries. Finally, was the simple fact that she was a woman. In that day, a man of any respectability at all would NEVER have spoken in public to a woman to whom he was not married—particularly to one with a reputation like hers. (Men really weren't even supposed to speak to their own wives in public situations.)

So, for any of several reasons, this lady didn't want this conversation. If this stranger was "coming on to her," that would only mean trouble for her—doubly so, since he was Jewish and she was a Samaritan. But she knew from experience that, were she stupid enough to continue talking with this stranger, she would likely end up being hurt or made to feel cheap and dirty. To her, the fewer people with whom she had contact, the fewer there would be to act disgusted, appalled, or irritated at her. That's why she was doubtful, suspicious, defensive, and nervous. She only wanted to be left alone, allowed to get through another day without problems, without one more humiliating rejection or show of disapproval or abuse.

Her grim resignation and coping with her limited life reminded me of an experiment done by a certain gardener. He said that, part way into the growing season, out of curiosity, he took an empty one-gallon jug and inserted the end of one of the pumpkin vines he was raising into the mouth of it. He left it that way and forgot about it. When, a couple months later, he happen to look at it, a pumpkin (of sorts) now filled the jug. It was, however, a very sad, distorted pumpkin. Despite having all the sunshine it needed and drawing the same nourishment from the soil as its sister pumpkins, life in the jug had been very constricting for the pumpkin. It was smaller than the others, was discolored for some reason, and it was obvious that there would be no further change or growth for it.

I get some of that "pumpkin-in-a-jug" picture regarding this woman in the story, and not only her. A similar constriction of people's spirits is quite common. Often people do it to themselves. Other times (like this gardener, creating this contortion in the life of the pumpkin), it is, at least partly, inflicted upon them. Either way, the results are about the same. Instead of unfolding and emerging as all that the person could have been, now his hope, his joy, his confidence, his ability to trust, and his "at-homeness" in his world are arrested and misshapen. Something like the pumpkin, he becomes resigned to existing in some confining role, some safe niche, or some obscure, dim corner of life.

> *I've screwed-up too many times. The only way to avoid another humiliation, further criticism, or still more regret is to stay out of sight and make no waves.*

> *I've faced up to the fact that I am not an interesting person, that I am intellectually mediocre, bland, and tediously predictable. The fewer people I bore to death, the better.*

> *With all of my terrible insecurities, hang-ups, and phobias, I have to keep my life safe and under very tight control. Otherwise, I'll behave badly and make matters still worse.*

Or, "Now that I no longer have a husband," or "Because I'm so overweight," or "Having aged as much as I have lately," or "Having so little money," or "Because of this hearing problem, ... I need to pull way in, to limit my exposure, and to accept that this is all that remains of my life."

As with that marginalized Samaritan woman, it becomes a way of life—actually, of "non-life." The person is shaped and limited, for example, by fear of other people's criticism and judgment. Or maybe she sees herself as a walking billboard, proclaiming some sin or failure in her past. Yet another, because of this-or-that weakness, disability, or deficit, sees himself as "being in the way" and needing to apologize for existing. Maybe it is someone whose only dream he ever had for his life has evaporated, so he now lives as a spiritual and emotional hermit, with little sense of worth or reason for being. Whatever causes it, it is a hellish state in which to arrive, and it happens to millions of us.

In moments of thinking clearly, the person even knows that his exile is self-imposed. The Samaritan woman probably had moments of saying to herself, "*I shouldn't have to tiptoe, worry, cringe, and doubt myself like this. Why am I doing it?*" But being able to say that, and even discuss it, doesn't keep it from stubbornly plaguing the person, does it? That's because (to go back to that pumpkin in a jug), for all of the constriction, limitation and distortion, after awhile, there is a certain security, protection, and (in the worst sense of the word) "peace of mind" to being confined and contained in that jug.

Slinking to the well alone to get water at the hottest part of the day was unpleasant, but it was safe and predictable. Lonely as it was, it was a way of getting by for yet another day. By not talking to, or even seeing anyone, her dormant hunger for friendships and closenesses wouldn't be reawakened. With the absence of human contact, nothing would challenge what she had decided was true of all the townspeople: that they were all snobs, were judgmental, and were cruel and merciless. Thus, her grim worldview, her sullen paranoia, her free-floating resentments, and her chronic petulance could stay unchallenged and intact. So, in a distorted way, it "worked" for her. It even gave her a form of control.

That's what's behind it for those who have, in effect, put

a straitjacket on their own spirits; those who have pulled the walls of their lives in close around them; those who now limit themselves to only the most narrow kinds of experiences; and those who have reached a final conclusion about who they are and what they are worth.

So this woman says to Jesus (liberally translated), *"Hey, fella, whatever you have in mind, I'm not interested. Buzz off and let me be."*

But Jesus won't! There had to have been more conversation than what appears in the scripture, but there was no one else there to record it. This much is clear, though. Jesus does not get sucked in—as is all too easy to do—by any of her peevish or antagonistic comments or put-downs. He patiently keeps working his way through barrier after barrier, allowing time for that sullen facade of hers to give way. Finally, she realizes that Jesus is unfazed by any of the stuff about her that has so bedeviled her: not her religious history, not her marital record, not the fact that she has recently been shacking up with some guy, and not the fact that everyone in town sees her as a bitter and anti-social wretch. As her conversation with him moves on, she begins to feel set free and forgiven—so much so that she runs back into town to tell all of those people (who as recently as this morning she wouldn't have dared speak to) that they owe it to themselves to come and meet this man who has made everything different for her.

They probably called it a miracle and, in one sense, it is. Insofar as a miracle is something no one expected to ever happen, it was definitely miraculous. But "miracle" in the sense of magical? No, unless we're talking about the "enchantment" of a noon-hour conversation that brings her to believe that, whatever were her old sins, her dirty little secrets, the weaknesses in her character, or her bad habits, instead of adding up to a prison in which she was sentenced to live, they were no more than a load of baggage for which she had full permission to drop, anytime she wished.

Her story does raise some important questions. They are ones like, "*What might I actually come right out and say, if I really thought that I had any business at all speaking out?*" or "*What might I do if I didn't think I had long since blown all my credibility?*" or "*What, once-upon-a-time, before I discredited myself, did I have to offer that was needed and important?*" or "*What difference, if I could ever actually be forgiven, would I be making by now in life and in lives?*" Or, in the case of the Samaritan woman, "*What could happen if I were to take the risk of holding up my head and making myself a part of that group, walking to the well at 7:00 a.m., instead of Noon?*"

What it comes down to is this: that it takes far more courage than one would think to turn one's back on the miserable, but familiar, security of settling for thinking of oneself as "washed up," or unwanted, or terminally mediocre, or obsolete, or discredited. The embarrassing-to-face part of this is, that NOT to break out of that is one's own choice, not a necessity. Even when it originally was something external that limited, confined, or squelched one's spirit, to settle in and stay there is a choice. For at every point, right to your or my last breath, God continues to have extraordinarily high hopes for us and the unique gifts that each of us has to give.

A poem by the Reverend James Forbes describes for me what Jesus seems to have awakened and restored that Noon in the soul of that Samaritan woman. Using music as a symbol for your and my own particular spirits, it says:

> There's a song inside of me
> And I can hardly wait to see
> What it is I have to say
> Or the music I will play.
> It has been so long in coming;

First the thought and then some humming.
But before I find my key
Something stifles it in me.
What keeps my song from being sung?
Past hurts, deep fears, a timid tongue?
What threat stands guard before my face?
What tyrant, what demons besieging my space?
Now it's tired of being repressed.
It demands to be expressed.
What a shame to keep a song
Cramped in silence, oh, so long.
"Release your song," said the spirit to me.
"You'll never be you 'till your song is free.
While you debate—decide to get ready to sing
Your song could die like a stillborn thing."
Struck by the peril of further delay
My song like a flood came forcing its way.
Up from within and down from above,
A kingdom built on the power of love.
Thank God, my song has been set free.
The rhythm and the word are right for me.
I'm finally ready to sing out strong.
My soul is saying, "This is MY song!"

Just so! Hauling water at noon, alone, is stupid and unnecessary. No matter who we are or what we've done, or have failed at, or have lost our way in, for God's part, there is absolutely nothing that requires us to repress our song of life, withhold our gift to life, or bury our particular wisdom or grace. Doing so is not humility or repentance. It is petulance. If you've drifted into doing that, then today—this week at the latest—give it up!

The Slob Who Came to Dinner

Matthew 22:1-13 (condensed)

The Kingdom of Heaven is like this. There was a king who prepared a feast for his son's wedding. But when he sent his servants to summon the invited guests, they did not come. He sent additional messengers to tell them that all was ready and to come at once. Still they took no notice. One went off to his farm, another to his business, and some even mistreated the messengers.

So the king said to his servants, "The feast is prepared, but those invited are unworthy of it. Now go out into the streets and invite everyone, good and bad alike." They did so, and the hall was packed with guests.

When the king came in to see them all seated at the table, there was one man who was not properly dressed for a wedding feast. He went to him and said, "My friend, how is it that you come here without wedding clothes?" The man did not reply. Then the king said, "Bind him hand and foot, and throw him out into the dark—the place of weeping and gnashing of teeth."

By the time he is finished telling it, this is not one of Jesus' simpler parables. The first part of it is reasonably clear. The people who are first invited to a great celebration are unresponsive or oblivious. They never get there. Whether too busy, too preoccupied, or maybe just bored with everything and everyone, they cannot be bothered with this invitation to celebrate, to be fed, and be refreshed.

But the king in the parable is resilient. If those whom he expected to respond won't, then he'll celebrate with whomever *will* respond. The invitation is thrown open to everyone. The banquet hall fills up, after all. So far, then, the moral of the parable is so simple it is almost trite; that is, *"Don't let yourself get so busy or distracted or self-important that you no longer are willing or able to celebrate life."*

But then the story takes a strange turn. The king looks out upon this hastily-recruited crowd and sees one fellow who did not bother to dress appropriately for the occasion.

He is sitting there in his torn jeans, skuzzy tee shirt, ragged running shoes, dirty fingernails, and greasy, uncombed hair under a dirty baseball cap. So, notwithstanding the fact that the fellow was one of those invited on very short notice, the king goes to him and demands to know why he has come so brashly unprepared to celebrate. The man offers no explanation and no apology. In fact, he doesn't say a word. He just stares back at the king, with a look that says, "*Hey, man, I showed up didn't I? What more do you want?*" Whereupon, the king has him hog-tied and pitched out into the alley behind the hall. Apparently, as the king saw it, "just showing up" was not enough.

As Jesus told this parable, the people listening to it undoubtedly enjoyed it, as long as he seemed to be criticizing those first people invited to the celebration. That first group were obviously the people who seemed to have everything going for them—the ones with all the opportunities, the privileged, the popular people, the well-connected ones, the attractive ones. His listeners were delighted to hear Jesus suggest that those who seem to get to do everything, to go everywhere, and to always have things their way, often do become so desensitized. They become so wrapped up in themselves that they no longer celebrate life or find much joy in it. "*You tell 'em, Jesus! Tell those fortunate people how spoiled, shallow, and self-absorbed they can get to be. Thank God, we're not like that! We're the good 'grass roots' folk. We've attended the school of hard knocks. We've learned to make do without a lot of life's joys and fulfillments. So, you're right, Jesus! We're the ones who really know the score and who, therefore, belong at the banquet of God's kingdom.*"

The crowd was just starting to nod smugly in agreement, when Jesus ruined the parable by going on to tell about the man who, though he did show up, missed out, too, because he came dressed in a fashion that got in the way. Smugness, perhaps, or reverse snobbery, or sullenness—we don't know for certain. Whatever it was, though, according to Jesus, it landed him every bit as much on the outside, as were those first invitees who were unresponsive. Jesus probably lost a few listeners at this point.

Obviously, what Jesus is talking about is the celebration of life itself, about your and my invitation to enjoy, to explore, and to be nurtured by the fulfillments, joys, graces, and opportunities for growth, amidst which God intends for us human beings to celebrate life. And, yes, the first warning is a very important one. It has to do with the insidious danger in some of our so-called "advantages": the comforts, protection, pampering, prestige, and social standing that are frequently seen to shrivel one's soul and destroy one's appetite for everything of worth in life. That is one real danger.

But the not-quite-so-fortunate, the strugglers, the humbled, and the not-so-successful are *not* automatically "home free." Spiritual sluggishness is not only the problem of snobs. True, it often IS persons for whom life has been the toughest and most troubled, that come dressed as the most grateful, large-spirited and celebratory of life, but it isn't always that way. Having had it rough in life can create its own brand of indifference, obliviousness, un-appreciativeness, and boorishness. People who, because of what they have been through, one might think would do better, nevertheless, often sullenly slouch their way into the precious days that are given to them, glib about the blessings on loan to them, half-hearted in human encounters, and, in general, oblivious to so much of what surrounds them.

In one scene of William Saroyan's play, *The Time Of Your Life*, the frustrated, discouraged policeman is talking to Joe in a waterfront saloon.

> "I think we are all crazy," he explodes. "Here we are in this wonderful world full of all these wonderful things—here we are—all of

us, and look at us! Just look at us. We're nuts. We've got every-thing, but we always feel lousy, irritated, and dissatisfied just the same."

Officer Krupp is on to it, there. Obviously, he senses that there is more to be enjoyed and appreciated. He is even hungry for it, but it doesn't happen. No, they sit there in a saloon, anesthetizing themselves, complaining, feeling de-prived, and working themselves into a snit over all that is wrong about the world. They've come dressed, one might say, like the fellow in the parable who gets thrown out of the feast: clothed in a dreary attitude, wearing his favorite set of hopeless assumptions, and draped in a cloak of resent-ments, all of which work directly against any of the joy, light-heartedness, the "at-home" feeling, or the inspiration that God intended for us. People do a lot of that to themselves.

For example, a common form of attire, that bars a per-son from celebrating the banquet of life, is that of coming clad in studied dubiousness and skepticism. They are the ones who just "know" that no matter where they look, what is there to be seen are ulterior motives, brazen hypocrisy, political scheming, and social climbing. For them, there'll be no celebration. Quite to the contrary, it will be all irrita-tion, indignation, and aggravation because, as we human beings do, they'll see it exactly as they come dressed to see it. And they will stubbornly persist in it, no matter how grim it makes them. They do so because they believe that theirs is the only intelligent and principled way to be in a world, a society, or a time like ours. In fact, they are often disdainful and irritated at the confidence, optimism, and lightheartedness with which others celebrate their lives, since it seems to them to be stupidity and naiveté. They end up somewhat similar to what is described at the end of Jesus' parable: not only kept from celebrating, but very much on the outside with all the others who moan and gnash their teeth.

Another very familiar way of clothing oneself—one that automatically blocks joy, hope, excitement, and virtually all else that makes life worth living—is the oh-so-familiar cloak of paranoia. God only knows why so many buy it, but more do all the time. One cannot possibly celebrate while wearing it. You've run into it. *"I am endangered. I am under siege by dread micro-organisms trying to take my health, by people who are at this very moment figuring out how to get my money, by social forces that rob me of my rightful status, by demonic technologies that are poised to rob me of my dignity, by conservatives or liberals who connive to undermine all that I hold dear. Don't try to tell ME that life is a banquet. It's a gauntlet. One must be on guard every moment, must trust no one, and must resist every change, because 'who knows what's really behind it?'"* It shouldn't take a genius to see what a total barrier that is to everything that could be good, fulfilling, and exciting about one's life, but some very bright people do come dressed just that way.

Yet another way some people keep themselves out of the celebration of life is by coming draped in their deficits, handicaps, hurts, and disappointments. One can certainly celebrate life, despite whatever his deficiencies or troubles, but NEVER if they are the attire in which he presents himself. Until he or she is through being a walking deficit or victim, that person will remain on the outside looking in. For here, too, this feast to which Jesus said that we are invited is inaccessible to some. That is because it celebrates what surrounds us now, NOT wallows in what is no longer accessible. It is fueled by forgiveness, NOT bogged down in excuses and defenses. It is buoyed up by hope, not stuck in resentments.

If you step back far enough to look at the total picture, the feast is always there and we all are invited. Whether we are graceful enough to be there, and how we come to it, are the only questions. It depends entirely on whether you or I take hold of life by the handle of hope and excitement, or by the handle of irritation and fear.

The facts, meanwhile, are these. Each one of us is an amazing, mostly unexplored and unused world of capabilities, complex senses, rich coloration of feelings, dreams, appetites, and unique capacities to heal, give, bless, and inspire.

On top of that, we are each surrounded by thousands of other human beings who are intrinsically related to us—are similar, but are yet fascinatingly different. Every one of those lives is a continent to be discovered and to be known. Each of them is a marvelous being, with whom to laugh, to cry, to hope, or to work; one from whom to receive and to whom to give love, joy, and understanding.

Then, too, by some miracle of grace, we have been set down in what is "a user-friendly" world (all floods, earth-quakes, and tornadoes notwithstanding). It is a place for us, replete with remarkable intricacy, unfathomable mystery, and breathtaking beauty which has scarcely begun to unfold and be enjoyed and appreciated.

Added yet to that is the fact that we have been placed here with amazing freedom. Unlike the other creatures with whom we share life, we are allowed to make astounding choices, to try all kinds of ways of being human, to be cre-ators, to change, to improvise, to experiment, to reinvent ourselves as many times as needed, and to reverse ourselves, if that is necessary.

Still, behind all of that, is this God of ours who knows us, identifies with us, cares about us, and even creates and acts and speaks through us, when we let that happen.

When one reflects on all that, and a lot more truth like it, don't the words of Krupp, that frustrated policeman in Saroyan's play, sound almost scriptural? He says, *"I think we*

*are all crazy. Here we are in this wonderful world, full of all
these wonderful things—here we are—all of us, and look at us.
Just look at us. We're nuts. We've got everything, but we always
feel lousy and dissatisfied just the same."*

No, that is not true of everyone all of the time, but one
can hear vital truth in it. It is precisely as Jesus' parable portrays: the banquet of life that God has spread before us is
always there. At least, in our best moments, we know that.
We are all invited to celebrate it in our own unique way. So,
if by any chance, we are missing it— if it isn't happening for
us—it is not because it can't. No, if we are out there with
those who moan, complain, and gnash their teeth, it has
entirely to do with our choices of clinging to some bad habit
of sullenness, for example, or shallowness, or false sophistication, or self-pity.

Really, what could be more self-defeating than that?

Revisiting Thanksgiving, Christmas, Epiphany, and Easter

Thankfulness Deferred

Luke 17:12-19

As Jesus was entering a village, he was met by ten men with leprosy. They stood off at a distance and called out to him, "Jesus, Master, have pity on us." When he saw them, Jesus said to them, "Go and show yourselves to the priests." It was while they were on their way to do so that they found themselves cleansed of the disease. Seeing that he was cured, one of them—a Samaritan—turned back, praising God. He threw himself down at Jesus' feet and thanked him. Jesus said to him, "Were there not ten of you cleansed? Where are the other nine? Were none thankful to God, except a Samaritan?" To the Samaritan, he said, "Stand up and go on your way. It is because of your faith that you are healed."

Before dismissing, as mindless and boorish, the nine lepers who did not come back to give thanks, we owe it to them to at least try to understand what they had been through as lepers—what it was that might have left them less grateful than one could wish. For a few moments, try to experience what it would have been like, back then, to discover in the midst of life, that you had leprosy.

It's several years before. Life has been going along quite satisfactorily. His job is progressing nicely. He is in a good marriage. His children are healthy. He is properly appreciative of all of this; is reasonably content, moderately generous, and a genial, respectable person.

Then one morning, as he steps out of the shower, he notices a blemish on the skin of one hand that is not like any skin problem he remembers having before. He hopes that it's poison sumac and will clear up in a few days. It doesn't. In fact, it becomes larger and there is a loss of sensation in the area around it. It begins to worry him. It is much too similar to what little he knows of the way leprosy begins. But, surely, it can't be leprosy. After all, he is clean and hygienic, leads a good life, and has never been around any lepers. So, he covers the area as best he can and tries to think positively. There is no improvement, though. The affected area gets larger.

He cannot keep it completely hidden any longer. A few friends have asked about it. There were, at that time, harsh punishments for people who concealed their leprosy. But were that not so, he'd still worry about infecting his wife or children. So, he knows that he has no choice but to go public with his problem, the leprosy.

What will that mean? It means moving out of his own home and, henceforth, being separated from his wife and children. It means losing his job, impoverishing his family, and becoming a beggar. It means joining all those other lepers out on the edge of town—a miserable assortment of suffering, subsisting humanity that he has always done his best to avoid. Most humiliating is the fact that, as a leper, one is designated as spiritually unfit, ritually unclean, and morally degenerate. So you are, in effect, excommunicated.

It is all so unthinkable, yet true. The priest at the local synagogue—the one in charge of identifying lepers—verifies it. That officially certifies the man as a leper. To warn people that a leper is in the area, he must now carry a leper's bell AND give vocal warnings to any non-lepers who get closer than a few yards from him.

What did he do to deserve all of this? Absolutely nothing. He is certain of that. But he knows that this is not what everyone else is thinking. Leprosy as a consequence of some sin or evil in the afflicted person, is part of their religious belief. Moreover, until it happened to him, he never doubted that to be true.

He tries telling himself that this is all a bad dream from which he'll awaken. It's not, though. All that he has worked for has collapsed. He is cut off from everyone he loves and who has loved him. He is deprived of every source of dignity, hope, and pride. His human contacts are now restricted to other lepers: pathetic, desperate people. He feels that he has absolutely nothing in common with them, other than leprosy.

That, then, is what life has deteriorated into, in the years leading up to his encounter (along with nine other lepers) with the Galilean teacher who is rumored to bring about remarkable healing. When it happens, that encounter is anything but dramatic. Jesus doesn't really do or say much. He just tells them to go show themselves to the priest. Incredibly though, halfway there, they find the leprosy to be gone.

They can barely believe it. They keep checking and rechecking the previously affected areas of their bodies. One of their group—a Samaritan fellow whom no one likes because he IS a Samaritan, is so ecstatic that he is insistent that, before going on to be certified as cured, they should go back to thank the Galilean teacher, Jesus.

No one else, though, sees any need for that. *This cure is nice enough, but even so, he still can't get past the fact that none of it should have befallen him in the first place. Yes, the leprosy is gone, but who is going to give back those wasted years that leprosy took from him? Who is going to restore the lost time with his family? What about his shattered career? Is someone going to catch him up to where he would have been by now? What about the psychological scars from being treated as a social outcast and a human throwaway? NO! This cure is a bare minimum. He is still an ex-leper, destitute, back on "square one" in life. There is a whole list of wrongs that are going to have be righted, injustices resolved, and entitlements restored before he's going to get all teary-eyed with gratitude. Let that Samaritan go give thanks if he wants to. Maybe a Samaritan should. Samaritans deserve leprosy or worse—the whole lot of them. But not he.* So he and the eight others, trudge on.

The exercise of imagining all of that is only to try to take us a little more deeply into how gratitude gets blocked or destroyed in us human beings. If it has never happened within you, you've probably seen it happen in others.

A most common barrier is precisely this one of my feeling that I'm a victim of a major violation of my minimum quota or my fair share of time, health, comfort, prosperity, appreciation, opportunity, and good outcomes. It is "entitlement thinking"—something that sneaks in upon us, without our realizing it. It may go quite undetected, until something evaporates to which I had come to believe I had a permanent "right." When whatever it is comes to an end, rage and bitterness become a dead giveaway that I have mistaken life's gifts for entitlements, and that I am no longer in touch with the fact that there are no entitlements.

Another serious obstacle to gratitude is triggered by other people. They are all of those for whom, though they are no better individuals than I am, their lives seem to sail smoothly upon the sea of life, pushed nicely along by the gentle, warm breezes of good fortune. Meanwhile, my life consists of one stormy episode after another. "As long as those undeserving fortunate are dangling right out there in front of me, and as long as nothing is happening to make it fairer, how can I possibly be grateful?"

Yet, something else that obstructs thankfulness is that awful habit some have of constantly borrowing trouble and sorrow from the future. In the case of this ungrateful leper, it would have been his dwelling stubbornly upon the fact that, since he'd had leprosy once, might he not get it again? It's true that it could happen. He could also get multiple sclerosis, cancer, rheumatoid arthritis, or Alzheimer's Disease. For those who insist on using the unknowns of the future to make themselves ungrateful in the present, there is more than enough material to keep them grim and thankless for the rest of their lives. Typically, the closest they'll come to gratitude is, "I'll be truly grateful if and when such-and-such or so-and-so turns out okay." Uh-uh! Gratitude with an "if" in it isn't gratitude. It is an attempt at manipulating God.

Perhaps the ugliest of the destroyers of gratitude, though, is one of the varieties of perfectionism. This is that mind-boggling quirk wherein, when surrounded with obvious reasons for gratitude, a person meets it with, *"Yes, BUT...."* The principle seems to be, *"How could anyone be thankful for something flawed, right?" "It would have been a time of profound happiness for me, but then she showed up." "Yes, the week could have been one of such sublime contentment, had it not been destroyed by that argument at breakfast on the second day." "I am still enraged that something so beautiful was obliterated for me by that crying baby (or by the man with the hacking cough six rows behind me or by what's-her-name wearing a dress identical to mine.)"* Worse yet, those with this problem are often evangelistic about trying to unravel the gratitude of others, by regaling them with the list of egregious flaws. It is "torpedoed gratitude."

Enough, though, about what destroys gratefulness in a person. What nourishes it, makes one a genuinely thankful person?

First, and maybe most obvious, it has very little to do with the external stuff: smooth sailing, good fortune, comfortable circumstances, and having a lot of fun. Our nation's Thanksgiving holiday, you'll recall, was started by a few dozen people who had none of that whatsoever. Their living conditions were extraordinarily harsh. Half their fellow pilgrims had died in the previous twelve months. Except for the welfare that they received from Indians, almost nothing worked out well.

Whether in those, or in others that you and I can bring to mind, gratitude in the most deeply thankful people seems to come, first, from a firm grasp of the meaning of that which they are doing. Second, it comes from excitement over the personal growth and expanded understanding that they experience. And, third, it seems rooted in a permanent reverence and awe for the whole, many-faceted adventure of being a living human being. Thankfulness at that level does not disintegrate because of setbacks, twists of fate, or even deep sorrow.

Another foundational part of being grateful has to do with what other people come to mean to us. An anonymous quotation that I jotted down, years ago, says, *"Life's greatest problem lies in the fact that the real food of the human being consists entirely of souls."* That's right. Despite the times when other people hurt us and wear us out, the real nourishment of human beings consists of souls! We are relational beings and our spirits languish in the absence of relatedness. There is no substitute. You've seen this in profoundly grateful people who require virtually nothing, as long as they have people to know and to be known by. Conversely, one can own everything imaginable and still be sullen, embittered, and sick, when detached and unrelated to other persons. Looked at carefully, there is very little deep thankfulness that is not based on other human beings.

Another part of it, though, has to do with knowing something about what we call "the grace of God." Herbert Spencer once wrote:

> When I remember how many of my private schemes have miscarried; how my speculations have failed, how agents proved dishonest, how my marriage became a disappointment; how I ended up impoverishing the relative that I sought to help; how my carefully-governed son has turned out worse than most children; how the thing I desperately fought as misfortune did me immense good; how the objects I ardently pursued brought me so little happiness when gained while most of my joys have come from unexpected sources—when I recall these and a host of similar facts, I am overwhelmed with how inept is my intellect to prescribe for society.

We're not concerned just now about "prescribing for society." But what Spencer is alluding to is the whole geography of God's grace that chastens and deepens and strains and heals a person, even though he blushes to think about much of it. Count on it: staying closely in touch with that kind of truth about oneself, and one's life, keeps one grateful. It is almost impossible not to be so, if we are honest with ourselves, honest about the sheer accident of birth that finds us here rather than in Albania, the stray bits of love or inspiration or forgiveness that happen to touch our lives at just the right time, the near-miraculous chance of being at certain right places, or not being at the wrong ones, at some point.

The 14th Century Christian mystic, Meister Eckhard, once said, *"If the only prayer you say in your whole life is, 'Thank You,' it would suffice."* When one reflects upon it, he's dead right. That's why we sense that the one leper (who returned to Jesus because he was so thankful that he just couldn't do otherwise) is ultimately going to be okay, no matter what happens to him in the future.

As to the other nine, they no longer had leprosy, but lacking anything useful in the way of gratitude, they were still very sick people.

The Joseph and Mary Story–Unembellished

Luke 1:26-32
In the sixth month, the angel Gabriel was sent by God to a Galilean town called Nazareth, to a virgin who was pledged to a man whose name was Joseph. Joseph was a descendant of the House of David. The woman's name was Mary. The angel said to her, "Greetings, favored one! The Lord God is with you." Mary, however, was troubled by this. She was concerned as to what it might mean. The angel said, "Do not be afraid, Mary, for you have found favor with God. Now you will conceive in your womb and bear a son. His name will be Jesus. He will be great and will be known as the Son of the Most High. ..."

In that first century B.C., the life of a young woman like Mary was an uncertain, insecure, and, in many ways, precarious thing. A woman had no rights. She had very limited choices and had virtually no control over her destiny. Her marriage was arranged by her parents at, or before, her puberty, usually to an older man. He was likely to be older because he had to be one who could afford to pay the price that the parents were asking. The young woman was expected to accept the marriage without question. Any rebellion against this arrangement, or any other deviation from her role as a wholly owned asset of her father (and, subsequently, of her husband), would result in harsh censure, if not brutal punishment.

Once married, the primary part of a woman's job description was to have and raise children. Childbirth was hazardous, particularly if there was the slightest complication, often costing the life of the mother, as well as the infant. The early childhood death rate was very high, which made motherhood often heartbreaking, even if one survived it.

That's some of the background needed as one reads that Mary "was troubled" when told that she was pregnant. She was troubled because she was young—maybe as young as 14 or 15—younger than is recommended for bearing a child.

She was troubled because she was unmarried and thus, was in danger of punishment, censure, and humiliation. She was troubled about what might be the response of Joseph, who, after all, was her only ticket to a reasonably secure life. And she was troubled because, even if what the angel said was true (that this was some kind of act of God), what was her preparation or her qualification for it?

Shortly, Joseph was troubled, too. In those times, a man worked a long time to acquire sufficient financial and vocational stability to enter into a contract for a wife. Joseph had finally managed to do so. Now there was indication that he had, in effect, "bought a lemon." But even if that wasn't so and her angel-story was true, who needed this? He was a carpenter. He wasn't looking for religious notoriety or anything else out of the ordinary. He wanted a simple marriage to a healthy, respectable young girl, who would then give birth to his children, would be his housekeeper, would do his books, would send out the monthly invoices for his carpentry business, and, along the way, maybe even become a compatible companion.

One should not have expected Joseph, then, to break forth with *"Praise God From Whom All Blessings Flow"* when word reaches him that Mary is wearing her robes without a belt lately, and that she's been skipping breakfast and vomiting a lot. Even after his own dream that seemed to support her extraordinary explanation, he still cannot help worrying. He has to wonder about how this will look in the community. He may believe in Mary, but that doesn't mean that others will. He has to be concerned about whether having a controversial wife might cost him some business. He considers the alternative of trying to cover this up by leaving Nazareth now and staying away until months after the birth, but how would they survive? The possibility that this has something to do with God is nice, but doesn't make it any less confusing, disruptive, and, in some ways, downright unfair.

The best hope he can come up with is the possibility that God might shortly arrange some favorable breaks. God might be poised to prepare a way for them, to take care of the problems, to protect them, and to shore up their morale in some wonderfully divine way. Who knows? Maybe, by the time the child is born, it will be unmistakable to everyone that he and Mary have, indeed, been favored by God, to the effect that all people and nations would look to them. He sure hopes so, but is far from certain.

They cling to that hope as long as they can. What they get instead, though, is an all-too-ordinary pregnancy, replete with nausea, swollen ankles, trouble getting comfortable, fatigue, back pain, and more.

Then, in Mary's third trimester, comes the announcement of a major taxation—bad enough by itself, but worse yet, a seventy-mile donkey trip in Mary's ninth month. The timing of it turns out as bad as they had feared. Mary starts into labor just as they arrive at their destination—a destination at which there are no accommodations. They grimly adjust as best they can, now willing to crawl into any kind of shelter whatsoever. So the baby—this child who, in some special way, was supposed to be of God—has to be born in a livestock shed. Bad as that is, what they don't know, because the news still has not reached them, is that this district has just been singled out to have all newborn babies exterminated in the next few days.

What are Mary and Joseph to make of this? Think it through with them. At this very moment, there are dozens of women around the country giving birth who, though they had no angelic visitations, are allowed to go through their deliveries in their home communities, under comparatively clean conditions, surrounded by their families, and attended by experienced mid-wives. So what is going on here? What happened to God? Is there no protection, no vindication, no respite, no exception made for the faithful, for the committed, for the caring? It is all beginning to feel absurd.

Someone envisioned the by-now-bewildered Joseph as going into the infamous inn and pleading with that innkeeper, *"I absolutely have to have a room. Can't you see that my wife is pregnant?"* The innkeeper replies, *"Hey, buddy, that's not my fault."* And Joseph says, *"Well, it's not my fault either!"*

Precisely. Though not having asked for any of this, he (they) are, nevertheless, doing their best. They have remained patient and have even tried to stay hopeful. They have paid their dues, in terms of working through all of the disruption and uncertainty. Surely they are entitled to better than this mess, are entitled, for example, to an angel-midwife helping out in that dark stable, or even a deep voice from heaven singing, *"Yes Sir, That's My Baby."* Something—anything—so that they'll know that they are not abandoned, forgotten, and/or that they have not committed some inadvertent error, for which this mess is their punishment.

Had you or I, on taking a short cut on the way home from a late dinner party that night, stumbled into that stable and ended up in conversation with this stressed-out, worn-out couple, what do you suppose would have been our response to their odd story and their bizarre predicament? What would be my reply when Joseph asks, *"If this has something to do with God, how come nothing has gone right?"* Or, when Mary demands to know what kind of a God would allow the "Son of the Most High" to be born in such filth, or when they point out that life was decidedly nicer and more coherent BEFORE they got involved with God, or when Mary, for the third time, agonizes about how their best apparently was still not good enough for God, or when they ask how they can go on believing in a God who appears unwilling to lift a divine finger to help.

I hope that I could muster enough humility and grace not to try to explain it to them; that is, not to throw a bunch of glib religious rhetoric on top of their stress and bewilderment. Most of us have heard that done, haven't we? *"Mary, Joseph, you shouldn't feel that way. Don't you see? This is God's way of testing your faith,"* or *"All of this is God's will, which you must accept and be thankful for it,"* or *"What you don't realize is how much worse things could be. Why I heard about a case down in Jericho where…,"* or *"Just believe and, any day now, you'll be gloriously rewarded,"* or yet some other such glib, pious bromide.

No! Those would-be explanations are not the answer for a Joseph and Mary. It would be nice if it could be that simple, but it is not. Huddling there in that pitch-black, cold, dirty stable, hanging on by their fingertips, it becomes as clear as any place in the entire Bible what faith really means.

Faith is NOT to be confused with the smug belief that God always blesses and protects those who are good. Faith is also NOT to be confused with believing that, IF something is the work or will of God, it will be obvious or that you'll always be certain of it. Also, turning out to be untrue is the assumption that feeling insecure, desolate, frightened, and worn down by the stress from that which you are trying to do or give, indicates a lack of faith and character. In fact, one thing that becomes clear is that, despite fervent prayer or tenacious believing, we still might not find the reassuring explanation that we believe we deserve—at least not for the time being.

Faith, seen in this ancient couple (next spotted tiredly trudging off toward a period of exile in Egypt) consisted of their continuing to trust, despite all of the considerable evidence to the contrary. They continued to bet their hopes, to bet their remaining scraps of energy, to bet their dwindling resources, and to bet their very lives that God, nevertheless, was doing something vitally important through them. This was faith at its rawest: an almost stubborn determination that, "come hell or high water," they would continue to act and work and struggle as if their dreams were of God. If they NEVER really understood how this made sense, that would have to be okay. STILL they would trust that, somehow, God would ultimately use this mess to create and bless. It didn't mean that they liked or welcomed morning sickness, or and blind frustration, or giving birth in livestock sheds, or tax increases, or curious shepherds, or immanent dangers any more than would you or I. But what held them together was the belief that, at some point and in some way, it would be woven into the fabric of God's grace and blessing.

Did they ever come to feel vindicated? Who knows? Joseph apparently died before Jesus reached adulthood. At least he is never mentioned again. But maybe he was the lucky one. Mary not only watched her son become very controversial, but saw him executed. Her faith was apparently "on the line" most of the rest of her life. It sometimes works out that way for the deepest and best of people.

If, by any chance, before she died, Mary wrote a best-selling scroll describing her "faith journey," undoubtedly one of the chapters would have been: "Faith is No Kid's Game." It can require living with a lot of doubt, frustration, despair, and confusion—even outrage—while still being everything that it should be. In fact, there is precedent for it turning the most ordinary of human beings (like you and me), full of flaws, weaknesses, hang-ups, and phobias, into God's Word made flesh.

That's the Gospel from Mary and Joseph!

Strange Epiphany

Matthew 2:9-11

The three astrologers then set out at King Herod's bidding. The star which they had seen at its rising went ahead of them until it stopped above the place where the child lay. ... Entering the house, they saw the child with Mary, his mother. There they bowed to the ground in homage to him. Then they opened their treasures and offered gifts: gold, frankincense and myrrh.

When they finally arrived, it was only a baby: two arms, two legs, having to be diapered like every other baby, helpless, needy, crying some of the time, and sleeping a lot of the time. The parents, though tired-looking, were nice enough people, but were not really anything to write home to mother about. It had to have been a bewildering—even disorienting—day for those three foreign dignitaries.

A quip that's been around for awhile is that in which someone says, *"There's nothing wrong with my weight. It's my height that is the problem. Someone of my weight is supposed to be eight feet tall."*

It was something like that for these astrologers, or wise men, or oriental diplomats, or however you wish to think of them. This baby and its parents were okay, in and of themselves, but there just wasn't enough to justify all those days of camel-riding, star-gazing, and gift-bearing, not to mention time away from the office.

And yet, they had been so certain that they were onto something big, that they were getting in on the ground floor of a world-changing event. They had done their homework, too: had researched the predictions and prophecies, had double-checked their figures, and had thoroughly discussed it from every angle, before reaching the decision that the time, the effort, and the cost would be worth it and would be appropriate. Taking with them appropriate gifts and formal-wear, they headed west with mental images of making their own majestic contribution to one of history's regal moments.

And THIS is all it came down to: very common people, ordinary baby, and in a country-and-western town. Had I been one of them, my stomach would have been in knots, palms sweaty, face flushed, rapid heartbeat, and all the other symptoms of the realization that I may have made a fool of myself, may have totally misjudged a situation, and that, moreover, there is no reversing it.

To me, it is a bit of a miracle that this story, instead of being about three wise men, isn't a story about "three frustrated men" or "three embarrassed men" or "three disgusted men" who had, at some point, reloaded the gold, frankincense, and myrrh back onto their camels and headed east singing,

> We three kings head home feelin' blue;
> Wasted time and spent a lot, too.
> Should've known it. Now we've blown it.
> Why? We haven't a clue.

Chagrin comes easily when outcomes are nothing like we were certain they would be. In fact, it does take a pretty "wise" man ("wise" woman) to do what it says those fellows did; that is, rejoice over what they found there, despite it being nothing like they expected; and THEN, even go ahead and give everything that they had to offer. Despite a dozen unanswered questions, to still embrace and to celebrate what they found there, showed an uncommon grace, trust, and even courage.

We find out a lot about a person at such times. When one of us finally arrives at what is supposed to justify all of our past effort; when the anticipated satisfactions and "fulfillments" are supposed to be there now, when one gets to what he assumed would be his time of well-earned bliss or of rest or of security, BUT IT'S NOT—we get everything from anger and petulance to astounding patience and graces.

So, when these three bone-weary, sunburned, saddle-sore, ancient pilgrims are now in the house with the child and his parents, and there is no choir of angels, no celestial light, no royal or priestly entourage hanging around—not even a gathering of reporters and curious neighbors—THAT'S when we find out that they are "wise men." Shallow, hollow ones would not have handled it well.

One of life's difficult-to-swallow lessons that has to be taught to us over and over, has to do with this. First, is the fact that there are no absolutely assured outcomes—not for anyone, ever. But there is this, too. No matter what we've dreamed and prayed and imagined of that great day or that glorious consummation or that shining victory or that total success, it will still consist of common, ordinary flesh and blood—of minutes and hours, of waking and sleeping, of frailties and limitations, and of all the rest of the common elements and processes of life.

In other words, there is nothing on up ahead, no goal that we'll reach, after which we'll finally be free of worry, struggle, complexity, and uncertainty. They may take different forms, but they will still be there.

The Christmas season itself ends up, for many, being this kind of a "strange arrival" experience. It was particularly so when we were young children and we discovered by the 26th of December that, as nice as were the toys we had so anticipated unwrapping, they were unable to deliver the sustained ecstasy that, for weeks, we had imagined and anticipated.

At another level, we, as adults, come to it (at least some of us do) year after year, hoping to be touched, enlightened, or moved by the message, the truth, or the light that we hope is there in the culmination of the Christmas experience.

When it is over, and the decorations are coming down, and January needs our attention, some always seem to feel betrayed, muttering that it wasn't worth the trip. It is the feeling that there was nothing of substance there. They are right about there being nothing magic or superhuman there, no built-in ecstasy, nothing uniquely other-worldly. No, it is a flesh-and-blood observance (as it was for the wise men), mostly dependent on what we bring to it, what we create of it, and how open we are to being touched by it.

At a more practical level, understanding this is what hangs in the balance with every young couple, as they, in effect, follow the star to the "Bethlehem" of their marriage. The expectations and hope are charming and endearing. Confident of their love and commitment, and of their eternal dedication to making every waking moment absolute and constant happiness for the other, they're convinced (at least the not-so-mature of them) that their marriage can only be the arrival at something downright heavenly. To a point, high expectations are important. Something like the wise men finding ordinary human beings at the end of their trek, so also will our love-struck couple. The important issue will be, *"Will you still believe, commit, give, and trust when what is found in the house just isn't what we were so sure would be there?"* Many handle it fairly well. But all-too-common are the marriages that immediately begin to crumble, because of the discrepancy between the glory of their fantasy and what is really required of them.

The end stage of child-raising can be a real "Bethlehem," in this story's sense. Quite often, one will hear someone say of their grown or nearly-grown children,

It wasn't supposed to be like this.

This was supposed to be the point at which I could enjoy the blossoming of my children's adulthood, not still have to lie awake nights worrying about dumb mistakes

they are making.

I had thought that, by this age, my sons would become appreciative of the sacrifices we made for them, not still be as self-centered as they were at age twelve.

I had imagined that, at some point, I could become a friend to my daughter, rather than still mostly her benefactor.

That Bethlehem, too, (as many can testify) can be shockingly different than the way it was pictured along the journey. Reforming one's hopes, reworking one's assumptions, and continuing to believe that, even if it has to unfold and mature the long, slow way, God is nevertheless at work in it and really does demand great wisdom: wise men and wise women.

Quite often, doesn't this hang over the matter of retirement? The problem and bewilderment that, for some, awaits arrival at that destination can be quite disorienting. Apparently, the problem is not with retirement itself. It is that some arrive at this "Bethlehem" expecting heavenly serenity to await them, envisioning a time of perfect indolence, and/or are looking forward to being blissfully free of demands upon them. When it's not like that (and it never is), they end up feeling that there must be some mistake.

How is it that I am so bored, am starting to feel stagnant, am becoming a disgruntled and dismal person?

Where is the contentment, the freedom, and the ecstasy that I thought would be mine after a lifetime of responsibility and hard work?

That dream of arriving at a glorious destination in life where, without doing much, without having to care about much of anything, there would nevertheless be vitality, that it would carry an automatic sense of worth, that it would confer plenty of stimulation and natural joy, turns out not to be what is there at this Bethlehem.

The wise men and the wise women, the ones who fill that part of their time with life, meanwhile, are those who expect to have to pour themselves into refreshing their own spirits, who reinvent their commitment, their love, their appetites, their passions, yet again, for the living of this segment of time that God has given them.

And it is like that all across the board in regard to ANY of life's destinations, for ALL mountaintop moments of achievement, for every one of those hoped-for gratifications or vindications. It makes it terribly important that we don't get our egos involved with things having to be the way we've dreamed. (They certainly weren't for the three easterners in the story.) Moreover, not only are those "arrivals" dependent upon what we bring to them, NONE of them are stopping places or ends in themselves. No. They, too, are part of a process. (Remember that the baby that the wise men found was going to have to grow up and develop before much would happen.) So, again, what our arrivals come to mean to us, and what they accomplish within us, has heavily to do with what we bring to them: in the way of hope, in the way of love, in the way of imagination and determination—even of celebration.

That, then, is the way we'll wind up the telling of the Christmas story: with the wise men NOT sullenly reloading their gifts and feeling cheated and misled. Instead, as it says:

> When they saw the child and Mary, his mother, they bowed down and worshipped there. Then they opened their gifts of gold, frankincense, and myrrh. And being told in a dream that they should do so, they went home from Bethlehem a different way than they came there.
>
> Matthew 2:12

Exploiting a Resurrection

Mark 16:1-8

After the Sabbath, Mary Magdalene, Mary the mother of James, and Salome purchased spices for Jesus' body. Early on the first day of the week, they went to the tomb. They were concerned as to who would roll the stone from the entrance of the tomb so that they could enter. When they arrived, the stone, which was very large, had already been rolled back. Entering the tomb, they saw a young man dressed in a white robe. They were frightened. But he said to them, "Do not be alarmed. You seek Jesus who was crucified. He has been raised and is no longer here. Go tell his disciples that they will see him in Galilee, just as he said." The women fled from the tomb, seized with terror and astonishment. They said nothing to anyone, for they were very afraid.

That was quite typical of the way the friends and followers of Jesus responded to rumors and reports that he was alive. Mostly, they reacted with fear, skepticism, obliviousness—anything but expectation, relief, vindication, or triumph. Looking at it now, long after the fact, that may seem odd. With some further thought, though, their reticence and restraint is probably understandable. It can be attributed to the fact that this resurrection was much too private, too subtle, too subdued.

Were we hearing the story for the first time, it might well seem like a badly missed opportunity. With only slightly different timing and placement, public attention and impact could have been so much greater. Even the most amateur public relations person would certainly have gotten far more mileage from it.

For example, as an act of God, shouldn't it have happened on their Sabbath—a holy day? That is, not have to wait until the day after? With a Sabbath Day resurrection, perhaps with Jesus followers at the temple holding a prayer vigil, praying for his safe return (rather than scattered, hiding, and demoralized, as most were) it would have been the public event of the decade. Right there in the temple court, amidst all kinds of onlookers, skeptics, and clergy, would have been a near-perfect time and place to have appeared. It would have publicly vindicated the faith of the disciples, and have made very clear to everyone else just *who* had God's backing and who did *not*.

As Herod and/or Pilate walked to the end of their driveways to pick up their morning papers on that Sabbath, *then* would have been another delicious moment for a risen Jesus to have appeared—scars, bloodstains, and all. Preferably, he would have appeared with an eerie glow to send icy shivers down their bureaucratic spines, maybe even giving them some unnerving chest pains, lest they ever forget their role in his execution. Wouldn't that have been a wonderfully gratifying, divine, *"I told you so!"*?

Then, why not a major Sabbath Day appearance in downtown Jerusalem—preferably thirty or forty feet above the street? There, masses of people would have been brought to a stunned halt, awestruck, and trembling—maybe even falling to their knees. It would have been a great time for some strong words from him about God's displeasure with the moral cesspool that the Holy City was becoming.

There, too (or at any other of the appearances), why not bring back the chorus of Heavenly Hosts that reportedly sang at the time of his birth, to sing also for this triumphant vindication?

And there are other possibilities—other ways that it could have been made so much more conclusive—turned into something so public and dramatic that everyone would have paid attention. If you are going to do something like this, do it right, for Heaven's sake!

But that's not the story, is it? Instead, it describes a resurrection that was very personal—in fact, experienced only by his followers. And it didn't happen until the first day of the week, our Monday. Yes, what has come to be called Easter was, in effect, a Monday! Small wonder that people weren't still hanging around, devoutly expecting it.

We know what a Monday after a tragedy feels like. It is the day when the whole, usual, dull routine starts up again for everyone except those who feel destroyed. The temple maintenance crew is picking up the trash left in the temple court by Friday's mob. The porch of the governor's palace is being swept and repaired, having become somewhat the worse for wear when the crowd pushed onto it, demanding Jesus' crucifixion.

The get-back-to-normal, Monday-type day of the week would have been when the wife of the soldier who gambled for, and won, Jesus' robe at the foot of the cross, takes the robe out to be cleaned and altered.

A farmer is filling the holes in the ground where the crosses were, so that his animals won't step in them, break a leg, and have to be put down. The crosses themselves have been rinsed off and put back in storage pending their next use.

The chief priests are back in their offices, reviewing the Passover evaluations. Pilate is working on his taxes. Herod is filling out his quarterly reports.

Do you see? It would have been getting, disgustingly, back to what is called "normal."

So, if you were one of those who had cared, hoped, prayed, and agonized, in some ways, it was the most depressing day yet, because of the unmistakable message it conveyed. The message was that the whole matter of Jesus WAS OVER, was finished, and that every trace would soon be carefully obliterated. Nothing would explain it, undo it, or even bring any good from it. NO. Shortly it would be forgotten by all, except a very few. They, who had cared and hoped and trusted, were each left to stew helplessly in their own solitary misery, despair, and disorientation, while the world around them obscenely adjusted, adapted, forgot, or shrugged it all off.

So, several of the disciples are totally withdrawn, cringing behind locked doors. A couple of others have left town. Three women have gone to the burial place, hoping that being there might get them to the rock-bottom finality of it all so that they could begin to get over it. A few disciples were discussing going back to professional fishing, thinking that returning to their past might make them feel better.

The question that hung over all of them, in the cold hollowness of this post-tragedy day, was "what would become of them?" Was it true (as felt likely) that each and all, through withdrawing, running, wallowing, cringing, and smoldering, would become an extension of Friday's tragedy—an additional human catastrophe?

That is when it happened! We are told that, at that lowest, most impaired time, each of them discovered Jesus to be alive again. Each in his own way and, in whatever was his or her own state of grief, hurt, and disillusionment, moved from death back to life.

It didn't come easily, but each, in turn, broke through his or her own grim resistance and discovered that last Friday had not been the final word. It happened along the road, to the two men trying to get away to Emmaus. It happened quite differently to the women who went to the tomb, intending to rub their noses in the absolute hopelessness of it. It happened to that group who were huddled in terror behind locked doors. It happened to the ones who thought fishing would make it seem as if none of it had ever taken place. Just as they hit bottom, determined to adjust to the cruel Monday-morning realities, one way or another, God, through Jesus, touched them and brought them back to life.

For many Christians, the main significance of this

reappearance of Jesus is that it demonstrated God's power to restore the life of Jesus. That's fine, as far as it goes, but I think there is more. Of equal, if not greater importance in this part of the Gospel, was the restoring of Peter and James and Mary and Thomas and Martha and John and you and me from the kinds of death that we sometimes are all too willing to settle for on *our* worst, most barren Monday mornings.

That the God of life and creation could open an empty a tomb is certainly intriguing. Striking much closer to home for me, though, is this matter of God's opening US to the empty tombs. For that miracle requires breaking through some of the fiercest and most stubborn human belief in finality, belief in inevitability, belief in the conclusions that we jump to, belief in the importance of sticking with it once we have "made up our minds once and for all," and belief in all manner of other absolutes with which we try to protect ourselves. Because of having been through too much, of now knowing too much, of having seen too much, and having been forced to adjust to too much, it often takes a miracle of God's power and intervention to drag us away from Good Friday afternoon, to discover what is coming to life (or could) on the first day of the week.

And it isn't only petulant "woundedness." There is often another kind of resistance to resurrection. It has to do with the matter with which we began: the fact that resurrection may not happen anything like the way we would think it should or need to. Note again, very carefully, what was NOT included in the Easter story.

For example, for all of the villains that could have been (and deserved to be) denounced, humiliated, and penalized as part of restoring the disciples to life, NONE WERE. As absolutely necessary to us as it may seem that the blame be firmly fixed, it didn't happen. Pilate, Herod, and the Chief

Priests went right on doing as they had been doing and were left free to go right on being the kinds of people they had been all along. One could infer from that, that you and I will stay dead or dying as long as one of our conditions for coming back to life is that of being able to see the evil-doers get their come-uppance.

Something else that did not happen was neat explanations and interpretations of "why?" Haven't you heard people in pain or grief say something like, *"If someone would just explain to me why it happened, why he did it, what allowed this to go on, or where this all fits together, THEN I think I could move beyond this."* That wasn't there in this story either, was it? There were issues and people and blind forces and timing and, for all we know, cosmic necessities that, while it would have been nice to have them spelled out, they weren't. So, if those disciples came back to life, they were going to have to let go of that, too; have to accept God's grace on Monday morning, without a shred of satisfactory explanation of last Friday.

As was mentioned earlier, glaringly absent, also, was the kind of public vindication and conclusiveness that would have felt so good and would have made it unmistakably clear to everyone that they had been right all along, and that all of the other unwashed masses had been wrong; if something had made it clear, as a minimum, that they weren't losers after all. But no, the resurrection appearances were personal, not public. *"How can I trust again, believe again, or hold up my head again without some saving of face, without being vindicated in the eyes of all of those who laughed or criticized or pitied me?"* Here too, if this says what it seems to say, I'd better find a way, or I'll remain permanently in the graveyard of bitterness or hurt or chagrin.

One of the messages is that, yes, while God's way is absolutely that of resurrection, restoration, and life overcoming death, we don't get to set conditions on it. When it happens for us, it will be on God's terms, not ours. Admittedly, that is a little hard to take. It didn't come easy, even for the disciples. But as we all know, they overcame their own resistance and ended up discovering, more powerfully than anyone in history, that while crucifixions (and the like) are atrocious, they are not decisive; that as much a fact of life as is physical death, it is not the end of us; that as awful as evil can be, it is no match for God or for good; and that hiding out, running away, submerging oneself in, or adjusting oneself to any of the many kinds of tombs that come along in life, is a stupid choice we make. It is NOT God's will or intention for us.

At a most down-to-earth, practical level, THAT is proclaimed by Easter: how crucial is our remaining "open" to the empty tombs.

I like this excerpt from one of John Masefield's plays. In it, Pilate's wife is bewildered and distraught when she hears that the tomb of Jesus is empty, and she asks a centurion, *"Do you think he is dead?"* *"No, lady, I don't,"* the soldier replies. *"Then w...wh....where is he"?* she asks, with mounting anxiety in her voice. *"Let loose in the world, lady,"* the centurion declares, *"where neither Gentile nor Jew can stop his truth."*

Exactly. ALIVE and UNSTOPPABLE! Let's pray that whatever happens to us—whenever, wherever—that *that* is precisely what will be seen to be true of you and me.

The "Fish Cookout" Resurrection

The Gospel of John, chapter 21 (*portions*)

Seven of Jesus' disciples were together. Peter had decided to go back to fishing. The others decided they would do so, too. They got into a boat that evening. Throughout the night they fished, but caught nothing.

At dawn, there stood Jesus on the beach, but at first they did not recognize him. He called out to them, "My friends, have you caught anything?" They said, "no." He said, "Throw your net to starboard and you will." When they did so, they caught so many fish in the net, that they couldn't bring the net aboard. It was then that Peter said, "It is Jesus!" Though stripped for the work, he wrapped his cloak around him, jumped from the boat, and waded the hundred yards to shore. The rest came in the boat, towing the net full of fish.

When they landed, there was a charcoal fire with fish cooking upon it and also some bread. . . . Jesus said, "Come and have breakfast." No one asked, "Who are you?", for they all knew. Then Jesus took the bread and gave it to them, and the fish in the same way.

All four of the Gospels—Matthew, Mark, Luke, and John—end with reports of Jesus appearing alive again. In some instances, his followers find it frightening. Other times, there is open skepticism, bewilderment, or confusion.

Small wonder! Encountering alive, someone known to have died, falls well outside normal expectations. It would be eerie and unnerving at best. The only exception to this seems to be this encounter reported in John's Gospel, in which their time with him seemed to turn out to be reassuring and comforting.

This one was several days later. The worst ravages of what Jesus' arrest, abuse, and execution had done to them, had abated somewhat. And while they didn't know quite what to make of them, there had been those ever-so-brief, almost ghostly appearances of a risen Jesus. While not at all the same as having him back—walking, talking, sharing and caring among them—it at least offered a sense that he was, somehow, somewhere, alive.

Still, though, the "now-you-see-him-now-you-don't" appearances didn't alter the bleak feeling that all the real good was over, was in the past, was out of reach. The hope, the inspiration, and the empowerment they'd felt in being with him had been snatched away on Good Friday. These ephemeral, ethereal glimpses of him didn't change that.

So, they'd better start adjusting, right? They needed to face facts, to retrench and resign themselves to being without the dreams, the spiritual nourishment and the inspiration that, for nearly three years, had so enlivened them. For notwithstanding these bewildering visits from beyond the grave, the bottom line was that, in every practical way, Jesus was gone. Their need, then, was to rid themselves of their former hopes and dreams.

(Many people know what it is like to be at that point, after the initial shock, when the dust and smoke of the loss or of the failure clears, and/or the hard, unyielding facts of the tragedy settle in. Now that the light is unmistakably gone, it seems to be the time to adjust to and learn to live with the darkness.)

So, Peter gives one of those tired sighs that are common to dispirited human beings at such times. He says to a handful of the others, *"Eeechhh, I guess I might as well go back to fishing. Anyone want to join me?"* The idea isn't exciting to any of them, but fishing is what they know best. It's better than sitting around thinking and remembering, so they go with him.

Not surprisingly, it doesn't feel at all like it used to. Unlike before Jesus, it now feels tedious, enervating, and boring. The sea air feels clammy, instead of invigorating. Every noisy creak of the boat, every soggy rope that brushes against them, every fly that buzzes near, and every droplet of the intermittent mist is worse than they'd remembered. The constant stumbling over each other in the boat is more irritating than they remembered. Worst of all, they apparently don't even know how to fish anymore. It gets to be 5 a.m. and they haven't a single fish to show for the entire night.

This boat full of men, who had spent three extraordinary years under the teaching and inspiration of Jesus, didn't look like they had. For they believed that, even if Jesus was alive in some way, THEIR lot was going to be just this: grimly rubbing their out-of-joint noses in the tough realities of what had turned out to be a very ugly world.

And right then, as they did their best to adapt their lives to joyless, colorless, desolate "god-forsakenness," comes this breakfast resurrection experience.

At earliest dawn, they spot someone on shore. They can't tell who it is. Then the person yells an inquiry as to how fishing is going. They tell him. He yells back that they should try throwing the net off the starboard side. They have their doubts, but they do it. The net is immediately filled with fish. That's dumbfounding. It causes one of them to wonder aloud if that isn't Jesus, there on shore. Initially, they resist the idea, not wanting to be hurt, yet again, by hope. But somehow, breaking free from their protective melancholy, they do head toward shore to find out.

It was Jesus. And not, this time, as the eerie, ethereal, mysterious, "out-of-nowhere" earlier experiences. This time, he was ministering—in very down-to-earth ways—to their worn-out, shivering, dispirited, and famished condition. There was nothing overtly religious about it. He has no exhortations or sermon or explanations. It's their fishing, their need for a breakfast, for warmth, and for reassurance that Jesus is attending to.

THAT, it seems to me, is a resurrection report that one can really sink one's teeth into. I don't know much about resurrections—at least, not in the sense of the resuscitations of corpses. Oh, I have no doubt that God can do such, if

God wants to, but as a miracle, it doesn't enthrall me.

That wasn't what this was about, though, was it? This was about the resurrection of these people, so busy dying within that "rigor mortis of the spirit" was setting in. I do know something about that kind of resurrection, because I have seen it happen. It's something marvelous, as well as miraculous—at least to me it is.

This, then, was SOME BREAKFAST! For as of then, this group of demoralized, dispirited, frustrated, all-but-lifeless men were immediately turned around to become more alive than they'd ever been. In fact, they went forth to transform their world and their time.

It's my favorite of the Easter stories. That's because I find myself much less interested in what God did with Jesus' body than I am in what God was able to do to return these disciples to life. Maybe it's just me, but I get far more excited, inspired, and moved by miracles that transform than I do by miracles that only dazzle and dumbfound.

Years ago, a recovering alcoholic reported being asked by a cynical, still-alcoholic acquaintance of his, whether, now that he was a part of Alcoholics Anonymous, he was believing all the religious stuff about Jesus walking on water, about multiplying bread and fish to feed thousands of people, and about it being said that he had turned water into wine. This new AA member replied that he hadn't given those miracles a whole lot of thought, just yet. He hadn't had time because he was too busy watching God turn vodka into furniture, cheap wine into groceries, his wife's fear of him back into love, and his children's embarrassment about him into respect. *"For the time being,"* he said, *"that is about all the miracles my mind can handle."*

That gets at it. Whatever was the miracle and mystery of Jesus' resurrection, it was certainly something deeper and better than only God demonstrating that God can reverse physical death, if God wishes to.

Yes! The more practical and important question with which Easter confronts us is: *"What is going to become of you and me following those deadly Good Friday-type experiences that happen to us from time to time?"*

Unfortunately, you see, it's those Good Fridays, NOT Easters, that are allowed to shape many of our expectations, to put a lid on our hope, and, in general, to define us. Terrible experiences of loss, exposure to depraved behaviors, being a spectator to travesties of justice, and outright betrayals of good can be fatal to human beings—especially when the person takes it as the final word and begins (like those disciples returned to fishing) to adjust to the darkness, smothering hope, passion, and the capacity to care any more. People do that all the time.

In the New Yorker sometime ago, a man told how, while he was stranded in Bosnia for awhile, he ended up helping with the grisly burial and disposal details, after the armed skirmishes and massacres. He said he and an older man were unloading bodies from a truck. One would grab the arms and the other, the legs. *"Then, suddenly,"* he said, *"the old man let go of this one body and just stood there staring down at it. I asked him what was wrong. In this flat voice, he matter-of-factly said, 'This one is my son.' But after only the briefest moment, he picked up the legs and we got back to work."*

That's scary, isn't it. It is tough to figure out, there, who was most dead—the father or the son? Good Friday's, all-too-frequently become that pivotal experience—that incident after which people bury everything that has been alive in them and about them.

A staggering, paralyzing, personal loss (like the one the disciples suffered on Good Friday afternoon, for example) becomes the rationale for never again allowing oneself to be so vulnerable, to hope so much, or to have such deep feelings. Over every really hurtful or hateful thing that one of us has to endure, hangs the possibility of our coming out of it as hurters and haters. The "Good Friday" of having been a victim of gross injustice or betrayal can easily leave a person permanently stuck in chronic distrustfulness and suspiciousness. In the most petulant of us, it takes no more than a string of scandalous headlines, exposure to major public corruption, disgrace, or hypocrisy to "do it" to them. They let it prove to them that evil is now in control of life, good no longer has a chance, and that makes it okay to give free rein to their cynicism, ridicule, derision, innuendo, and malice. Good Fridays can do that, and worse, to people. They are permitted to be more than only a terrible experience. They become a rampant, fatal infection of the spirit.

Reversing that all-too-common form of death is a major miracle—to me, a MORE important one than the miracle required to revive a corpse.

And, somehow, this story of Jesus and the breakfast at dawn embodies that. The real meat of that breakfast was not fish. It was the coming back to life of these grim, depressed victims of that first Good Friday. What did it? Oddly enough, it was them seeing Jesus in the common, natural, "at-homeness" of that breakfast. By the time the breakfast had ended, they realized that there was a whole lot more going on than they'd thought, as of a week ago, last Friday. God, it seemed, knew and cared after all; cared even about their lousy night of bad fishing, cared that they needed warmth and nourishment, cared about what was happening to their morale. If God were really that personal, and that knowing, then there was, indeed, hope!

No, it didn't reverse or undo any of the injustice, brutality, or agony of Good Friday. But, here on the beach this morning, in Jesus' appearance amidst the fishy smells and charcoal smoke, they'd encountered God marvelously present in ordinary human closeness. They'd encountered a God who understood more than they had thought, a God of real kindness, and, above all, a God who was very personal and involved. That's what put them back on the road toward being alive again—more alive than they'd ever been.

Do I know what all went into that? No, I don't. But I do know that God works that way, appears that way, seems to move people like you and me to be there on the shore, making that kind of difference for those who've been through a dark, hopeless, fruitless wilderness of the soul. In fact, some of you have been used by God in just that way—have been the ones who, in your common acts of nurture, caring, and companionship, have been the reason people came back to life. Nothing could be more important.

That's one part of it. But think about this story, too, when you are one of those dying of a Good Friday. Remember that those disciples, that morning, who understandably didn't wish any further hurt or disillusionment, could have sailed their boat in the opposite direction. They didn't do that, and one mustn't. Instead, they risked hoping one more time. Remember, too, that no matter how a "Good Friday" has hurt, crushed, victimized, or exhausted us, and—even when we have strong doubts—staying open to the fact that there is more going on in this world and life than it may appear just now, is important. There are kinds of healing and bases for hope and astounding miracles of grace to which we remain blind, until we move toward them—this has everything to do with our spiritual survival.

Our world and life has never lacked for miracles. It has only suffered from people too cynical or small-minded to open themselves to all that is mysterious and miraculous. There is no lack of returns from being dead. There is only a shortage of people graceful enough to let it happen to themselves.

And yes, one could argue that it is unfair that anyone should be faced with a life and death decision, when already flattened by anguish or despair. But we are. Simply put, it is the decision between being "Good Friday people," of which they are many millions, and "Easter people," who are in somewhat short supply. God knows we don't need even one more of those grim, churlish, spiritually "dead behind the eyes" types who are stuck in the muck of Good Friday. What it comes down to is, that Easter is really the only "live alternative."

Some Interesting Light From Other Sources

Cinderella: Selling Oneself Short
(Scripture: Matthew 5:13-16)

One of the fables that we hold in common, in this part of the world, is that of Cinderella. In addition to being a generations-old children's story, a popular film, and a video, Cinderella has become a common metaphor for a person breaking free from one persona, to blossom forth in unexpected ways. It is, then, a fable about human transformation, which is, in turn, a very spiritual matter.

To refresh your memory, Cinderella was a sweet, attractive, young woman whose mother died while Cinderella was still in early adolescence. Her father remarried. His second wife had two daughters who were close to Cinderella's age. You certainly remember them, don't you? All references to those stepsisters and to their mother are preceded by the adjective, "wicked." Portraying them that way (that is, as congenitally and instinctively "wicked") may be simplistic and unfair. They did, though, behave badly in regard to Cinderella.

Their doing so could have been a result of compensatory closeness and affection shown by Cinderella's father, for this daughter of his now-deceased, beloved first wife. (It would not have been the last time in history that a second wife or husband came to think of children from the former marriage as spoiled, as adversaries, or, at least, as competition.) Cinderella's stepmother, then, favors her own two daughters in every way possible, at the expense of Cinderella.

Cinderella's father, maybe out of a blind wish to believe that everything is just fine and that they are one big happy family, oozing love and good will toward each other, stays oblivious to what is really going on. There is no evidence in the story that he ever intervenes on Cinderella's behalf. For the stepmother and stepsisters, that makes it "open season" on poor Cinderella. She becomes the target for all their resentment, insecurity and jealousy.

Curiously (and now we get into some important "meat" in this story), Cinderella seems to cooperate with it. She dutifully accepts as legitimate, her crummy treatment at their hands. She cringes by the hearth, we're told, as if this mistreatment by these three women is okay—is "meant to be." She acts just as mousy, withdrawn, and unattractive as they wish her to be. Their spite for her is quietly accepted by her as an indication that she is despicable. She obediently and passively operates on their humiliating script for her. That sounds strange, even neurotic, but it happens—and not just in fairy tales.

Now enters the fairy god-person. Fairy god-persons, as everyone knows, can make anything happen that they choose to make happen. She could, for example, have simply zapped those three mean, petty, spiteful women and rid poor Cinderella's world of them, once and for all. She doesn't do that, though. Possibly having majored in psychology at God-person University, she shows important insight and judicious restraint.

What she does, however, is arrange for Cinderella to experience a very few hours, in which she will have a chance to get another sense of herself, where she might, ever-so-briefly, know herself as an acceptable, interesting, and attractive person. The fairy god-person does this by dressing her up and transporting her to an elegant event at the local palace. Maybe—just maybe—she will come away from that palace ball with a sense of herself as being other than that picture she's gotten from her stepmother and stepsisters.

That godmother-arranged experience is, though, a very limited one. In fact, Ms. Godmother mandates that Cinderella be in before midnight (a requirement which may indicate that this fairy godmother had previously been a housemother in a dormitory at a church-related college). Nevertheless, for Cinderella, the time at the palace ball is one of absolution and rebirth, as she discovers that there might actually be a version of her, other than that of being a punching-bag for other people's hang-ups or a lightning-rod for their jealousies. She is so innerved and inspired by it all, that she cuts the midnight deadline very, very close.

She wakes up back at home the next morning to all the same injustice, humiliation, and resentment from those three women. Now, though, we sense that change is finally on the way. Thanks to having seen herself, however briefly, in a most redeeming light, she knows what she knows about her own worth, and we just know that she will never be quite the same.

A day or two later, an attractive, successful, single man appears at the door. His last name is "Charming" (if you can believe that). He has been going door to door, trying to find the owner of the slipper that Cinderella lost, while trying to make curfew that night. Despite attempts to confine her to her place in the kitchen, while her stepsisters fawn over Mr. Charming, Cinderella asserts herself and makes her presence known to him, much to his delight. Her sense of worth has blossomed just enough that she is able to muster the courage to present herself to Charming. It works. In fact, she ends up married to Mr. Charming. They live happily ever after, notwithstanding the fact that they probably were not invited to very many of the family reunions.

This, however, doesn't solve everything in this story. Her coming back to life like this does nothing to cure the jealousy, insecurity, or irresponsibility of her stepmother and stepsisters. It may have made it worse. That is something she will have to accept. Though she obviously had not understood this, Cinderella was the last one who would ever be able to assist those women in becoming decent people.

Sweet person that she was—and notwithstanding her willingness not to challenge their jealous behavior, and notwithstanding her willingness to make excuses for them in her own mind, and notwithstanding her cherishing the fantasy that she was slowly, but surely, inspiring them to become nicer—it wasn't going to happen. If they became well, it would be triggered by something or someone other than Cinderella. She was an unwitting contributor to what was disordered about them.

It is not, though, the bad behavior and character problems of the stepsisters and stepmother that we most need to understand. We all know quite a bit about that.

The more subtle, but nonetheless important, matter is Cinderella's inadvertent effect upon those women, during all those unhappy and unpleasant years.

Some might mistake her way of handling her persecution as a singularly Godly approach to her situation; that is, some might consider her willingness to accommodate their meanness, defer to their tyranny, accept the injustice, and, in general, cooperate with their inappropriate behavior as being a devout "suffering servant" of Biblical proportions.

It is true that there can be times when non-resistance and patient forbearance—carefully and intentionally applied—are Godly and are truly Christ-like.

Didn't Jesus say in his Sermon On The Mount, for example, that one should try turning the other cheek when assaulted, that it would be good to go the second mile, when a first mile is forced upon us, and that we should try offering, also, one's sport-coat when strong-armed for our raincoat? That IS what he said. Looked at carefully, however, that was never a commandment that we must become knee-jerk, chronic, Cinderella-like victims. To the contrary, what he was asking for was some imagination, intelligence, and ingenuity to be brought to this very serious matter of troubled or broken relationships between human beings. Offering the other cheek, the second mile, or your cloak in addition to your windbreaker, were out-of-the-ordinary, possible alternatives to merely getting sucked into a stupid fist-fight, or plunged into permanent resentment, or trapped in bitter enmity. Not at all was it a commandment that, in every such case, we automatically embrace the role of victim. Doing so only reinforces the wrong behavior of people like the stepmothers and stepsisters in the fable

So, again, Cinderella's accepting and adjusting so nicely to mistreatment was not exemplary. It was not, as she may have been telling herself, a way of being loving toward these women. To the contrary, accepting their abuse contributed to their emotional and spiritual delinquency. That was no favor to them.

Worse yet, to relinquish her own self-respect and allow resignation, cringing, and blind submission to become her approach to life, was to waste a good-size hunk of the very life and time that God had given her to live.

This is a most crucial understanding. It figures heavily in what happens when in a marriage, for example (or any other love relationship), one person is jealous and possessive. To go along with that, to humor it, to adjust to it, to make excuses for it, or to buy into his or her claim that the jealousy is a sign of especially strong love, are nothing but well-meaning ways of helping the jealous or possessive person remain sick.

Physical spouse abuse is another, all-too-familiar way that this comes into focus. It isn't that the victims prefer the abuse, but they will, in many instances, accommodate it and, thereby, support it. Some will do so by blaming themselves for their own abuse. Others will cling stubbornly to their fantasy that each mistreatment is the final one—that it'll never happen again. Most upsetting of all, some will accept and adjust to it, telling themselves that this must be God's will.

The same unfortunate dynamic is often there in those excruciating dilemmas where, for example, the parents of a troubled teen-ager feel as if the most loving and helpful thing to do is to bite one's lip and accommodate the misconduct and irresponsibility, lest the child become angry and break off contact with them. Here, too, absorbing the wrong can feel a lot like love, forgiveness, and Christian forbearance. Like Cinderella, though, and her adjustment to her disordered family, it sends precisely the wrong message. The unintended message it sends to that young adult is that you are infinitely adaptable and abuseable, that you have few boundaries (if any), and it even hints that you are committed to making it appear to turn out okay, no matter what distortion is perpetrated, or how much your integrity gets mangled. That message is a disorienting one, not an inspiring one.

Taking up the slack for, running interference for, or coming up with excuses for another person's bad temper, her self-centeredness, his laziness, or her manipulations are yet other serious, but familiar, Cinderella-type errors. They come with making oneself believe, *"It's my fault. I made him jealous,"* when that simply isn't true. Other abuse-inviting fictions: *"I failed to protect him from the things that upset him. That's what's causing him to be like this." "My expectations of her were too high, and that's probably what made her insecure and so hostile." "I just didn't do enough to make her happy."* However, those sacrificial-sounding words are the language that keep the wicked stepmothers and stepsisters wicked.

None of this is permission to become vengeful, insensitive, or judgmental regarding those people whose emotional, character, or personality problems are such that they bring chronic confusion and pain to their relationships. No, this is only to clarify what it is that we ARE ABLE to give to them (which is honesty, insight, empathy, friendship, and tough love) AND also to make it clear what it is NOT good to try to give to such a person (such things as their self-respect, inner peace, protection from the consequences of wrong, or blind acceptance and approval). Like everything else that is powerful in life, forgiveness, sacrifice, acceptance, and forbearance can be destructive, as well as redemptive. So one cannot just pour them on heedlessly and assume that they are bound to make things right.

After Cinderella finally understood how the healing and transformation happened for her, I would like to think that she did much better with subsequent troubled or exploitative relationships. Her transformation came the night that she rediscovered, at that palace ball, her own worth. It came that evening, when she was shown what a source of life and light she could be. It reached her through that experience in which she got some sense of how exciting it might be to "be all that she could be." Having understood that, I'd like to think that, never again, did she let anyone or anything obscure or distort that—not even Prince Charming.

That's not a bad lesson for any of us, of whom Jesus proclaimed that we are created to be the very light of the world and are intended to live as the salt of the earth. It is also a warning to us to not let anything obscure that.

Pinnochio: To Be or Not To Be a Puppet

The land of a rich man produced abundantly. He asked himself, "What should I do now, for I have no more room to store my crops." Then he thought, "This is what I will do: I will demolish my barns and build yet larger ones, where I will store all my grain and other goods. Then I will say to my soul, 'Soul, you have ample goods laid up for many years. Now relax, eat, drink, and be merry.'"

But God said to him, "You fool! Your life is being demanded of you this very night. And all of this which you have prepared, whose will that be?"

It is unclear whether Carlo Collodi's story, *Pinocchio*, is still a popular children's book or not. I've not heard it mentioned in recent years. As a child, it was, by far, my favorite fable. Someone had given me a hardback edition with dark brown covers and gold lettering. It was, moreover, the long version of the story which, nevertheless, I read over and over.

The story, in case you were never exposed to it, or have forgotten it, is about the creation of a person. A lonely, childless woodcarver named Geppetto crafts a boy-sized wooden puppet, to which he gives the name Pinocchio. There follows a magical intervention by a good fairy, through which the puppet comes to life. He is still made of wood, but with no strings attached. He can walk and talk. The plan is that he would be like a son to the old woodcarver. Geppetto does, indeed, love him and care about him as if he were a flesh-and-blood son.

Pinocchio has a lot going for him. He has the ability to wish, to dream, and to hope. He even has a conscience of sorts—albeit, an external one. His conscience is a hard-bitten cricket named Jimminy, who does his best to stay with Pinocchio and help him sort his way through temptations. This cricket/conscience, though, is alternately respected and avoided by Pinocchio—something that most of us understand all too well. That "good fairy" that gave him life adds one other intriguing innovation. It is that his nose visibly lengthens anytime that he tells a lie or is deceitful or duplicitous. (It was a fascinating addition—one which, were it so for of all of us, would undoubtedly push the revenues of the cosmetic surgery business way ahead of the automotive industry.) Also, the possibility of Pinocchio ultimately becoming a "real boy" had been hinted at. What that would require is not made clear—only that it would take time and that it would hinge on the way he lived and developed.

It is touch-and-go through the whole middle part of the story. There is much that conspires to encourage him to remain a puppet—a bright, amusing, active puppet who, again, can walk and talk and dress himself, but, nevertheless, is still no more than that: an animated puppet. He has one close call after another, as he lets himself get tempted and manipulated into one misuse and abuse after another. There turn out to be many who are anxious to turn him into a commercial entity.

Some might say he was naughty (crafted from knotty pine, perhaps.) At one very low point in this saga, his self-indulgence, his immature ricocheting from one impulse to another, and, in general, his trivializing of himself has become so bad that his ears grow long and hairy and he grows a tail. So, at that point, he is not only a puppet, he is a jackass of a puppet. Yes, for awhile, it appears that he'll never come close to becoming a real person.

The story, as you may recall, finally resolves itself when (a little like the Bible story of Jonah) Pinocchio finds himself in the belly of a whale. He is not alone there, either. His creator and father, Geppetto, who has pursued him in hope, concern, and love, in case he might rescue him from the messes in which he's embroiled, has also been ingested by the whale. So now, reunited with Geppetto in that impossible, hopeless situation and soon to be digested, it finally dawns on Pinocchio how asinine and self-defeating his life has been—how he has made himself, by the stupid choices he's made and because of the forces and appetites he has allowed to rule him, more (not less) a puppet than when he started out.

He determines that, if nothing else, he is going to get Geppetto out of the belly of the whale. The effort is successful, but, in the process Pinocchio drowns (or, I suppose in his case, becomes water-logged). At that point, having finally shown some depth, the "good fairy" appears once more and turns him into a real boy—a fully alive human being like any other (except that he had no one to whom to send a card on Mother's Day).

Even after all these years, I still find that to be a remarkable children's story (if a children's story is what it really is). The question and issue at stake throughout the fable—through every dilemma, error, and failure—is, "Will he ever be more than a puppet?" Given the delectable temptations, the dehumanizing forces, and the intoxicating distractions that swirl around Pinocchio, will he ever really come to life (in the deepest sense of the term "life")? Or, will he, instead, fall into some reasonably workable 'puppet situation' and wait out the coming of dry-rot?

When you think about that, isn't there a sense in which we all go through a "puppet" stage? The earliest form of us is quite "other directed," is tightly managed, and controlled (just as is a puppet). Also, much like Pinocchio, we start out very self-centered, self-absorbed, and with little, if any, depth to us. It isn't that we are not, even then, inherently good creations. We are. It is just a phase that is part of life. Moreover, we are given, or surrounded by, everything necessary to move us on from the puppet stage; that is, to become sons and daughters of God, in the image of God. But with us, as with Pinocchio in the fable, it may or may not happen. That's what's up for grabs in the life and unfolding of every single one of us.

Something very close to this is also what was at stake in Jesus' parable of that man who arrived at a point in life where he had accumulated major personal resources. That story did not turn out well. The man was still so much a puppet that he could not bring himself to break out of it. Having spent his time accumulating, he had failed to develop the appetite, imagination, vision, or inventiveness to do other than just go build still more storehouses, so that he could accumulate yet more. And there would be still more store-houses after that—sheer puppet-like banality!

Mind you, his storehouse-building was not evil. Nor was there anything inherently evil about his accumulation of resources. It was tragic, though, for the way it had locked him in as a one-dimensional person. Talk about a puppet, is there any better symbol of it than this ancient fellow who is so controlled by what he owns that *that* is all that moves him, all that occurs to him anymore, to which to apply himself?

It is a serious problem, this one of human beings ending up arrested in a stage of life that ultimately trivializes the grandeur with which we were created. One has to be concerned about what is, at every juncture and opportunity, now becoming of him or her. Over and over again, hard questions have to be asked that have to do with coming to life, versus slipping back into being one of life's tragic puppets. They are questions like:

As I move through each stage of my life, each transition, am I steadily becoming a larger-spirited person, or am I one whose spirit keeps becoming more and more constricted, rigid, and congealed? (For a lot of people, that is a "dead heat" by middle age.)

Are the experiences toward which I gravitate, ones which demand constant growth from me—the ones that forcibly keep recreating me? Or, are they repetitive, puppet-like ones which tie me to the same ways, thoughts, routines, fixations, and conventions?

What is my vision for myself—what will my life have meant when it is completed? It is to be hoped that it is something more than having been an empty builder of full storehouses, or worse yet, that I reached a point where as little of me was required as possible.

It says, at another point in the scripture, that, without a vision, people perish—not necessarily physically, but absolutely spiritually. One of the hymns we sing from time to time has a line in it that says, *"I ask no dream, no prophet ecstasies, no sudden rending of the veil of clay, no angel visitant, no opening skies."* Overall, it's a good hymn, but I've never liked that line. That is the puppet talking, and we do not need even one more puppet-minded, pragmatist in our world.

Are my encounters with evil, my disillusionment and the hurtful things that happen in my life hardening me, making me more suspicious, distrustful, and cynical (as happens automatically with puppets)? Or, have I, with God's help, extracted from them a greater resiliency, stronger empathy, and more in the way of personal grace?

Is my response to my own stupid mistakes, to failures of mine, to being faced with the wrongs I've done, that of honest, open contrition and of accepting forgiveness, or is it that mindless, puppet-like defensiveness, petulance, or blame-shifting?

As I hope we are all aware by now, the Bible is not anywhere near as concerned about the fact that we have flaws and that we sometimes get caught up in stupid, sinful, shallow, weak, cheap behavior, as it is concerned over what we make of that, and what it is allowed to then make of us.

What is the general drift of my life? In what overall direction have my typical, recent decisions moved me? Has it been toward some cutting edge, toward making some unique difference, toward embodying some truth that needs to be lived, toward holding out for some justice, or toward unfolding some kind of excellence? Or, are my decisions those that make me as similar as possible to those made by as many others as possible?

And there are still other hard questions like those. Their answers are less a matter of what we usually think of as bad versus good, as they are of life versus death.

They are necessary, because part of being created in the image of God includes the awesome freedom we have been given, including this freedom to never "get off the ground" in our living, OR (in the language of the Pinocchio fable) to remain little more than an animated, wooden, humanoid puppet.

It doesn't take a "spiritual genius" to recognize the tragedy in the stunting of a human being who was created to grow, the inherent sacrilege in confining of minds and spirits that were intended to flow freely, or the sheer waste when one turns his back on these unique, implicitly sacred capacities of ours.

Are there pitfalls in moving beyond puppetry? Yes, there are. The almost inevitable false starts, the embarrassing mistakes, the bruising temptations, and just getting lost from time to time, can be very unpleasant. It is all a part, though, of what creates us, of what carves some depth to us, of what puts us ever more firmly in touch with God's grace and forgiveness, of what brings us to where—far from being puppets—we are sons and daughters of God, the creator, something very much like we saw in Jesus.

So, lets keep right on bugging ourselves with those difficult questions about what—even at this moment—is becoming of you and me. Something IS, you know.

Metamorphosis: That "Cockroach Feeling"

(Scripture: Job 1:6–2:9)

I recently reread portions of Franz Kafka's eerie work, *The Metamorphosis*. If you are not familiar with it, it is a weird story about a man named Gregor Samsa.

Gregor, a mediocre salesman for a cloth manufacturer, awakens one morning and discovers that, during the night, for no reason whatsoever, he has turned into a giant, human-sized cockroach.

The rest of the story is the description of what he experiences in the days and weeks that follow this unhappy transformation. At first, as one can imagine, there is shock and denial. Denial, though, is not easy in a case like this. When one has literally become an honest-to-goodness giant cockroach, denying it is denial at its very toughest. (People tend to notice something like a 160-pound cockroach, and don't always handle it well.)

So the realization dawns fast and hard that this is not just a bad dream. Almost immediately, as a giant insect, Gregor Samsa is isolated from, and rejected by, everyone who had meant anything to him (including his family). There is no human intimacy, almost no communication, and what little contact he has with others results in revulsion on their part. As the days move on, his despair deepens. His "cockroachness" remains unchanged and, by all indications, is permanent. There is no glimmer of hope. He withdraws into his misery. The withdrawal becomes the prelude to his dying. And, die he does.

It is not a very upbeat story and it is certainly a bizarre one. People don't turn into cockroaches—not even those whom you would swear are trying to.

In certain ways, however, it is not so far-fetched. Powerfully portrayed in this troublesome fable is a kind of human "exile" that can happen to a person, right in the middle of life and living. It can be almost as bad as Gregor Samsa's awakening that morning suddenly to discover that the way he is seen by others, the way he sees himself, his control over his life, the limits with which he must live, the shape of his future, and, virtually all else is turned upside down and has become utterly foreign to him.

One doesn't have to be turned into a cockroach, or even a toad, in order to have that experience. In a much less freaky fashion, the parable of Job in the Hebrew Bible describes it happening to someone. In that story, almost overnight, Job's livelihood evaporates, his children's lives are taken, health problems begin, and his relationship with his wife begins to fall apart. Each of those troubles would, in itself, have been excruciating. But, all happening together, it is as if Job has been snatched up by some giant hand and plunked down into a totally different world, right while remaining there in the same town. Other people relate to him differently, if at all. All of that in which he has found satisfaction and has taken pride is gone. The future has suddenly switched from being very bright to very bleak. His very life seems to have become a totally unreliable and unfriendly place in which to try to live.

According to the scripture that tells the parable, this was all part of Satan's attempt to destroy Job's faith—to reduce him to a cynical, embittered, cringing non-entity. Nine times out of ten, it would have worked. If one wishes to thoroughly disorient, intimidate, and demoralize a person, just deprive him, like that—of the "given" of his or her life, the familiar sources of joy, reassurance, and self-esteem. Then, hot on the heels of that, cause the working assumptions, on which she depends, to seem shaky or even wrong. Finally, do everything possible to make the future either bleak or incomprehensible. It will feel a lot like Gregor Samsa waking up and discovering that he is no longer a cloth sales-man, but is now a cockroach.

There seem to be echoes of it in the plaintive words of one hospital patient, a corporate executive who was under-going his first-ever hospitalization. He found himself im-mobilized by IV tubes, a catheter, and restricted to bed pan use. On his second night there, he said to his wife, with some anguish,

"Do you have any idea what it does to a person to have been 'W. J. Hamblin, Senior Vice President and Chief Executive Of-ficer' one minute, and merely 'the ruptured gall bladder in room 4903, bed #2,' the next moment?"

That has just a tiny taste of what we are talking about. He'll survive the gall bladder problem and, in a day or two his life will become familiar again. But suppose that, rather than a gall bladder problem, W. J. Hamblin has been told that his is a seriously life-shortening illness. Not always, but much of the time, getting that kind of information in the midst of life is very much like being plopped down in an exceedingly strange, frightening, disorienting world. It is to wake up to find yourself at an all-but-unintelligible place where, for example, something that has always been as simple as the concept of "a year from now," has now become a pain-ful thought. It's now a world where all priorities are sud-denly scrambled, a world where people relate to you differ-ently—some of them actually avoiding you, because of what you are going through. It is a world where you find that you are now relating differently to your own body; that is, to the twinges or aches that you always shrugged off. It throws ev-erything out of kilter.

For some, the experience of going through a divorce can be similar to that of Gregor Samsa. I've seen it, and so have you: a person who, because of her marriage ending, experi-ences a shattering, completely unnerving feeling of exile.

The self that she so recently thought she knew, that she had enjoyed being, and that she was able to feel proud of, has now become, if only in her own eyes, a social embarrassment. She may start believing herself to be a hurter of her children, a danger to other marriages, a negative statistic, or a devalued being with no decipherable future. Here again, it is because so much about her life has been jerked apart at the same time. It feels like more than merely going through a problem. It feels like she IS a problem. So, without any actual change in surroundings, she feels like an alien.

Once in awhile, suddenly losing one's job has turned out to be the "cockroach experience." True, a person's job is supposedly only one segment of his life, but as we all know, for some, a job becomes the total definition of their lives: the source of one's friendships, of one's concept of herself, shaper of the hopes that he has for himself, and the only real arena of her dreams. So the day he walks out, after cleaning out his desk, he, too, is confronted with an almost totally unfamiliar world.

For some of the same reasons, retirement occasionally leaves a person in a foreign place, not knowing who he is. To have been jerked, overnight, out of a world where there was never enough time and always too many demands upon you, into a world in which there is little or nothing of urgency and more time than you have any real purpose for, has been a horribly destructive shock for some.

One can see that this has to do with something more than merely getting through some temporary trouble or embarrassment. This is the overpowering feeling that one's whole world and identity has suddenly been dismantled. It is to not have the faintest idea how to go about living, in what has come to be (and, maybe, no longer feeling that it is worth trying).

If, incidentally, you should be unfortunate enough to

happen to land in some such place in life, you'd better hope and pray that you are not surrounded mainly by smug people. They are the ones who haven't the faintest concept of how heavy or brutal life can suddenly become for someone. Such people can further disorient you. They are the glib, insensitive dolts who believe that anyone should always be able, instantly, to lift himself up by his own bootstraps. They are the ones who will say, or will strongly hint that, if you aren't able to do so just now, it is because you are a wimp or because you have a negative outlook or because you enjoy being in the pits. They are the kind of people who would have told Gregor-Samsa-the-cockroach, that it was all in his head. They haven't been there. They don't know what they are talking about, so avoid them or ignore them.

But, meanwhile, what does it take to survive at such times? There are several understandings that need to be firmly in place in our thinking, long before it ever befalls us.

For example, despite whatever doubts and self-torturings haunt you, hold on to the fact that whatever it is, you are NOT being punished by God for some terrible thing that you have done or left undone. Nor are you being made an example of for assorted wrongs you may have committed. Yes, in some instances, a part of it may have something to do with a mistake of some type, but God is NOT doing it to you! It is only an unfortunate collision with some of the most jarring of what is always possible with us, as fragile, vulnerable human beings in this throbbing, on-the-move, changing world. So don't lose sight of the fact that, no matter how dramatic is the contrast between now and the way things recently were, no matter how ugly the problem, or how deteriorated the situation, you are no less a worthy son or daughter of God than anyone else. Nothing has turned, or can turn, you into Kafka's hopeless cockroach.

Another is the understanding that, however undesirable

and unpleasant it is, for now, you are called to live it. You and I are called to be just as fully human, just as determinedly alive, just as doggedly persistent in the search for meaning in this,

which is chaotic and outrageous, as in those nicer times when you knew who you were, knew where you were going, and knew just how it was going to work.

You may be wracked with pain, full of self doubts, and scared half to death, but unless you settle for letting that be all there is to you, there is still far more to you. Whether it feels like it or not, you are still a person capable of full hope, deep joy, and profound good—notwithstanding the fact that, just now, you have some extraordinarily tough weeks or months with which to work.

You may, for example, have that illness that will substantially shorten your time here, but right now you are fully alive, fully human, and have a whole array of alternatives for applying yourself and for making up in depth what you don't have in length. Don't then, fall into seeing yourself as some kind of walking billboard about death.

Yet one more understanding is this. It is not your responsibility or calling to "keep up a good front" or to "stay out of the way" or to set a perfect example, or to contrive any other kind of heroics. Christians sometimes think that this is what is required of them: to create the impression that their faith has removed all doubt, confusion, grief, or rage. Note that Job, in the depths of his agony, screamed (in effect), "*God, I defy you to show me that I deserve to be going through all of this. God, show me how this makes any sense!*" On the cross, Jesus yelled out, "*My God, why have YOU forsaken me?*" The point is, that any God worthy of our faith and belief has to be capable of understanding whatever wrath or doubt or irreverence or self-pity or resentment that may overwhelm us, when circumstances conspire to terrify and disorient us. What could be more absurd than trying to pretend something for God's benefit?

Obviously, we hope and pray that jarring changes and cataclysms will not pile up for any of us, in a way that plunges us into seeming to be in exile in our own lives. But it does happen.

So again, etch into your consciousness, in such a way that it will be there (should it ever happen), the fact that God is never more at work, never more present, never more involved with you and me than when all has become impossible, not credible, and out of control. Again and again, it has been out of the ashes of those "cockroach experiences" that one's identity, her capacity for appreciation, his sense of calling, her empowerment, or his most eloquent living have risen.

"Flatland"–Breaking Out of It

Matthew 13:53-57

Leaving the district where he had been teaching, Jesus came to his home town and there taught in their synagogue. They were astounded at what he was saying, and they said, "Where does he get this wisdom and such power? He is the son of our carpenter, isn't he? Is not his mother the one called Mary? Are not his brothers James, Joseph, Simon and Jude? Do not his sisters live here among us? Where does he get all of this?" And the people there would not accept him. Jesus said, "A prophet is only despised in his own country and in his own house."

That was curious, wasn't it? One might have thought that the return of a local boy who had become a well-known teacher, prophet, and healer around the country would have gone quite differently than that. But, no, he is met with irritation and incredulity. *"Who does he think he is, anyhow?"* was their reaction to him. *"He's just another kid who goes off for awhile and then comes back, thinking that he's smarter than the folks back home."* In Luke's version of the same incident, it says that the local people were so incensed that they not only chased him out town, but were ready to kill him.

But then we are aware, aren't we, that people tend to be resistant when their presuppositions are messed with, their worldview challenged, or their beliefs put under scrutiny? Sometimes, it is particularly irritating, coming from one of their own. As a local boy, shouldn't he have shown more reverence for the faith of his fathers, more respect for the wisdom of those who, after all, had known him as a toddler?

The intensity that boiled in that abortive return of Jesus to his home town reminded me of a little book written more than a century ago. The book is entitled, *Flatland*, and was written by a Victorian author, Edwin Abbot.

The whole book is a parable, in which "Flatland" is an imaginary world where all of the beings are circles, squares, triangles, trapezoids, hexagons, and other geometric figures. Flatland has a whole class structure, in which circles are the priests, squares and pentagons are the professional class, hexagons are the nobility, and triangles are a lower class.

One night, one of the squares has a disturbing dream in which he finds himself in a different world—one called "Lineland." In Lineland, all of the beings are either lines or points. The men are lines and the women are points. In Lineland, obviously, there is no such thing as area, only long lines and shorter ones, plus all of these dots or points. In his dream, this visiting square from Flatland tries to explain to the citizens of Lineland that there is this thing called "area" where there is width as well as length. The lines and dots of Lineland cannot make any of *their* kind of sense of what he is saying. He tries and tries to get through to them about how lines can connect and create figures—figures with area. But the residents of Lineland are so conditioned and so certain that they are in touch with all there is to which one can be in touch, that they find ridiculous the idea that reality could contain anything more.

The dream of that "square being" finally ends. But he wakes up from his dream very frustrated. His dream of having tried to enlighten those unimaginative lines and points, leaves him exhausted and upset. *"How could those dots and lines be so stupid and obtuse"?*

Before too long, however, this same square citizen of Flatland, who dreamed about Lineland, is somehow transported into another realm. You've guessed it. He lands in a bewildering realm called "Spaceland." Here the beings are cubes, spheres, pyramids, cylinders, and cones. Because he isn't used to the nuances of light, shading, and perspective that are part of this additional dimension—because he has always seen everything only in terms of flat figures—he doesn't perceive the difference at first, but then he begins to. He encounters and talks with one of the beings there in Spaceland, a sphere, who then patiently introduces him to the dimension of depth. At first, he is resistant to it, but after a bit (thanks to having had his mind somewhat pried open by his dream about Lineland), he begins to realize that there could even be more to reality than length and width. It is an astounding discovery for him.

Filled now with excitement and enthusiasm, he is anxious to bring back the good news to Flatland that there is this whole other dimension to life. He returns there to do so. It does not go well—not even with his own family.

At first, the citizens of Flatland try to be patient and tolerant with this crazy idea of his, but they soon become irritated with his fervor, his persistence, and his certainty. Not only do they fail to understand, but after a time, they decide that he and his ideas are dangerous. They imprison him permanently, lest he spread this weird heresy or fantasy of a dimension of depth.

He says, moreover, that there in prison, with no one now to talk to, after awhile he finds that his memories of Spaceland, and of all that he discovered and understood while there, are weakening and his excitement is fading. That's the unhappy way that the parable ends.

One of the questions this undoubtedly raises is, *"Why are we using up half a sermon on this odd-ball story?"* The reason is that, in its strange way, it offers some interesting tools or images for thinking about our lives, our faith, and the whole matter of spirituality. For when I, at least, am at my shallowest, I think I get to be a lot like those citizens of Flatland—at best, blasé and, at worst, resistant to the idea that there is this other, even more important dimension to you and me than the practical, bottom-line, utilitarian one that claims so much of my attention and energy.

And it is not that we haven't seen and grieved over some

pathetically one-dimensional people (as did the square in his nightmare about Lineland). Most of us have seen and have been dismayed over lives, not only stuck in self-imposed tedium, indifference, and shallowness, but who, like the citizens of Lineland, were stubborn about staying that way. If nothing else, they make us grateful that, built into our living, are our various accomplishments, competencies, and areas of interests, entertainment, and activity.

But this is where this strange Flatland story gets a little unnerving, if not annoying. Whether accidentally or deliberately, it asks the question, *"What if, in our own way, you and I have a blind spot, a stubborn "closedness," or habitual resistance that is not very different from those beings of Flatland who were so sure of themselves and so certain that they knew the absolute limits on what could be real, that they dismissed the possibility that there could be a depth dimension, also?*

For me, this suggests yet an additional way of looking at the Christian Gospel. Being Christian (to stay a moment longer with the images of the story) is obviously thought by some to be mostly a matter of being a more dedicated "Flatlander." It is seen as no more than bending ourselves around to be yet squarer squares, sharper triangles, rounder circles, or larger hexagons, to get all the angles right. But what if, instead of, *"Try to do a little better," "Try to be yet nicer,"* or *"Try to cover more area,"* the REAL message is that there is more to you and me than we were thinking and that you and I were also created for this depth dimension, for a "spiritual realm" that goes much deeper than accumulating and consuming and triumphing and keeping ourselves busy, connected, and amused? What if THIS were what Jesus meant by life more abundantly?

As you can see, quite unlike the easy-to-measure surface dimension of our lives—the standard achievements, acquisitions, notoriety, prestige, power, etc.—this "depth dimension" or the dimension of "spirit" is more difficult to describe. But "hard to describe" doesn't make something any less real, does it?

If one COULD measure it, the depth dimension would be measured, for example, in how much one appreciates, rather than how much he controls.

It might be determined by how much he is growing, rather than how good he has it.

It pertains to how much he manages to give, rather than how much he accumulates.

It is seen in her being less interested in the cost of things, than in the meaning of them.

If there were such a way to measure it, it would be the measure of someone's personal warmth and empathy, rather than his personal influence or authority.

We'd know it was there in that person who found it strangely easy to choose against what was most practical, productive, and expedient, if whatever it was included something not very humane.

We'd be able to spot it in one's overall level of gratitude—gratitude just for the total, incredible adventure of being alive.

Without any question, the depth dimension would be evident in the person who has learned to love people and use things, rather than use people and love things.

Similarly, they'd be the ones who could feel genuinely "rich" because they have fewer needs, not because of their acquisition of more comforts and conveniences.

It is the dimension in which one seems driven by an appetite for getting close to as many others as she can, rather than coming out ahead of as many as she can.

It would be that "kingdom of God" (referred to by Jesus) where wisdom is infinitely more important than mere intelligence, where being open is more important than being right, where adding (in the deepest sense of it) life to your years is more exciting than adding years to your life.

Best of all, it is the dimension that makes holy, one's passion, imagination, ecstasy, hope, and the like.

It is all of that and more than that. It was, I suspect, what Le Baron Russell Briggs was talking about when he wrote,

> Now and then we meet a person who seems to live high above the little things that vex our lives, and who makes us forget them.
>
> He may speak or he may be silent. It is enough that he lives and that we are around him.
>
> When we face such a person, we feel somewhat as we feel when we first see the ocean or Niagara or the Alps or Athens, or when we first read the greatest poetry.
>
> Nothing is more like great poetry than the soul of such a person. For when he is good, when he loves everything that is beautiful and true, when he makes life like that which he loves, his face becomes transfigured; for the soul within is the light of the world.

That may be a bit flowery, but I suspect that most of us do have some intimation of what Briggs is referring to: that most of us have known people who, like that, were much larger than life; ones who, for reasons hard to explain, really seemed like residents of that "Kingdom of God" repeatedly mentioned by Jesus.

The point in all of this is, though, that this is not the way certain people were born to be, while others were not. This is a way of being for which you and I were created. It is something we choose for or against, over and over again, in all manner of little ways, every day of our lives. You and I remaining (in effect) stuck in Flatland, rather than going for depth, is at stake in every tiny decision regarding our use of time, for example, between alternative ways of spending our resources, having to do with the handling of our relationships, pertaining to issues or concerns to which we expose ourselves, and in which we might immerse ourselves.

And it is not that being a part of Flatland is all wicked or destructive or of no significance. It is just that God created us for a lot more than our only "getting by" and surviving, killing a few decades of time, collecting a few toys, and then jumping into our coffins and calling THAT a life. We were created as potentially spiritual beings, capable of "abundant life"—that is, of understandings, of creations, of intimations, of kinds of beauty, of meanings, of kinds of joy, and of the kinds of profound experience that become the very work and presence of God.

Flatland is fine as far as it goes. But that becomes precisely the point. It doesn't go far enough! Not only this whole Bible of ours, but something deep inside of us screams at us, that we were created for more than consuming, competing, protecting ourselves, and getting by as long as we can. There are real limitations on how much of that we can do, but there is no limit to how deep we can become, anytime— every time we go beyond "Flatland."

Index of Scripture

Bibliography

Coffin, William Sloan. Sermon at Riverside Church.
New York City, 1986.

Freeman, James. "Rivers." Internet: personal communication,
multiple forwardings.

Child and the Icecream. Internet: personal communication,
multiple forwardings, narrator not identified.

Tillich, Paul. *The Shaking of the Foundations.*
Charles Scribners Sons, 1948.

"I Keep the Rules for Being Good." Internet: personal communication,
multiple forwardings, narrator not identified.

Boyer, David. *The Sidelong Glances of a Pigeon Kicker.*
Viking Press, NY, 1968.

Bettleheim, Bruno. *The Uses of Enchantment.* Alfred Knopf.

Kazantzakis, Nikos. *Zorba the Greek.* Simon & Schuster, 1952.

Silverstein, Shel. *Where the Sidewalk Ends.* Harper Row Collins, 1974.

Keillor, Garrison. *Prairie Home Commonplace Book: 25 Years on the Air
with Garrison Keillor.* Audio Book. HighBridge Co., 1999.

Van Buren, Abigail. "Dear Abby." *The News Journal,* Mansfield, OH.

Stevens, Paul. *Married for Good.* Regent College, 1997.

Remarque, Erich Maria. *All Quiet on the Western Front.*
Little Brown, 1930.

Lewis, C. S. "The Shaping of a Self." St. Mary's College Press.

Fulghum, Robert. *Words I Wish I Wrote.* Harper Collins.

Hillesman, Etty. *An Interrupted Life.* Excerpts from the journal.

"This World is Not My Home." Rodeheaver, Homer, ed.
Songs for Service. Rodeheaver Gospel Music Co.

Nelson, J. M. *Between Two Gardens.* Pilgrim Press, 1983.

"Around the Corner I Have a Friend," Internet: personal communication, multiple forwardings.

Katzenbach, John. *In the Heat of the Summer.* Ballantine Books, 1983.

Hugo, Victor. *Les Miserables.* Penguin Putman Trade, 1997.

Shaw, George Bernard. *Saint Joan.* Penguin Putnam Trade, 1989.

Guenther, Max. *The Weekenders.* J. B. Lippencott Co.

Forbes, James. The 1981 Beecher Lectures, Yale Divinity School, New Haven, CT.

Spencer, Herbert. "Coming of Age." St. Mary's College Press.

Briggs, Le Baron Russell. *In the Stillness is the Dancing.* Argus Communications.

The Reverend Clifford Schutjer has enjoyed a ministry of 39 years at The First Congregational Church in Mansfield, Ohio. He is a 1958 graduate of Anderson College in Anderson, Indiana, and a 1961 graduate of Union Theological Seminary in New York City, New York.

The First Congregational Church in Mansfield is a church with a membership that is broadly diverse in age, occupation, and religious background. It is a theologically inclusive church, determinedly open to the full spectrum of ways in which individuals can approach their own spirtual growth and expression.

• • • •

Another thought-provoking book by Clifford Schutjer
Calling in...WELL!

A group of employees, distressed and sickened by deceptive, morally-repugnant work being required of them by their employer, framed an innovative response. Instead of a "sick-out"—a familiar kind of work stoppage—they staged what might be called a "well-out."

One day, they each called in to report that they were no longer sick enough to come in and do the kind of inappropriate work that was being required of them. They were..."calling in well"!

This image/perspective is a solid tool of thought for grasping what God in Christ calls us to consider doing for the restoration of our souls, the reclamation of our freedom, and the return from the many kinds of deaths that can subtly overtake us.

Calling in Well is available for $10.00 (plus shipping & handling) from the First Congregational Church, 640 Millsboro Rd., Mansfield, OH 44903; (419) 756-3046 or New Concord Press, PO Box 8016, Zanesville, OH 43702; 800-659-9442 • http://www.newconcordpress.com